W9-ANH-414

JANE CAMPION

INTERVIEWS

CONVERSATIONS WITH FILMMAKERS SERIES
PETER BRUNETTE, GENERAL EDITOR

JANE CAMPION

INTERVIEWS

EDITED BY VIRGINIA WRIGHT WEXMAN

UNIVERSITY PRESS OF MISSISSIPPI / JACKSON

http://www.upress.state.ms.us

Manufactured in the United States of America

02 01 00 99 4 3 2 1

The paper in this book meets the guidelines for permanence and durability of the Committee on Production Guidelines for Book Longevity of the Council on Library Resources.

Library of Congress Cataloging-in-Publication Data

Campion, Jane
Jane Campion : interviews / edited by Virginia Wright Wexman.
p. cm. — (Conversations with filmmakers series)
Filmography: p.
Includes bibliographical references and index.
ISBN 1-57806-082-6 (cloth : alk. paper). — ISBN 1-57806-083-4 (pbk. : alk. paper)
1. Campion, Jane—Interviews. 2. Motion picture producers and directors—New Zealand—Interviews. I. Wexman, Virginia Wright. II. Title. III. Series.
PN1998.3.C3545A3 1999
791.43'0233'092—dc21 98-46090
CIP

British Library Cataloging-in-Publication Data available

CONTENTS

INTRODUCTION

HAVING DIRECTED ONLY FIVE feature films to date, Jane Campion has given relatively few interviews. Most have clustered around her visits to the Cannes film festival, where her work has been shown on several occasions. As might be expected, the release of her most widely acclaimed production, *The Piano,* which shared the top prize at Cannes in 1993 and won three Academy Awards, generated the most published conversations, especially in the United States where Campion went on a brief tour to promote the American release. Otherwise, most Campion interviews have been published in Australia. While French film journals like *Cahiers du Cinéma* and *Positif* as well as German publications like *Filmbulletin* and *EPD Film* have printed several question-and-answer sessions with the director, surprisingly none of the major English language journals, *Sight and Sound, Film Quarterly,* or *Film Comment,* has thus far published a Campion interview. In part this is due to the director's attitude toward the press, for she claims that she dislikes personal publicity. "It's all right for actors," she told *The Australian* in 1986, "they have to promote their image. But I'm just a maker of products."

Most of Campion's interviews have been held in hotel rooms, though a few have taken place in the director's apartment in Sydney, Australia. In most of these sessions Campion has impressed her questioners as open and unaffected; one or two, however, have found her shy. A tall, fair-haired, attractive woman (Carrie Rickey described her as "robust, broad-boned and radiantly horsey"), she laughs often and frequently reveals a sense of humor about her extraordinary success. "I can't work well if I get too serious," she confessed to *The Sydney Morning Herald* in 1990. "I don't want to be a child emotionally or in terms of responsibility, but I do think that playfulness can be very liberating."

A few interviewers have conducted multiple sessions with Campion, notably Australian critic and writer Andrew Urban and Michel Ciment, editor of the French film journal *Positif.* Urban's brief, journalistic profiles are packed with information about Campion's career. Ciment's more scholarly question-and-answer sessions, are detailed, probing, and knowledgeable, with an emphasis on matters of technique. The respect Campion has for Ciment is evidenced by her thoughtful responses to his queries and by his evident ability to influence the direction her work has taken. In 1989 Ciment compared the director's films to the writing of Emily Dickinson and asked if she was familiar with this poet. Campion responded in the negative. However, by the time she was being interviewed about *The Piano,* Campion was citing Dickinson as an important influence on this production. "Dickinson led such a secret life, and my main character, Ada, does as well," she told the Australian journal *Cinema Papers* in 1993.

The Cannes interviews suggest the debt Campion owes to that festival, where in 1986 her early films were screened in the category "Un Certain Regard," an honor arranged by festival scout Pierre Rissient. As a result of this exposure, the Palme d'Or for best short film at Cannes that year went to Campion's *Peel.* Andrew Urban, writing in 1989, called this debut "unprecedented," and it led to her first interview with a non-Australian publication, the prestigious *Positif.* Urban had previously reported in 1986 that on this, Campion's first visit to Cannes, the festival's director Gilles Jacob told Australian Film Commission chair Phillip Adams, "You must give her lots of money so she'll be in competition with a feature film in two years." As a result of Adams's support, Campion was able to make *Sweetie,* which was accepted for the festival's feature film competition in 1990. The Cannes screening of *Sweetie,* however, represented a major setback for Campion; she has told several interviewers how devastated she was when audiences there reacted to the film with boos and stamping. Following this disastrous screening, a number of journalists cancelled previously scheduled sessions with her. Nonetheless, the faithful Rissient subsequently put Campion in touch with CiBy 2000, a French film financing entity which bankrolled *The Piano,* giving her total freedom to make the film as she wished. With this project Campion staged a major comeback at Cannes in 1993, sharing the festival's top prize with Chen Kaige's *Farewell, My Concubine*. This victory and the worldwide publicity it generated led to international interest in Campion and her views. Given her tumultuous history with the festival, however, it is understandable that the filmmaker harbors a somewhat skeptical view of it.

As might be expected, Campion's interviews with the Australian press emphasize her antipodean heritage more than other such pieces do. In these conversations the talk often turns to New Zealand, where she grew up. "In New Zealand you say 'small is beautiful' because everything in New Zealand is small," she told Hunter Cordaiy in an interview conducted for *Cinema Papers* in 1990. To Katherine Tulich of the *Sidney Daily Telegraph*, she commented, "Going [to New Zealand to make *Angel at My Table*] made me realize what an influence the country had on me. . . . It's quite a Presbyterian work ethic country. Thinking you're better than anyone else is a cardinal sin. New Zealanders believe in modesty at all times and we all thought Australians were vulgar and coarse."

Campion's 1993 film *The Piano* reflects her desire to explore issues related to the European colonization of her native land. She has frequently commented on what it was like working with New Zealand's indigenous people on this film. In a 1993 *Cinema Papers* interview the director described searching for information on the Maori in the photographic section of the Turnbull Library in Auckland, "which documents, from the earliest days of photography, the ways in which New Zealand became colonized. . . . how the Maori people adapted to European clothes, in combination with their own dress, which became such a graphic metaphor for their understanding of Europeanism—and vice-versa." Campion also made dramatic use of the New Zealand landscape to create *The Piano's* wild, romantic atmosphere. In the same interview with *Cinema Papers* she explained, "For me, and for many New Zealanders, the relationship with very wild beaches, especially the black sands of the west coast beaches around Auckland and New Plymouth, and the very private, secretive and extraordinary world of the bush, is a kind of colonial equivalent of Emily Brontë's moors."

Campion has offered mixed impressions of Australia, her professional home base, to the press there. On more than one occasion, she has indicated how much she enjoys living in Sydney. "I enjoy the way Australians are," she told the *Sydney Morning Herald* in 1989, "I moved to Sydney twelve years ago and really developed my creativity there. I wouldn't have had the same freedom in New Zealand." She has, however, expressed reservations about the Australian filmmaking scene. "A lot of Australian films are cynical," she told Kristin Williamson in 1985, "People believe that the honorable thing to do with a movie is to make money from it. I think the idea is revolting, but someone has to fill the K-Mart gap."

Campion generally presents a rosy portrait of her early homelife in these conversations. "If my family was really weird, I think I'd have found it very hard to tell stories about what went wrong with the family unit," she told Sandra Hall in 1993. In 1989 she reflected more generally on family life in an interview published in *The Sydney Morning Herald*: "What I think about families is that they're incredibly funny at times, and yet there is a tragic underbelly." The nature of this tragic underbelly came out in a 1995 interview with Sue Williams granted on the occasion of an Australian television documentary on depression. Campion revealed in this interview that her mother Edith had been hospitalized for this disease during Campion's youth and that Campion had thought at one time of helping her mother commit suicide. "I had to get away," she confessed. I couldn't breathe. I couldn't see for myself my own optimism any more because [the depressed state is] so seductive."

To escape and to enlarge her perspective Campion went to Europe where she briefly attended art schools in Venice and London. This period in her life has not evoked pleasant memories. In Venice a friend was arrested for drug trafficking. "I had no idea what was even going on," she told Lizzie Franke of *The Guardian* in 1997. "I just thought, I'm going to be arrested and put in jail, and no-one is going to listen to me. I felt that I really had the confidence knocked out of me." Eventually, the young Campion moved on to London, where she was equally unhappy. "I had to hide my personality," she told Carla Hall of *The Washington Post* in 1990. "I was too much for them."

Campion has frequently described her development as a filmmaker as a gradual process. "I'm a late developer," she told the *Sydney Morning Herald* in 1986. "Until I was twenty-five I didn't have a proper career." Her years in art school represented a process of self-discovery for her. "Art school is where all the learning I did took place," she told Carrie Rickey in 1990. During this period she became immersed in the aesthetics of minimalism.

She has also mentioned Joseph Beuys and Frida Kahlo as strong influences on her at this stage of her development. In the 1990 interview with the *Sydney Morning Herald,* she said, "At art school everything is really pondered and thought about. You're just talking about one shot or one image usually, so it's a very thorough examination." She still relies heavily on her background in art to translate her ideas into filmic terms. "I'm not nearly as verbal as I am visual," she told Donna Yuzwalk in 1990. "I have a very strong visual recall."

At a certain point Campion began to move in the direction of filmmaking. "I decided I wanted to do work about things I was thinking about and involved in, which were generally relationships and love . . . and sex!" she told *Cinema Papers* in 1984. "Previously I would go to art school and draw and I couldn't wait to get home and gossip about the intricacies of relationships and so on. Then I thought, 'Why am I not doing my work about these things?' So I started making story paintings and it clicked that I was trying to tell stories."

The narrative Campion has created about the emergence of her technical moviemaking skills in these interviews suggests a process that began relatively late. To *Premiere* in 1996 she confessed, "I could never have dreamed I'd become a director. I wasn't even that interested in movies." *Tissues,* the short film that got her accepted into the Australian School of Film and Television, represented a turning point for her. She often recalls her astonishment at hearing someone comment that it contained no wide shots. "I said 'wide shots? What are they?' " she told Katherine Diekmann in 1992. "That comment kind of blew my world apart, and I realized that I did not have any idea what I was up to."[1] As she told *Cinema Papers* in 1993, her time at film school represented "years of preoccupation" with the craft of filmmaking, though she claimed to Mark Stiles in 1984 that she found the school itself "boring and feeble." However, she was grateful for the freedom that was offered her there. "You could do any story you wanted to without having to argue for it," she told Mary Cantwell in a lengthy profile that appeared in *The New York Times Magazine* in 1993. "You had a chance to see how your ideas would turn out."

The names of numerous filmmakers come up in these pieces as having been influential on Campion, most frequently Buñuel, but also Antonioni, Bertolucci, and Polanski. In 1996 Rachel Abramowitz reported that Campion's mother had taken her to see *Belle de Jour* when she was thirteen. "It is funny to see those movies at an age . . . when you couldn't possibly grasp the moment," Campion mused. Lina Wertmuller is another of the director's favorite filmmakers. "*Seven Beauties* is an absolute classic," she told Vicky Roach in 1994. She also likes Peter Weir, as was evident in her 1985 interview with Kristin Williamson. "Weir has a sense of mystique, a depth, another layer," she said. "It's good to work below what you know consciously." To Mary Cantwell in 1993 Campion praised Spike Lee ("He's great, with a good, clean style") and claimed that she watched *The Godfather* "at least once a year."

Campion invariably speaks warmly about her collaborators and is generous about their contributions. Unable to attend the Australian Film Institute ceremony in which she was awarded the AFI's Byron Kennedy Excellence in Cinema Award in 1989, she sent a short film which showed her sitting on the floor surrounded by numerous pairs of shoes. As reported in a *Sydney Morning Herald* interview published in 1990, she then proceeded to introduce each of these pairs of shoes by the names of her collaborators on *Sweetie*. "When your collaborators really get high on something—when they've entrusted you to direct the film—that's one of the best moments," Campion told Sandra Hall in 1993. There is evidence to suggest that Campion has used her growing popularity to her advantage; Veronika Jenet, who edited most of Campion's films, observed to *The New York Times* in 1993, "Jane always surrounds herself with people who are very supportive and give her free range." In return, the director treats her collaborators with respect. "I felt really protected by her," actor Martin Donovan told Kennedy Fraser for a *Vogue* profile published in 1997, "yet also pushed really hard."

Many of Campion's closest collaborators have been women, including Jan Chapman, cinematographer Sally Bongers, and writer Laura Jones. Campion told *Cinema Papers* in 1993, "Jan Chapman and I have known each other for many years and we like each other immensely." To Michel Ciment she described her relationship with Sally Bongers. "I am good friends with Sally Bongers, which does not prevent us from arguing," she said, "but the reason is always the control each of us wants to exert." Campion has frequently been asked about working with Holly Hunter on *The Piano*. "I was lucky to have such a passionate collaborator," she told Michel Ciment in 1993, "because she really had a lot of work: mastering sign language, playing music. It wasn't easy."

Some of Campion's relationships with her male co-workers have been intertwined with love affairs. She wrote the script of *Sweetie* with Gerard Lee, a former boyfriend. "Gerard and I had a screaming match in a car park once—a humorous one," she told Sandra Hall in 1993. "He said, 'You've ruined the movie. It's a mess.' He'd been looking at it without sound. Then when he finally saw it, he really did adore it." *Sweetie* was co-produced by another boyfriend, William MacKinnon, who travelled with the director on her United States publicity tour in 1990 and contributed comments to *The Washington Post* interview done at this time. Campion subsequently married the second unit director of *The Piano,* Colin Englert.

Campion has always been aware of her position as a woman filmmaker. "It's harder being a woman director because on the whole women don't have husbands or boyfriends who are willing to be wives," she told the *National Times* in 1985. As a female director, she is aware of creating a different atmosphere on the set. "There is a different kind of vulnerability when a woman is directing," she told Marli Feldvoss in an interview for the German journal *EPD Film* in 1989. "It also makes a difference that there are more women on the set than usual." She is also conscious of creating a different kind of film from those of most male directors. "There are not a lot of films where the heroes are women," she told *Cahiers du Cinéma* in 1993. "And I think I know things about women that men cannot express." At the same time, she bridles at being narrowly identified as a feminist filmmaker. "I think it's quite clear in my work that my orientation isn't political or doesn't come out of modern politics," she told *The New York Times* in 1993.

Campion's comments on individual productions frequently bring up autobiographical connections. About the 1983 *A Girl's Own Story,* her remarks have been somewhat contradictory; while she has often denied that the film is autobiographical, she remarked in an interview in the *Sydney Daily Telegraph* in 1990 that she used a dress belonging to her mother in the production. "Mum never noticed," she commented, "until my sister said, 'Don't you see. We're all in that film.'"

Sweetie is the film about which Campion has acknowledged autobiographical elements most freely. She has frequently remarked that of all of the characters in her films, Kay resembles her most closely. "Kay is closest to what I was," she told Thomas Bourguignon and Michel Ciment in 1993. "What is part of me is a certain sense of the absolute and a desire to control things. I always had trouble understanding the separation between myself and the world; the mystery of sexuality, of hate, of passion, has always been a problem." She has also suggested that the film's plot relates to experiences she shared with Gerard Lee, the co-writer of the screenplay. "It was an experience that both Gerard and I had with somebody, so it was fairly familiar," she explained to *Cinema Papers* in 1989. In the same year she told Michel Ciment, "The character of Sweetie was inspired by a man. For family reasons, we changed gender."

Questions about *An Angel at My Table* have frequently prompted Campion to reminisce about the affinity she felt with the experiences of New Zealand writer Janet Frame. She read Frame's autobiographical *Owls Do Cry* at age thirteen. "I was shocked to find out how normal she was," Campion confessed to the *Sydney Morning Herald* in 1990, "and how much my childhood felt like hers."

Campion's interviews suggest that *The Piano* may represent the deepest strain of her sensibility, though it is perhaps her least obviously autobiographical work. Unlike her other full-length features, *The Piano* was created from a screenplay credited to her alone. "It's more difficult writing alone," she confided to Vincent Ostria and Thierry Jousse in 1993, "but at the same time it was a very personal subject and I wouldn't have had an idea about how to write it with someone else." Her interviews document the long period of development the script went through, for she began to speak of the idea for the film in her 1984 *Cinema Papers* interview. To *The Observer* in 1993 she described wanting to tell a story about her New Zealand heritage. "*The Piano* is me trying to come to terms with the fact that I'm a colonial," she said.[2]

Campion's statements about *Portrait of a Lady* have brought out yet other autobiographical connections. "Coming from Australia or New Zealand now makes one more like Americans going to Europe were then than Americans going to Europe are now," she observed to Mary Cantwell in 1993. "They're much more sophisticated, whereas we have more of a colonial attitude about ourselves, a more can-do, anything's possible attitude. I felt so much like Isabel as a young woman, a sense of having extraordinary potential without knowing what the hell to do with it." Some of the director's more specific associations with Europe, and in particular Italy, came out in an interview with Michel Ciment in 1996, where she alluded to "the dark face of beautiful Italy, which is like that of

Madame Merle and Osmond, whose sunny disposition is the only thing that [Isabel] sees at the beginning. I discovered this Italy myself when I was twenty-one and I left to study art in Venice. I passed the winter there profoundly depressed by the cold, the humidity, the imprisonment, and also my terrible loneliness since I didn't know anyone. It was my first existential experience of isolation. That helped me a lot to understand Isabel's feelings." A few interviewers have suggested yet another autobiographical connection: Isabel's tragic loss of her baby, an experience Campion had undergone in 1993. By the time filming on *Portrait* began, however, the filmmaker had given birth again to a little girl called Alice. "My identity as a big time director is not enough," she told the *Christian Science Monitor* in 1997. "When Alice walks in the room, that's the best thing."

Because actors figure so prominently in most people's perceptions of what movies are about, questions about casting arise frequently in Campion's interviews with mass market publications. Her early films mostly employed non-professionals or semi-professionals. About her 1982 short *Peel,* she has explained that the film was inspired by the family of Australian fashion designer Katie Pye, all of whom played themselves in the production. To Kristin Williamson in 1985 she said, "*Peel* is about very tough people who don't understand each other. [Katie Pye] and her family were quite angry with one another at that time. But they were honest because when they read the script I wrote about them they laughed and said, 'yes, that's us.' Not many people would admit that." Campion also likes to tell the story about how she came to cast Karen Colston as Kay in *Sweetie.* "By the time she was shortlisted, she was in Sweden on an indefinite holiday," Campion told Andrew Urban in 1989. "With great cool and characteristic strong faith, Karen flew back, auditioned twice and got the part."

When she graduated to directing features that were internationally financed, Campion began working with highly trained and visible American stars. She has admitted on occasion that she sometimes resisted casting these actors in part because they intimidated her. The prospect of working with the strong-willed Harvey Keitel on *The Piano* was especially daunting. Campion was also initially reluctant to consider Holly Hunter for the leading role in this film. "In the romantic tradition I was originally working toward, most of the women are tall, strikingly beautiful, almost fearsomely so," she told Paul Freeman in 1993. "When Holly auditioned,

I realized she had an equivalent, if different, strength."[3] The director has described similar hesitancies about casting Nicole Kidman in *The Portrait of a Lady.* "It's something I'm a little ashamed of because you should think very, very deeply before you get as far as I got with Nicole," Campion told *Premiere* in 1996. "But it worked out very well for us in the end. We worked together for two days and I was blown away by her courage and honesty and development."

Issues of style and technique in Campion's films are less frequently raised themes in interviews conducted by the popular press, but they often come up when she is questioned by representatives of film journals, especially in her sessions with *Postitif*'s Michel Ciment. In 1989 she described *Sweetie*'s visual style to Ciment. "The artistic director deliberately created drab and ugly sets," she said. "What is ugly can be viewed with elegance." In an interview with Andrew Urban in the same year she described the effect of the film in terms of editing and cinematography. "It's the way it's made, I think, that's different," she said. "The links between scenes are surprising, and the way it's shot."

Campion described the structure of *An Angel at My Table* in a 1990 *Cinema Papers* interview as having been inspired by the workings of memory, "the idea of how your memory develops. I wanted the first bits to be like little slides, visual impressions. If you look back to your very first memory, you can't even put a story together: it's just a picture. So I wanted Episode I to build up the storytelling with very short scenes that get longer and longer, as would a memory. By Episode II, it's normal storytelling." The production's intimate, televisual style is another of Campion's favorite topics when asked about this film. "The subject didn't lend itself to an experimental style like *Sweetie,*" she told Michel Ciment in 1990. "On the contrary. For me the story as told by Janet Frame imposes the square format of the TV screen. Sometimes you lose the substance of a film when it's on television, but not in this case. There are a lot of close-ups, for example, but they are suitable for a story which is of an intimate nature."

According to Campion, *The Piano* began with a piano and only gradually evolved from a Gothic tragedy into a modernist fairy tale. She has often spoken about her conception of the piano as the center of the story. "I wanted to tell a story around an object," she told *Cinema Papers* in 1993. She found further inspiration in the desolate, doom-filled novels of the Brontë sisters, especially *Wuthering Heights*. In her interview with Thomas

Bourguignon and Michel Ciment in 1993 Campion discussed the changes the script went through during its long incubation from a blood-and-thunder action story to a character-centered fable. "Originally the ending was very traditional," she recalled, "with the resolution of the drama in a violent action." Campion has also spoken about her concern that *The Piano's* cinematography reflect her emphasis on character development rather than appear to be imitating the style of conventional epic cinema. As she explained to *Cinema Papers* in 1993 she wanted "to photograph a story that has epic qualities without seeming a clone of David Lean—to still have my identity but also have a feminine epic quality and to recreate it so that the epicness didn't feel like it relates back to other big-look movies."

Campion's most recent film, an adaptation of Henry James's *Portrait of a Lady,* posed the challenge of recreating a literary classic in cinematic terms. Speaking with Michel Ciment in 1996 about the process of writing the screenplay with Laura Jones, the director recalled, "We even wondered at the beginning whether it was even possible to do such an adaptation, until the moment I realized while rereading the novel that we weren't going to shoot *Portrait of a Lady,* but simply the story of *Portrait of a Lady,* interpreted by me, with some of the original dialogue." In the same conversation she discussed the visual strategies she had adopted to express the heroine's interior feelings, something James did with prose. "Some of these choices reflect the dilemma of the story's central character," she explained to Ciment. "She believes she's looking for light when she is attracted by shadow, by a somber adventure that is going to swallow her up."

As her career has progressed, Campion's technical concerns have been subsumed into larger questions of character and theme. "I'm finding myself less and less interested in what you can do with shots and things," she confessed to Katherine Diekmann in 1992. "There's probably only about twenty different possibilities in the end. I'm more after what sort of sensations and feelings and subtleties you can get through your story and can bring out through performances—although at the same time I'm always wondering about style, trying things out."[4]

Campion's world view as revealed in these pieces is nothing if not idiosyncratic. "I like bizarre underground things," she told Andrew Urban in 1986, "things you're not supposed to like." In the same year she told the *Sydney Morning Herald,* "We all have bad thoughts and unpleasantness in us. If we make films of people who don't have those things we make ourselves lonelier." Over the years, however, Campion's vision of the world has mellowed. "As a very young filmmaker I was particularly committed to what was nasty, what isn't spoken about in life," she told Kristin Williamson in 1985. "Now it's a bit more balanced." In 1997 her mother offered another appraisal. "If Jane hadn't done anything I think she may have become a great criminal," Edith Campion commented to Lizzie Franke. "She likes to set things in action and see what happens. But then, that's rather like being a movie director."

A collection of unedited interviews such as this is bound to feature considerable repetition, but such redundancy can provide readers with a sense of where Campion's interests lie. Because some of the most in-depth interviews with the director have been done for French and German publications, I have arranged to have these pieces translated back into English for this volume. Readers should bear in mind that, inevitably, these interviews may at times reflect the gist of what the director said rather than reproducing her original words exactly. I am very grateful to Michele Curley and Andrea Riemann for their excellent work on these translations, and to my colleagues Peggy McCracken and Helga Kraft for arranging to have this done. This volume also owes an enormous debt to the tireless efforts of my research assistant Tobi Jacobi, who gathered much of the material and obtained the necessary permissions. As always, my husband John Huntington provided invaluable support and wisdom at every stage. Finally, a special thank you must go to Gerald Peary, who collected a great deal of material on Campion including copies of all of the Australian interviews while he was visiting that country; because of his generosity, this volume contains much material that would otherwise have been unavailable to me.

Endnotes

1. Katherine Diekmann, "Jane Campion," *Interview,* 1992.
2. Ruth Picardie, "Notes on a Grand Winner," *The Observer,* 17 October 1993.
3. Paul Freeman, "Keys to Fulfillment," *Chicago Tribune,* 14 November 1993.
4. Diekmann.

CHRONOLOGY

1954 Born April 30 in Wellington, New Zealand, the second of three children, to Richard Campion (opera and theater director) and Edith Campion (actor and writer), both second generation New Zealanders.

1975 Graduates from Victoria University in Wellington with a B.A. in Structural Arts (Anthropology).

1976 Travels in Europe. Attends Chelsea School of Arts in London.

1977 Begins studies at Sydney College of Arts in Australia.

1979 Graduates from Sydney College of Arts with a B.A. in Painting.

1980 Makes her first short film, *Tissues.*

1981 Enters Australian Film and Television School.

Makes a short video entitled *Mishaps: Seduction and Conquest.*

1982 Makes the short film, *Peel,* which wins her international recognition.

1983 Writes and directs *Passionless Moments* with Gerard Lee.

1984 *A Girl's Own Story,* a tale of youthful incest, is released.
Joins Australia's Women's Film Unit.
Graduates Australian Film and Television School.

1986 Directs *Two Friends,* a telefeature about adolescent girls.

	Directs an episode of "Dancing Daze" television series.
1989	The black comedy *Sweetie* is released to initial controversy. Wins Bryon Kennedy Award, Australian Film Institute.
1990	Directs a TV adaptation of Janet Frame's autobiography, *An Angel at my Table,* subsequently released theatrically.
1992	Marries Colin Englert, second unit director on *The Piano.*
1993	*The Piano* is released to worldwide acclaim. Son Jasper dies at twelve days old.
1994	Daughter Alice born.
1996	*The Portrait of a Lady,* an adaptation of the Henry James novel, is released to mixed reviews.

FILMOGRAPHY

1980
Tissues
Director: **Jane Campion**
Super 8

1981
Mishaps: Seduction and Conquest
Director: **Jane Campion**
video

1982
Peel—An Exercise in Discipline
Australian Film and Television School
Producer: Ulla Ryghe; Writer/Director/Editor: **Jane Campion**; Cinematographer: Sally Bongers
Running Time: 9 minutes
Cast: Tim Pye (Brother/Father), Katie Pye (Sister/Aunt), Ben Martin (Son/Nephew)
Cannes Film Festival, 1986: Palme d'Or, Best Short Film

1983/4
A Girl's Own Story
Writer/Director/Producer: **Jane Campion**; Cinematographer: Sally Bongers; Original music: Alex Proyas; Editor: Christopher Lancaster

Running Time: 27 minutes
Cast: Paul Chubb, Jane Edwards, Colleen Fitzpatrick, Joanne Gabbe, John Godden, Geraldine Haywood, Marina Knight, Gabrielle Shornegg
Sydney Film Festival, 1984: Rouben Mamoulian Award; Australian Film Institute (AFI) Awards, 1984: Best Director Award (Non-Feature Section)

1983/4
Passionless Moments
Australian Film and Television School
Producer/Writer/Director (with Gerard Lee): **Jane Campion**; Cinematographer/Camera Operator: **Jane Campion**; Editor: Veronika Haeussler
Black and White
Running Time: 9 Minutes
Cast: David Benton (Ed Tumbury), Ann Burriman (Gwen Gilbert), Sean Callinan (Jim Newbury), Paul Chubb (Jim Simpson), Sue Collie (Angela Elliott), Elias Ibrahim (Ibrahim Ibrahim), Paul Melchert (Arnold), George Nezovic (Gavin Metchalle), Jamie Pride (Lyndsay Aldridge), Yves Stenning (Shaun), Rebecca Stewart (Julie Fry)
Australian Film Institute Awards, 1984: Best Experimental Film

1984
After Hours
Writer/Director: **Jane Campion**
Running Time: 97 Minutes
Cast: Anna Maria Monticelli, Russell Newman, Danielle Pearse, Don Reid
Melbourne International Film Festival, 1984: IXL Elder Award

1985
Dancing Daze
Director: **Jane Campion**
Episode of Television Series

1986
Two Friends
Producer: Jan Chapman; Director: **Jane Campion**; Writer: Helen Garner; Cinematographer: Julian Penney; Editor: Bill Russo; Original music: Martin Armiger; Production and Costume Design: Janet Patterson
Telefeature

Running Time: 75 minutes
Cast: Kris Bidenko (Kelly), Emma Coles (Louise), Peter Hehir, Kris McQuade (Louise's mother)

1989
Sweetie
Producers: William MacKinnon and John Maynard; Director/Casting/Co-Writer (with Gerard Lee): **Jane Campion**; Cinematographer: Sally Bongers; Editor: Veronika Haeussler; Original music: Martin Armiger; Costume Designer: Amanda Lovejoy
Cast: Geneviève Lemon (Dawn aka Sweetie), Karen Colston (Kay), Tom Lycos (Louis), Jon Darling (Gordon), Dorothy Barry (Flo), Michael Lake (Bob), Andre Pataczek (Clayton), Jean Hadgraft (Mrs. Schneller), Paul Livingston (Teddy Schneller), Louise Fox (Cheryl), Ann Merchant (Paula), Robin Frank (Ruth Bronwyn), Morgan (Sue Sean), Callinan (Simboo), Diana Armer (Melony), Emma Fowler (Little Sweetie), Irene Curtis (Mandy)
Los Angeles Film Critics' Association, 1990: New Generation Award; American Independent Spirit Award, 1991: Best Foreign Feature; Georges Sadoul Award, 1991: Best Foreign Film; Australian Film Critics' Association, 1991: Best Film, Best Director, Best Actress (Geneviève Lemon)

1990
An Angel at My Table
Producers: Bridget Ikin, Grant Major, John Maynard; Director: **Jane Campion**; Writers: Janet Frame (autobiographies) and Laura Jones; Cinematographer: Stuart Dryburgh; Original music: Don McGlashan and Franz Schubert; Production Designer: Grant Major; Costume Designer: Glenys Jackson; Editor: Veronika Haeussler
Television Miniseries (Subsequently Released Theatrically)
Running Time: 157 minutes
Cast: Kerry Fox (Janet Frame), Alexia Keogh (Young Janet), Karen Fergusson (Teenage Janet), Iris Churn (Mother), Kevin J. Wilson (Father), Melina Bernecker (Myrtle), Timothy Bartlett (Gussy), Dymock Hamish McFarlane (Avril Luxon), Edith Campion (Miss Lindsay), Andrew Binns (Bruddie), Glynis Angell (Isabel), Sarah Smuts Kennedy (June), David Letch (Patrick), William Brandt (Bernhard), Martyn Sanderson (Frank)
Venice Film Festival, 1990: Silver Lion and Grand Jury Prize; Sydney Film Festival, 1990: Most Popular Film; Australian's Film Critics' Circle, 1990:

Best Foreign Film; Festival of Festivals, 1990: International Critics' Prize; Valladolid Film Festival, Spain, 1990: Best Actress; New Zealand Film and Television Awards, 1990: Best Film, Best Director, Best Screenplay, Best Female Performance (Kerry Fox), Best Performance in a Supporting Role (Martyn Sanderson); Berlin Film Festival, 1991: Otto Dibelius Film Prize, Most Popular Film; Union of Critics, Belgium, 1991: Best Film

1993
The Piano
CiBy 2000
Producers: Jan Chapman, Alain Depardieu, Mark Turnbull; Director/Writer: **Jane Campion**; Cinematographer: Stuart Dryburgh; Original music: Michael Nyman; Production Designer: Andrew McAlpine; Costume Designer: Janet Patterson; Editor: Veronika Jenet
Running Time: 120 minutes
Cast: Holly Hunter (Ada), Harvey Keitel (Baines), Sam Neill (Stewart), Anna Paquin (Flora), Kerry Walker (Aunt Morag), Geneviève Lemon (Nessie)
Cannes Film Festival, 1993: Palme d'Or, Best Feature, Palme d'Or, Best Actress (Holly Hunter); Academy Awards, 1994: Best Actress (Holly Hunter), Best Original Screenplay, Best Supporting Actress (Anna Paquin); British Academy Awards, 1994: Best Film, Best Director, Best Actress (Holly Hunter), Best Original Screenplay, Best Original Score; Directors Guild of America, 1994: Best Director; Golden Globe Awards, 1994: Best Film (Drama), Best Director, Best Actress (Drama) (Holly Hunter), Best Supporting Actress (Ann Paquin), Best Screenplay, Best Original Score; Independent Spirit Awards, 1994: Best Foreign Film; Los Angeles Film Critics Association, 1994: Best Director, Best Actress (Holly Hunter), Best Supporting Actress (Anna Paquin) (co-winner), Best Cinematography; New York Film Critics Association, 1994: Best Director, Best Actress (Holly Hunter), Best Screenplay; National Society of Film Critics, 1994: Best Actress (Holly Hunter), Best Screenplay

1996
Portrait of a Lady
Producers: Steve Golin, Monty Montgomery, Mark Turnbull, Ann Wingate; Director: **Jane Campion**; Writers: Henry James (novel) and Laura Jones; Cinematographer: Stuart Dryburgh; Original music: Wojciech Kilar and

Franz Schubert; Production and Costume Designer: Janet Patterson; Film Editor: Veronika Jenet
Running Time: 144 Minutes
Cast: Nicole Kidman (Isabel Archer), John Malkovich (Gilbert Osmond), Barbara Hershey (Madame Serena Merle), Mary-Louise Parker (Henrietta Stackpole), Martin Donovan (Ralph Touchett), Shelley Winters (Mrs. Touchett), Richard E. Grant (Lord Warburton), Shelley Duvall (Countess Gemini), Christian Bale (Edward Rosier), Viggo Mortensen (Caspar Goodwood), Valentina Cervi (Pansy Osmond), John Gielgud (Mr. Touchett), Roger Ashton-Griffiths (Bob Bantling), Catherine Zago (Mother Superior)
Los Angeles Film Critics Association, 1997: Best Production Design (Janet Patterson), Best Supporting Actress (Barbara Hershey); National Society of Film Critics, 1997: Best Supporting Actor (Martin Donovan) (co-winner), Best Supporting Actress (Barbara Hershey)

JANE CAMPION

INTERVIEWS

Jane Campion

MARK STILES/1984

How did you get involved in films?
I was at Sydney College of the Arts, which is probably my greatest teaching influence. I had a fantastic time at the school. I had very old-fashioned ideas about art which I had picked up at home—you sort of drew things—and that was what I wanted to learn. Art was all very mysterious; there were these wonderful paintings and you wanted to look at them for a long time without really knowing why. Art school knocked a lot of that out of me. It is not so much that it really changed me but that it made me rethink everything, which was pretty monumental at the age of 25.

After that, I decided I wanted to do work about things I was thinking about and involved in, which were generally relationships and love . . . and sex! Previously, I would go to art school and draw and I couldn't wait to get home and gossip about the intricacies of relationships and so on. Then I thought, "Why am I not doing my work about these things?" So I started making story paintings and it clicked that I was trying to tell stories.

Did you start writing?
Yes. I started writing plays, little performance pieces, and began putting them on. They were pretty wild. I was in some of them but I was so humiliated when I saw the videotape I said, "Never again." And I thought how crummily the videotape was shot and that it was a shame.

From *Cinema Papers* (Melbourne), December 1984. Reprinted by permission of MTV Publishing, Ltd.

The next thing I decided was that instead of doing it live I would make it on film or video. That is how I came to make *Tissues* and how I became totally obsessed. I got this great Super-8 manual and I just taught myself. We did it double system Super-8 sound, which is really quite complicated, but it didn't seem to be any trouble at the time. I don't know why.

Did you shoot it?
No. People just seemed to turn up. I had imagined I would have to do it all myself. I went somewhere to find out about Super 8 and there would be someone else there and he would say, "Oh, I'll do sound if you like." I didn't even think about that to be honest—to put the microphone on a chair or something—and suddenly there was a crew.

How did you feel about having a crew?
I was always worried about whether they would come; the arrangements were terribly casual. Sometimes they didn't!

Tissues is one of my favorites actually. The subject matter and the tone is exactly the same as what I am doing now, but with a bit more style. It is a bit disturbing—I haven't made much progress!

And after that you went to the AFTS . . .
After I made *Tissues,* I tried to get some money from the Australian Film Commission (AFC) and I also tried to get into the AFTS. I did a test scene for the AFC but they didn't like it. The AFTS wanted me, even though they didn't like what I had made. They couldn't understand the humor in *Tissues*: "Are we supposed to be laughing?" they asked.

What was your experience at the AFTS?
I fell in love with Gerard Lee in my first year which was just great because I think I would have gone mad otherwise. The AFTS was so boring and feeble; the relationship was wonderful. We sort of kissed and held hands all through classes and drove everybody mad.

I made an experimental video called *Mishaps: Seduction and Conquest* about two brothers: one is climbing Mt Everest—that is Mallory in the 1924 expedition—and the other is his fictional brother, who is trying to seduce a woman who is not very interested in him. It is the two styles of conquest. I was very moved by the way the men on the expedition talked about the mountain as though it had the qualities of a temptress: the closer you got to it the less you wanted it. It just seemed so much like the nature of desire.

I quite like the finished film. It has a nice feeling and is more sophisticated than some of my other stuff. But I hated it when I first finished it. I made it in a very open-handed way and everybody came in and told me what a heap of shit it was. So I just kept working, trying to make it the best I could.

Your films are all very funny. There is a lovely sense of humor in "Peel" . . .
The people at the AFTS loathed *Peel* when they saw a first cut of it. They told me not to bother finishing it. I was quite vain so I found that really upsetting, but it was good for me. I cut out everything that was remotely extraneous and made the film a lot better. The AFTS people thought I was arrogant and not particularly talented. There were people there more talented than I was, but my talent wasn't the kind they were ever going to understand, which was one of the luckiest things for me.

Why?
They tend to wreck the people they think are talented: they overfeed them. But if they are critical of you, or don't like you, they leave you alone and that means you educate yourself. They don't stop you; they don't say, "This is too rude. Don't put it in your film." There is no censorship at the AFTS; there is just harassment.

I don't mean to be too harsh about the AFTS. Everyone wants the AFTS to exist; one just wants it to be better.

Peel *is about a red-headed family who go for a drive in the country, have an argument and are too stubborn to give in and go home. What was it like working with red-headed actors?*
At a certain stage things happened rather quickly. Katie Pye said, "You have to do all the rest of my shots in one day because I am not coming out here again!"

What was great about the actors was that they were honest enough to play themselves. I have a lot of respect for them because of that. We are all much closer for what we went through.

How did you cast the children in A Girl's Own Story?
After *Peel,* I learned the lesson that it is really good to have people who are really interested in a career in film. Otherwise, no matter how good they are, if you can't afford to pay them they get terribly pissed off.

So, on *A Girl's Own Story,* I went to all the drama groups in Sydney. I also rang up some secondary schools and talked to their drama teachers, went to school plays and things like that. I met one girl in a coffee shop. It took a long time. A few people didn't want to do certain roles, like the girl who gets pregnant to her brother. The girl I originally cast couldn't handle it. She was a very innocent girl, which was what the part called for and she would have been perfect, but I didn't want anyone who was going to feel like that. She ended up with a consolation part instead.

There is a very unexpected humor in it. All of a sudden it takes these lovely digressions. What one has been absorbing as social realism becomes very baroque . . .
Yes, I am a great digressor!

Why did the obsession with relationships manifest itself in a visual way on film rather than by your writing it down?
I come from a certain background, inasmuch as my father is a theatre director and my mother is an actress. It is loathsome to go and do exactly what your parents did, so I avoided it for a long time. But I have always been interested in acting, always read a lot of scripts and plays at home to myself, and always gone to the theatre and thought about performance. So I knew a bit about performance and film was probably my favorite medium anyway. I am also a girl and I thought that if very clever, ambitious boys do this stuff, then why shouldn't girls? It sounds corny, but I really did think like that.

I had a very low opinion of what sort of career potential I had as a person, anyway. The idea that I had never admitted to myself consciously was finding a husband whom I respected and whose work I thought was wonderful. Until I went to art school in Sydney, I was undirected, mostly because I was confused about a woman's role. I am quite directed now but it has made me very sympathetic to women who are still looking for a career. I can understand being in that situation.

When did you realize that that was a problem?
When all my boyfriends ran out. There was nobody and I was by myself. I realized I could no longer attach myself to someone else and be just that: an attachment. So I said, "Okay, I'll have a go myself." And I suddenly felt this incredible new interest in life and this great excitement. I was going to dare to make mistakes, I was going to dare to put myself on the line. I started doing these crude, pornographic paintings, kind of funny as well as being pretty awful, but nobody told me off. I was working like a demon 12 hours a day and slowly they became more sophisticated. But it really was the first raw gesture, the first clues that I was starting to say anything I felt like saying. And once I got the work done, I began to see my potential. I started to give it a chance and it became really exciting. And it has been hard to stop working ever since.

Do you want to continue writing?
Not particularly. I like it if I have an idea I am excited by, but I find it difficult. I have a lot of ideas but it is a real art to tease those ideas out well. I hate to see things done badly. I worked with Gerard on *Passionless Moments.* The tone of that is much more sophisticated than anything I have written.

Did he write and you direct?
We thought up most of the scenes together and he wrote the narration. We thought it was important that only one person write it, to maintain the tone. We actually directed it together. It was a simple, little collaborative film to make, with five or six people in the crew.

How important is audience reaction to you?
I find the audience terrifying, actually! It is the making of the film that is important; the feeling that I have pulled it through and I am satisfied with it. I figure I am harder than most people to satisfy. If I think I have done as good a job as I can, that is my satisfaction. I hope an audience gets something out of it; everybody does, but I can't control it. If people see the film and like it, I feel grateful, but in a way I wish it weren't up there and I could just go on and make the next film.

Your films have already had theatrical distribution . . .
Yes, through the Dendy Cinema in Sydney. Barbara Grummels has been very supportive. It is very encouraging to think that an independent

exhibitor like her takes the trouble to support short films when there is really nothing in it for her economically.

What are the other films you want to do?
The idea I would like to do next has to do with everything I feel about being a New Zealander in New Zealand and being an expatriate New Zealander going back. It has to do with concealment and why families are separated, and with the first bad or dishonest moves in terms of the settling of New Zealand which have never been acknowledged. I will probably be working with John Maynard, who produced *Virgil*. I want to keep living adventures. I am really only ambitious as far as the next idea. I would like to think that that will one day be a feature, but who knows.

The New Filmmakers

KRISTIN WILLIAMSON/1985

"I'M NOT COMMITTED TO niceness. I'm committed to seeing what's there," said *Jane Campion.* "As a very young filmmaker I was particularly committed to what was nasty, what isn't spoken about in life. Now it's a bit more balanced."

Campion's short films have the same honesty, sensibility and visual strength as Gillian Armstrong's early films.

Peel is a blackly funny story about a red-haired family going for a miserable drive in the country. *Peel* is about very tough people who don't really understand each other," said Campion. "Katie Pye (the fashion designer) and her family were quite angry with each other at that time. But they were honest because when they read the script I'd written about them they laughed and said, 'Yes, that's us.' Not many people would admit that. The Pyes all have red hair; there's an amazing similarity. I saw the film as a family portrait."

The Pyes agreed to play themselves being stubborn, manipulative and yet loving in a cruel sort of way. It is a wonderful comment on family relationships.

Campion says the Australian Film and Television School thought *Peel* was so bad it wasn't worth finishing. But she was "arrogant" enough to believe in it and later it was a finalist in the Greater Union awards.

Next she made *Passionless Moments* with Gerard Lee. "I was living with him at the time and it was great fun to make. It's about the moments in a

---

From *National Times* (Sydney), 20 June 1985. Reprinted by permission of the author.

person's life, mostly shy unsuccessful people, when their minds drift off into silly fantasies." It won the AFI Best Experimental Film for 1984.

A Girl's Own Story, a starkly honest look at the sexual awakening of a group of convent girls in the 60s, won the Rouben Mamoulian Award at the 1984 Sydney Film Festival. This film, like several other Campion films, had a commercial run at the Dendy Cinema in Sydney.

"Are awards important to you?"

"Yes, they are really," Campion admitted with an embarrassed laugh. "It seems to make life much easier for me. Other people feel my films are worthwhile."

Campion is directing one of the dance series for the ABC at present. She is hesitant to call herself a film director until she has directed a feature. But she radiates confidence and a sense of self worth, talking often of truth and the need to "work into people's hearts."

"I've found that by doing what I want to do, even if people don't understand it, they have something to think about. Their spirits have been touched."

She admires Bunuel and Australian directors Weir, Beresford and (Mad Max) Miller. "Peter Weir has a sense of mystique, a depth, another layer. It's good to work beyond what you know consciously. I do that."

But Campion says she would never introduce herself to Weir or Beresford. "I feel very shy about talking to those establishment people and very aware of their need for privacy. I'm happy just to see their films. I don't like mentors.

"A lot of Australian films are cynical: People believe the honourable thing to do with a film is make money from it. I think that idea is revolting, but someone has to fill the K Mart gap."

She concedes that many film directors compromise on quality as they grow older, and is aware of the dangers of becoming obsessed by filmmaking. "People close to me have said I'm too obsessed. I tell myself film doesn't come first. I do.

"It's harder being a woman director because on the whole women don't have husbands or boyfriends who are willing to be like wives. I'm not looking for that type of man. I don't think I'm looking for anyone any more. I want to be quite open to whatever happens.

"I recently read a script I totally loved, a telemovie by Helen Garner. It's very exciting to find something like that. I'm particular about what I do. Honouring myself is the most important thing in the end."

Getting It in the Cannes

YVONNE PRESTON/1986

JANE CAMPION HAS NEVER been to an international film festival before. At her first, which opens in Cannes this week, the young film-maker from Australia is set to make a striking debut. Four of her films, three of them shorts she made while still at the Film and Television School, have been chosen for showing in various parts of the festival, including one in competition.

Her achievement is unprecedented and she still admits to being surprised by it as she recalls the 6 am phone call one morning in Sydney from Pierre Rissient, French film distributor and publicist, extolling her work and inviting her films to a Cannes showing.

New Zealand-born Jane, 32, doesn't quite know what to expect but she is making preparations for Cannes. She wants to know if it's pronounced Cans or Carns. As she talks at the Australian Film Commission's London office her Walkman hangs around her neck ready-loaded with a *French for Beginners* cassette. She says she has no plan of how to use her Cannes opportunity to her best advantage. "All I want to do is to make good films."

She may be young and unknown—she completed her course at the Film School just two years ago—but she has few doubts about her philosophy as a film-maker. It is essentially a philosophy, no doubt enunciated by dozens of young film-makers before her, but nonetheless firmly held, of making good films without compromising commercially.

From *The Sydney Morning Herald* (Sydney), 7 May 1986. Reprinted by permission of the author.

"I'm not committed to niceness," she says. "I am most interested in seeing the world as it really is, a world with a lot of bad, threatening, confronting things in it, and I don't believe in not seeing them there."

She dislikes work that puts the shutter on reality and sweetens it falsely. "We all have bad thoughts and unpleasantness in us. If we make films of people who don't have these things then we make ourselves lonelier. We must be honest with ourselves.

"I don't look in terms of things being good or bad, I say, that is what I see."

Much of her approach reflects a determination to present on screen the feelings of people who don't have control. Most of us are like that, she says, so it arouses automatic sympathy. A lot of people have no resources to get out of a situation and are frightened. She grins at the notion of Sylvester Stalone being too scared, in the aftermath of Libya and the threats of terrorist bombs, to go to Cannes.

Her first film, *Peel,* entered in the important official short competition at Cannes is just nine minutes long. It features a red-haired, obstreperous, belligerent family based on the family of fashion designer Katie Pye.

Her second, *Passionless Moments,* is also fully nine minutes long and in 10 little stories, tells of a succession of moments in a person's life when the mind drifts off into meaningless fantasy.

A Girl's Own Story recalls the sexual awakening of a group of 60s teenagers. And, her 75 minute feature, *Two Friends,* based on a Helen Garner script, follows the dissolution of a friendship between two young girls and will have the Australian premiere at the Sydney Film Festival. She loves Garner's work. Another film could emerge from the collaboration between the two.

At 21, Jane Campion left New Zealand for Australia and the Sydney College of Arts with a degree in anthropology. At that stage she had no clear idea of a career or even interest in one. "I'm a late developer. Until I was 25 I didn't think of a proper career."

She enjoyed the luxury of support from her parents in Wellington where her mother is an actress, her father a theatrical director. "They thought every little finger painting I did was just wonderful."

She admits that awards are important. "So long as you don't over inflate your own idea of yourself." At the moment there seems little chance of

Campion doing that. She still fronts her success with modesty and genuine amazement. "We were going to tour Europe anyway," she says. And now she finds herself en route to Cannes and perhaps even international recognition for her work—just two full years out of film school.

The Contradictions of Jane Campion, Cannes Winner

ANDREW L. URBAN/1986

JANE CAMPION, WHOSE MOVIE *Peel* has won the Golden Palm for the Best Short Subject Film at the Cannes Festival, says she is ashamed of her own propensity for contradicting herself. But in keeping with her paradoxical nature, she also likes contradictions in people.

New Zealand-born but Australian resident, Campion is in Cannes for the screenings of no fewer than three of her films in the festival's Un Certain Regard section as well as the fourth, which has just won her the main competition section. *Peel* is her first short film and was made while a first-year student at the Australian Film and Television School. Her first feature, *Two Friends* which was made for ABC TV is programmed with two short narratives, *Passionless Moments* and *A Girl's Own Story* in Un Certain Regard.

Campion, 32, has contradictory views about the praise this sort of selection attracts. "I feel some responsibility to Australian films, and they need to be visible," she says. But she doesn't think her films are fantastic. She is reluctant to pose for photos, "not because I have a small ego, far from it, but because it simply doesn't fit with what I perceive as my role. It's all right for the actors, they have to promote their image, but I am just a maker of products."

By the same token, Campion is a perfectionist; "There are lots of films better than mine . . . but they show a quirky sort of talent I suppose, an

---

From *The Australian*, 21 May 1986. Reprinted by permission of the author.

individual view." The sort of recognition gained at Cannes, she says, may bring a benefit in that "people might have more faith in me."

"I like bizarre, underground things, things you're not supposed to like," she says.

Campion says festival director Gilles Jacob has told Australian Film Commission chairman Phillip Adams: "You must give her lots of money so she'll be in competition with a feature film in two years." She is one of the most exciting talents Jacob has seen, it seems.

It was in fact the Australian Film Commission which pushed very hard to get Campion's films accepted at Cannes. Campion sees herself very much the beginner in film, and despite her tendency to be a paradox, she has clear ideas about it. When asked what sort of film she wants to make, she is adamant that there are lots of reasons for making films. "It's just a medium. People define it each time they make a film.

She says she is easy going, fascinated by Zen and she meditates, which she admits seems at odds with being a perfectionist. "Yes, I know... you have to be philosophical about perfection. The Japanese consider perfection to need a flaw. I meditate to be more relaxed and more serious about life, if you can understand that."

Campion says she doesn't like to try too hard—it shows in the work, she feels. "It's better if you aren't trying so hard... things you really badly want often go wrong; I find it best to take it easy." Her attitude is all embracing of her life, and her big, sharp blue eyes look directly at you as you speak. "I just want to be free to do anything—if I want to make an exploitation film, I will. There's nothing wrong with just entertaining people. But the way the general public is entertained is not the way I am. Sometimes it is." She says with a little smile in recognition of her contradiction. "I'll do that a lot... contradict myself... but I don't mean to."

Campion: Cannes She Do It?

ANDREW L. URBAN/1989

THE RED CARPET STRETCHES from the edge of the pavement to the top of the long, wide stairs leading into the Palais des Festivals, between thousands of people held back by rows of gendarmes.

Scaffolding holds two large platforms for the dozens of photographers on either side of the carpet just below the stairs, and the long arm of a television camera crane swoops down as the limousines pull up one after the other in the gentle warmth of the Mediterranean evening.

As each car deposits its formally dressed occupants, cheers and applause break out over the music that plays on the public address system. Cameras flash, the tv crane pans past the smiling faces, curiosity and respect blend into euphoria—this is the scenario at the Cannes Film Festival when a film is screened in the Official Competition. The sense of occasion is heightened by the public announcement of the film and its director, and by the officials greeting the VIPs at the top of the stairs. Once inside, spotlights follow the director, producer, writer, stars—whoever is there—to their specially allocated seats, as the 2000 strong audience claps. And that's BEFORE the movie starts.

It's a big moment, very different in mood from the Oscars. Here, the art of cinema is paid tribute. Here, it is the director who collects the award. Here, it is the director who is revered. Each year there are only 20 films chosen from the thousands made around the world, to come and compete at Cannes for the Palme d'Or. One of those 20 films this year is *Sweetie,* an

---

From *The Australian,* 13 April 1989. Reprinted by permission of the author.

Australian film directed by Jane Campion, who will walk up that red carpet in May as one of the celebrities of the Cannes Film Festival—which effectively means the whole darned cinema world.

Campion, while "very excited" is also very modest, and feels somewhat dwarfed by what she calls "the big boys," like Fred Schepisi, whose film *Evil Angels* (under its foreign title of *Cry in the Dark*) is also in Competition. (The Festival runs from May 11 to 21.) "I'm not a very complicated person . . . I don't see myself as working to the art house market really . . . I'm not a deep intellectual, I just have my ideas," she says.

New Zealand born but Sydney based for the past 11 years, Campion tends to undersell herself; her producer John Maynard says of her that "she's got an acute, modern sensibility and a rare honesty."

Maynard himself is chalking up an impressive track record as a producer, with *Sweetie* being his third consecutive film selected for Competition at Cannes. The first two were by another New Zealand born, Sydney based director, Vincent Ward, titled *Vigil* and *The Navigator.*

Campion too, has in fact already won a Palme d'Or, with her short film *Peel,* in 1986. That year, she also had a program of three films in another 'by invitation' section of the Festival, Un Certain Regard: it was an unprecedented debut for any film maker.

It was coming to Cannes in 1986 that gave Campion "a lot of confidence" and although she was subsequently offered several projects, "nothing else tempted me." *Sweetie* was an idea that engaged her; it has something to do with contemporary relationships, she says with characteristic imprecision. "I felt I hadn't fully realised—in the sense of achieved—what I was moving towards, until *Sweetie.*"

Campion describes it as a film about meetings and relationships, and "more of an experience than a story." By the same token, there is a story, and it's about the love affair between Kay and Louis, two bank clerks, and Kay's older sister Sweetie, "the one who is very heavily deluded."

Campion made her central characters bank clerks "so people wouldn't come to easy conclusions. One day I saw a story in the paper about two very square looking brothers—salesmen, I think—and the caption said they spent a lot of time meditating. It just reinforced what I think . . . people don't wear uniforms to say what's underneath . . . we're all as complex as each other." The film also has "an Australian flavour. I love Australians, there is a kind of frankness about them, especially out of the cities, they are so warm and genuine. I find them totally adorable." But above all, she says, "*Sweetie* is me trying to work out what's going on in the 80s, and in a way it's about new age spirituality, love and delusions . . . and occasional moments of reality—and how these are precious.

"It's the way it's made, I think, that's different. The links between scenes are surprising, and the way it's shot."

Cinematographer Sally Bongers is the first woman in Australia to shoot a 35 mm feature film: it was Bongers who shot *Peel,* too. The film was written by Campion with Gerard Lee, with whom she studied at the Australian Film Television and Radio School, where they co-wrote another award winning short film, *Passionless Moments.* It was also at the School that Campion made *Peel.*

Genevieve Lemon plays Sweetie, Tom Lycos plays Louis, Dorothy Barry (of the singing duo The Barry Sisters) makes her acting debut as Flo, John Darling (actor, poet, photographer, carpenter, bush lover) plays Gordon, and Karen Colston plays Kay.

Colston trained at the Q Theatre in Penrith, but "when she first auditioned for Kay," says Campion, "Karen was working as a salad bar assistant in David Jones. By the time she was short listed, she was in Sweden on an indefinite holiday. With great cool, and characteristic strong faith, Karen flew back, auditioned twice, and got the part."

The whole casting process was performed by Campion and her small creative team, not given out to a casting agency. "Because we were naïve to that area, yet open, I think we came up with a very distinctive cast, none of whom had been in a feature film before."

It was typical of Campion's preference for working under-planned: she prefers to work on intuition. This also influenced the way the script was written, to provide maximum freedom. "We consciously wrote Sweetie for a low budget," says Campion, "to explore areas a big budget film can't. So we had no obligation to look big. I thought if we didn't ask for a lot of money, people would let us try something unusual. And I thought it would be fantastic to make the film with the generation of film makers I had grown up with. For most of us it was our first feature."

At around $1 million, it will probably be the cheapest film in competition this year. "Perhaps it means I can make a film with a bigger budget," says Campion.

In fact, Campion is going on to direct *To the Island* a three part drama, coproduced by John Maynard and New Zealander Bridget Ikin, based on the internationally famous autobigraphies of Janet Frame. It will also be released as a 150 minute feature film and will be shot in New Zealand, beginning in July, by which time Campion will have had the red carpet treatment at Cannes.

Jane Campion

PHILIPPA HAWKER/1989

SWEETIE, THE FIRST THEATRICAL feature from director Jane Campion, has been selected for the main competition at Cannes. Written with Gerard Lee, her collaborator on *Passionless Moments,* it tells the story of Kay and Louis, whose relationship is disrupted by the arrival of Kay's sister, Sweetie, and the events that follow. Four of Campion's short films were invited to Cannes in 1986, and *Peel* won the Palme d'Or for the best short film. She has also directed a telefeature, *2 Friends,* from a script by Helen Garner.

PHILIPPA HAWKER: *Where did* Sweetie *begin?*

JANE CAMPION: Last time I was invited to Cannes with the four short films and it was a big surprise to me—it came out of the blue. I had been thinking about some feature ideas but I just didn't know how possible it was to pursue my own line. I thought I'd have to start making my features look like normal ones. I think the Cannes Film Festival and other festivals I attended, where I watched the audiences watch the films—something I hadn't done very much previously—made me aware that they seemed to like that kind of work. It gave me the confidence to want to give them more and to experiment with my own style. I also felt intuitively, that I wanted to do something modern and something that pursued the interests of my own film generation, the one I went through film school with.

From *Cinema Papers* (Melbourne), May 1989. Reprinted by permission of MTV Publishing, Ltd.

Slowly, during the year I was overseas, I kept going back to that thing. I had some projects in front of it and I pushed them aside saying, "I don't want to do them now, it's time to do something modern, something about the Eighties."

One of those projects was a piece called *The Piano Lesson,* which I felt was a mature work and also more expensive, whereas *Sweetie* could be done quite cheaply, and I thought that would be an appropriate thing to do first—and I could work with people my generation on it. People probably wouldn't take that sort of risk with *Piano Lesson,* they wouldn't want to use someone from my generation as a DOP, for example.

Sweetie itself started with the idea of trying to talk about relationships that don't work, particularly relationships where people feel they're in love but it's not happening, or they feel love but they don't want to have sex any more. I wanted the lead girl, the main character, to be extremely superstitious, so she had a sort of uncertainty or fear of the world and the only way should could control that was through superstition. It's not abnormal though, it's the normal level of superstition that many people have.

And although we don't go into it very deeply, I thought it would be good to have it that people meditate, not as an unusual thing but as a matter of course—part of the fabric of life. I'd been involved with meditation and workshops and I found it was very prevalent, though people don't admit it. So many of my friends were searching for some depth in their life, trying this and trying and that and it always seemed incredibly humorous when we looked at it. That's what it started with but it's not so heavily in there now.

When did the character of Sweetie *come in?*
The character was conceived at the beginning. I read one of those stories about how you put a script together, a manual really, and it said that you write out the storyline in three or four pages. I think I was about ready to do it then, so I ran downstairs and sat at the table and wrote it out. She turned up then. It was an experience that both Gerard [Lee] and I had with somebody, so it was fairly familiar. There was a dark side and a funny side to it, which I liked. And since I'd had such fun writing with Gerard before, and I really love his writing. It's a lot faster writing with somebody else. I was overseas at the time and I came back and rang up Gerard and asked

him if he'd like to work with me, because I felt he knew a lot of the ideas, and because we'd lived together before and shared experiences—it would only be fair to offer it to him. When he came into it obviously it changed again and he was invaluable. You can't underestimate what it is to occupy another human being's mind with a project, you're renting space in their brain basically. He made endless contributions in terms of characters, scenes, dialogue, ideas about how to get round problems, encouragement...

How long did it take to write the script?
It didn't take very long. We started in February '87 and we had a final draft by the end of May. And we didn't work together all that time, we did it in bursts. We rented a beach house for a couple of weeks and talked it out to start with. I tried to make it as fun as possible.

Did you have particular strategies, or difficulties in the writing?
We felt that getting the right tone was the key so we wrote lots of scenes until we felt we had them speaking in the right way. There are so many other things that affect tone, of course: the way they speak, the dialogue, heaps of things help to create it and change it and mould it. Gerard and I kept on writing scenes until one of us hit on something that we thought had a good feeling about it. Once we understood what that was we could just keep doing it. And all along the way you find actors that are going to fit that tone. It changes slightly as you go on, of course.

You're always trying to raise your expectations all the time, raise the game with those various elements and make yourself beyond what you were, raise your aspirations in all sorts of ways at once.

Other people make that possible. I was very keen to work with cinematographer Sally Bongers on the film because we have a very complementary ways of seeing things and it's easy for us to understand each other. We talked quite a bit about how it would be write to shoot it. The art department contributed a lot, and Peter Long put together a lot of visual references for me and that was very stimulating.

[Producer] John Maynard was there from the beginning, He had said he was very keen to produce something with me and we'd known each other for years, before I'd even thought about making films. So we had his support right from the beginning, and got the funding and was really encouraging. The other producer, Billy MacKinnon, was the script editor.

What does the transition to a 35mm feature involve for you?
A lot of people who had been making short films at the same time as me were making their first features and feeling dissatisfied with them. They didn't have enough time, they were pressured into budgets that weren't adequate: not enough shooting time, not enough pre-production, not enough time to make it special. I was very aware of that. You have to be canny enough to know what you need.

I hyperventilated for about two weeks after I found out we'd got the money. I felt really frightened—not that I looked frightened, but I felt it deeply somewhere. It took me about two weeks to settle down. *Two Friends* gave me the confidence to know that I could get through a five-week shoot, but I knew *Sweetie* was going to be more difficult.

How did you go about casting it?
I wasn't hard to find Sweetie. We came across Geneviève Lemon early on, and realized there would only be one actress in every generation and we had to try and keep her; she's the most wonderful actress and gorgeous girl.

We did the casting ourselves—me and Tina Andreef, my assistant. Neither of us had done it before and we thought we couldn't afford a casting agent, so it was a huge learning job for us. I'm working with casting agents at the moment, and I don't think I'd ever appreciate what they do as much if I hadn't had to do it myself.

The hard thing was learning what we needed. It was very difficult, because you think you know things and you don't. I'd think about Kay and who she should be, but every actress I met seemed to come up with something good. In the end I let the people suggest themselves to me, I tried to stay open, and I began to learn what was appropriate.

When Karen Colston came in I felt very excited about her because she had this really great innocent quality, earnest and innocent. She's got a gorgeous sense of humour as well, but she was cunning enough not to let to know me about it. I wrote out what I was expecting for Kay, and one of the things was that I thought she should be really pale-skinned, and I thought Karen had put something on her face, she was so white, I thought she must have read what I'd written.

It was hard with the older actors, because when actors are 60 or so and have been working a long time you can hear that in them. At the same time our older people had really big parts, and we wondered how people who hadn't had much experience would handle it. Flo [the mother of Sweetie and Kay] ended up being a country'n'Western singer who'd never acted before, but she had such a lovely quality, we all adored her right from the beginning. We wondered if she could make those darker moments, but there's always that question—you can't see everything at the beginning.

It was the same with Gordon [the father]—we went with this guy who had these amazing eyebrows, and this ability to seem fresh all the time. We were really concerned about his memory, whether he'd be able to remember the lines, and he was too, it turned out. He'd stay up all night worrying about it. But he was great. I think once you've decided to go with someone you feel so relieved that the choice is made, and they start to shine. You've got to expect that they will work to get something, you got to trust them to do that, which is quite hard because directors don't like to trust anything.

How did things change in post-production?
The script's one thing, and then you get everyone into rehearsal and they add something, and then when you get there on the day you've had time to add even more, and then when you get into the editing room, you think, "Why didn't I do that, why didn't I add something more?"

There were surprises in the editing room when it came to dealing with the material. I'd never dealt with that much material before, and the editor, Veronika Haussler, who edited *Passionless Moments* with me, had never done drama before, let alone 35mm; but she's got a fantastic instinct, and we just figured it out for ourselves.

I expected to push the material round and tell it what to do but I found that it was the other way round. The best way was simply to respond to what the material told you it wanted to do—I had a very small will in the matter. By far the best way to go was to be honest about what was there and feel out of that what could be there. If you tried to go against it, everything would go wrong.

You never knew what it was going to feel like next. You'd do all these cuts which seemed like the obvious thing to do and you'd screen it and you'd never have imagined what the result would be. I'd no idea how the relationships would come up and they came up a lot stronger than I thought they were going to: the dynamics of the characters was what led the story in the end, and the more you fixed up characters and made them stronger, every scene they were in started to sparkle or would start to really stand out. I never expected it to be that way, but it's a very character-led story, I suppose. I expected to be able to predict the feeling that came out, but I found that I couldn't.

Where does that element of surprise fit in with the need for control?
In the end you have to drop all your schemes and plans and respond to it. Obviously I'm still the manipulator of tone, and if I think the tone is not clear I can try to clarify it. Or if I think something can be taken two ways and that's not a good thing, I can try to make the material make a stand one way or the other.

You can't recreate the tone, you have to go with what's there. But at the beginning of the film I felt there was an ambiguity, people could think we were very serious and we were actually quite tongue-in-cheek. The whole film perhaps has got a bit more gravity than the script, and because of that the early stuff looked like you could mistake it for us being serious, not knowing what we were doing. I was very clear that somehow I had to alter that tone. People had to know that the voice of the filmmakers was that we knew we were being ironic. In the end we chose to do it with music. There are lots of ways you can alter things, but you have to know you need to. In the editing room I could feel that it was ambiguous. But the music added humour and irony.

I had the idea that I would like to have accapella music in it, that everything had to be hand-made sound, and someone put me onto a group called the Cafe at Gates of Salvation. They sent us a demo tape, and we just loved it. They write their own stuff too and that was wonderful, because we couldn't afford copyrighted stuff. I love accapella because I feels very straightforwardly emotional—just human beings singing. It gave something that was what we were aspiring to with *Sweetie,* something very humble.

Campion Goes Out on a Limb—Again

RUTH HESSEY/1989

JANE CAMPION SEEMS SO down to earth. The countrified lilt of her New Zealand accent, her clear eyes, straight hair and easy way of speaking belie the unsettling originality of her work. She made three short films which established her reputation—*Passionless Moments, A Girl's Own Story,* and *Peel* which won the Palme d'Or for Best Short Film at Cannes in 1986—before she even graduated from the Australian Film Television and Radio School.

She emerged into the international limelight as a film-maker with a unique vision before anyone in Australia quite realised she was here. In fact at Film School where Campion and cinematographer Sally Bongers were regarded as people whose films were going to be forgotten as soon as they were made, Campion resigned herself to the idea of being unemployable.

Now she is working on a new mini-series in New Zealand based on the autobiographies of Janet Frame, and she has finished her first feature film, *Sweetie,* which once again attracted a great deal of baffled interest at Cannes.

Unlike the first feature film attempt of most whiz kid short film-makers, *Sweetie* is as daring in its unconventionality as any of her earlier work.

"With *Sweetie* I wanted to create a film that had more interior to it, because I think we all have an interior life," she said during a quick trip to Sydney.

From *The Sydney Morning Herald* (Sydney), 5 July 1989. Reprinted by permission of the author.

"You can have a terrible day, and your boyfriend can leave you, but you look in the mirror and you look the same. What's happening inside is so big for you, yet on the surface you are making cups of tea. You don't want anyone to know what's going on in there. I think the surface reality most of us end up living can be quite dominating and oppressive. There's a lot going on below that."

Consequently this film, which was made for a modest $1 million, entirely eschews the tested formula which people like Yahoo Serious have used to impress Hollywood backers and mass audiences alike.

"I find the Australian version of the big film doesn't relate to me in any way," Campion said. "I feel a bit let down when I go to the movies these days. I don't really feel they relate to how I feel about life."

Not that there is anything particularly eccentric about the way Campion feels about life. Her films are filled with the most banal images of the ordinary world. But in the way they are lit and shot, everyday settings assume the alien quality of subterranean caves. The unexpected lurks behind the Hills Hoist. In *Sweetie* it's as if a bolt of lightening has struck the backyard and something strange and unnerving is coming up among the cracks.

"Money is so conservative," Campion said. "I felt that with a budget the size we had, we had a right to take a risk, to make something that is thoughtful and different. Just to do anything we thought would work without really knowing if it was going to."

In fact *Sweetie* embodies the sort of luxury most film-makers won't risk, even when reputations are firmly established. But the risk is irrelevant. Campion says she did not enjoy her one stab at making a "normal film," *After Hours,* which won the IXL Elder Award at the Melbourne International Festival in 1984.

"I just don't like that film. I can feel the worminess in it, and I really learnt my big lesson with it. I've got to do work that is right for me. With all the energy that went into it I kept feeling I was robbing myself or cheating myself.

"It's like the difference between how you might speak at a party to a group of people where you are more on guard and how you might open yourself up with friends. You know how that feels inside yourself. How much more rewarding that really close or interesting conversation is."

This is quite a good description of Campion's work. In some ways, it's difficult because it's so personal, and refuses to spoon feed the viewer with the stock vocabulary of commercial film. Yet it's far from elitist in its concern for the reality of humdrum suburban life.

In *Sweetie,* Kay, who appears to be the central character for the first half of the film, finds her attempt at happiness and an ordinary life thwarted by the inner truckload of secret fears. After visiting a fortune teller Kay decides that Louis (Tom Lycos), who has a curl in the middle of his forehead like a question mark, is the man she has been looking for. Kay and Louis move in together.

It's a fairly ordinary situation, but halfway through it starts to change. What starts out as a personal odyssey opens out to embrace the dynamic of a family, and Kay's story becomes much more interesting in the context of the stories of her sister, Sweetie, and father and mother.

"Everybody has a family and there's a legacy you carry from that. I was lucky to have good, encouraging parents, but it wasn't until my late 20s that I realised how similar I was getting to Mum," Campion said. "Suddenly you realise that you haven't left your family behind at all, that you've been carrying them with you, and you've been living under the illusion that you haven't. What I think about families is that they're incredibly funny at times and yet there is a tragic underbelly."

In *Sweetie* the underbelly is personified by the rampant libidinous Sweetie herself, played with wonderful humor and willfulness by Genevieve Lemon.

"Sweetie," said Campion of her semi-monstrous creation, is so wild and able to be intimate and warm and sexual with people—things that her sister Kay is very frightened about. But then she was ludicrously encouraged as a child performer with probably very moderate ability, and loved for it, and she's addicted to that sort of attention and love and she's never able to get enough of it."

Sweetie's insatiable appetite for life becomes a headache for her family, even leading it to crack up under the pressure. But it's the kind of crack, like the one in the backyard where the uprooted Hills Hoist once lived, that can bring forth good.

Apart from Lemon, Campion took as many risks with her casting as her shooting and scripting. Some don't pay off in conventional terms, but they do contribute to an unusual suburban authenticity.

"The casting was a bit scary," Campion admits. "With the Mum and Dad for example we found actors in their age group were just too theatrical. They didn't have a naivety, an innocence, and openness that Dorothy

Barry and Jon Darling had. Dorothy and Jon weren't very experienced but I responded to them as people. I felt they had a quality which was really special if we could get it."

Karen Colston, who trained at the Q Theatre, had no film experience when she stepped into the role of Kay, but she appealed to the director because she was "very instinctive, she worked right from her feelings."

There is something heroic about Jane Campion's low-key willingness to go out on a limb in the pursuit of some special feeling or quality in a story, or a character, or even a moment on film. It seems fitting that the ideas for her next film have been inspired by that diadem of feminine aesthetic, *Wuthering Heights*.

"The boys at Film School all dreamed about making epics, which at that stage, was my idea of a horror story," Campion said with a laugh. "I like to start with details and get them right—but I can feel myself moving towards that.

"I love the Bronte sisters—the tragic vein of their work. I want to explore that romantic tradition. I don't mean in a soppy way, but in the true meaning of the morality of that tradition—the right for people to decide to follow their passions.

Jane Campion's approach to casting was recognized last night when *Sweetie* was nominated in five categories of the 1989 AFI Awards. The nominations include Best Lead Actress and Best Supporting Actress.

Two Interviews with Jane Campion

MICHEL CIMENT/1989

THESE TWO ENCOUNTERS WITH Jane Campion took place three years apart from each other. The first was in Paris a few months after the presentation of her shorts and her work for television *Two Friends* at the Cannes Film Festival 1986 (in the "A certain glance" section), which had amazed us with the audacity of their style, their extreme sensibility and the singularity of their universe. The second was in Cannes last year after the projection of *Sweetie* which confirmed her immense talent.

Jane Campion has the impertinence, the vivacity, the charm of her films. She often accompanies her comments with a crazy communicative laugh; this moviemaker knows how to look at the world with warmth, but also with a humor that is sometimes cruel. Whatever the very real qualities of *Sex, Lies and Videotapes,* there is no doubt that *Sweetie* (completely ignored in the list of award winners) deserved the Palme d'Or given the criterion that Wim Wenders and his jury had chosen: spotlight a very personal first feature of modest budget. Such a choice would have without a doubt created controversy, but also would have shown true audacity. But with or without awards, Jane Campion will make her way and *Sweetie* has already established itself as a work of originality and mastery.

Interview: Cannes, 17 May 1989. From *Positif,* January 1990. Translated by Michele Curley. Reprinted by permission of *Positif* and the author.

Short and Medium-length Films

You were born in New Zealand. What kind of environment were you raised in?
My parents were in theater and their families had lived in New Zealand for many generations. My mother was an actor, my father a director, and they had both trained in England. They formed a company in New Zealand which put on Shakespeare and they toured the country. When I was born they stopped and settled in Wellington, the capital where I grew up. Then they did farming because they were tired of dealing with problems of theater where they didn't earn very much money. From time to time they got back on stage. At home, conversation revolved around classical plays they put on and the role of actors. I myself was passionate about theater and I tried it in high school. My brother, my sister and I competed for the attention of our parents, but we were all good friends at that age. When I was sixteen I went to the university. I grew up both in the city and in the country because cities are near fields in New Zealand.

Why were you never attracted to the theater?
Little by little I became very critical of the theater. The actors I met seemed artificial, unnatural. I decided to attach myself to something more serious and I wanted to go to university in Australia. It's the kind of decision you make when you're sixteen. I studied anthropology after having tried psychology and education which didn't really please me. My degree didn't really lead me anywhere but we had a fantastic professor, a Dutchman by the name of Power. He had studied with Lévi-Strauss—and we discussed structural anthropology and linguistic problems. What interested me about anthropology was to be able to "officially" study what I was curious about anyway: how our thoughts function, their mythic content which has nothing to do with logic, human behaviors. I believe, moreover, that I have an anthropological eye, a sense of observation. In anthropology I loved both the theory and the poetry.

Nonetheless, your short films are different from a lot of Australian films which take into account the presence of Aborigines, the role of myths. You are closer to a behavioral study of characters.
I don't think that the great myths of the Aborigines are really a part of Australian culture. People talk about them, but superficially. I'm very interested in them as in everything that touches humans, but they are not

a part of my universe. On the other hand I think that humans believe themselves to be rational beings when they are not, they are governed by something completely different. And that's what interests me. So I finished my studies and got my degree. But I realized that if I continued in that field I would have to express myself in a way that would only be understood by other anthropologists. But I wanted to communicate with people and find common symbols, which you can do by telling stories. So I decided to go to Europe. It's there my heritage was located, the history I had learned in school. I was curious to discover what it really was like. I also wanted to learn how to paint, which I did in London while working as an assistant on a film. But I didn't much like that city, though I stayed for a year. I returned to Australia because the tuition at the School of plastic arts, as well as the cost of living in general, was too expensive in London. Everybody seemed a little lost when I was studying art, even the professors! On the other hand, my experience at the College of Arts in Sydney was marvelous. The teachers were young. They had a clear idea of what they wanted and, they weren't burdened by all the traditions that prevailed in England. What interested me was the relationship of art and life, how one reacts visually to an experience.

What style of painting did you do?
I wanted to paint what was important to me and I ended up telling little stories on canvas. It was figurative. Since I also loved writing, I made my paintings into legends. At the same time I put on plays that told stories of love, of disappointing experiences. They were filmed on video and I played the roles. I realized they were very bad and I didn't like myself as an actor. So I decided to make some movies myself in super 8 by directing actors in roles I had written for them. It was very ambitious on my part since I knew nothing about film, everything came from a manual. But I was very motivated because I insisted on telling my stories. The results were hardly satisfying since the super 8 demanded a lot of precision and I lacked experience. So I made two films. One was called *Tissues* and ran about twenty minutes, the second *Eden*—I never really finished it since I never added sound. *Tissues* announced *A Girl's Own Story.* People liked it because I put a lot of energy into it, but visually it was horrible because I didn't really understand what a shot was!

What were your tastes in cinematography?
I wasn't really a cinema buff. I went to the movies at random. But I remember that I was completely crazy about Buñuel, I tried to see everything he made. I also loved people like Antonioni and Bertolucci. On the whole I was more attracted to European cinema or people like Kurosawa than the world of Hollywood.

After the College of Arts, what did you decide to do?
I didn't know what would be the next stage. I didn't see how I could connect with film industry people or with people from the Australian Film Corporation. One day they seem to have faith in you and the next they no longer believe in you . . . So I decided to attend the Australian Film and TV School and I tried from the first day to make as many short films that I could during the three years that I was there. I made *Peel* the first year, *Passionless Moments* the second and the third year and *A Girl's Own Story* the third year.

What was the idea behind your first film Peel*?*
I knew a family which was extremely unusual, and I thought it would be interesting to film them. They were people who didn't seem to be able to control themselves. I would suggest scenes for them, and since they were very honest, they realized that they revealed their true nature in these scenes. It's a very short film of about nine minutes.

Passionless Moments *was more elaborate.*
It was the result of a collaboration with one of my friends, Gerard Lee. It was his idea at the beginning and we wrote and directed the film together. Once we had the frame of the film—a series of playlets—, we tried to imagine the maximum number of stories that would be told with a certain ironic distance. We finally wrote ten of them. Gerard and I wanted to show sweet, ordinary people that you rarely see on the screen and who have more charm than better known actors. The film was shot in five days, two episodes per day. I was also responsible for the photography and I realized the benefit of film school where in two hours I had learned how to light and to exploit the possibilities of the camera.

All these short films have in common the sense of observation, the choice of moments, of epiphanies where behaviors reveal themselves.

That always interested me. I remember that at film school my classmates wanted to make big movies or spectacular scenes with car crashes. That was the last thing I wanted to do.

You love Katherine Mansfield, your countrywoman, who was also interested in the observation of details?
Yes. I love her books. When I was a child in New Zealand, I played next to her monument which was in a park near our house.

To what extent is A Girl's Own Story *inspired by your childhood and adolescence?*
I wanted to pay homage to that period of our lives when we feel lost and alone. It's very characteristic of youth. It's a very curious stage in our development where we feel adult emotions but we lack experience. With experience it's easier to face our emotions. The smallest things seem immense obstacles when you are very young. I had lived many experiences that I had never seen represented. For example in class everybody kissed each other and as soon as we grew up we stopped doing it. Everyone pretended that it had never happened. I also wanted to talk about the Beatles whose music touched my generation since I was born in 1954. The episode of incest wasn't a personal experience but I remember a very young neighbor who got pregnant by a classmate and the scandal that it created.

Did the actors bring you material or was everything written from the start?
Of course the actors always contribute a little. But in this particular case the adolescents thought I was very bizarre and swore they had never done anything similar. In fact they essentially recited the text. I had a hard time finding actors. The first one I chose did not feel at all at ease with the incest. She was too immature and I had to get someone older but who appeared younger than her age. The shooting officially ran ten days, but I was able to "steal" extra time. The whole crew was formed by students and we didn't have a lot of experience but the film was well-received in Australia and even won some prizes. When it was shown in theaters, the reaction was very good, people laughed a lot, so much so that it was hard to hear the dialogue. That moved me because my professors had never supported my work. They were very conservative people who thought that type of film was too strange to allow me to get a job.

It was after leaving school that you made After Hours.
Yes. On the basis of my short films, the Women's Film Unit suggested that I write and make this film. I don't like *After Hours* a lot because I feel like the reasons for making it were impure. I felt a conflict between the project and my artistic conscience. The film, commissioned by Women Production Unity, had to be openly feminist since it spoke about the sexual abuse of women at work. I wasn't comfortable because I don't like films that say how one should or shouldn't behave. I think that the world is more complicated than that. I prefer watching people, studying their behavior without blaming them. I would have preferred to have put this film in a closet but it toured the world! I like making movies that I would like to see as a spectator and that's not the case with *After Hours,* but it was important for me to do it.

You then made an episode of Dancing Daze *for ABC.*
It was a commission, light entertainment for television. I was in the process of writing a project for a television series on the New Zealander writer Janet Frame and I wanted to know what it was like to work for television. It was an interesting experience, even though I don't care much for the film. However, it allowed me to meet Jan Chapman who later produced *Two Friends.* I was obliged to work fast and to make a fifty minute film in seven days with songs and dance numbers. It was the classic story of a group of young people who in 1986 want to form a dance troupe. I had to be visually inventive, which amused me and gave me confidence that I could do commercial films.

A little later you made Two Friends.
It had to be quick, because ABC had a crew available and an opening in their production plan. The preparation was short. Helen Gardner's screenplay was proposed to me by, as I told you, the producer Jan Chapman. We agreed on objectives and we had a relationship of trust. I also liked the script a lot even if the idea of telling a story by going back in time was not what I would have chosen. What I loved was the freshness of observation and the truth of the situations. I felt I could get something out of it. Helen Gardner had been inspired by the experiences of her daughter and one of her friends. I went to Melbourne to meet them. The student who played the role of the daughter had blond hair and we thought she wasn't serious

enough. We gave her brown hair and cut it like a boy's. I think that on the whole it's not too difficult to work with adolescents even if there are certain days when their emotions are very confused.

How do objects, which are numerous in your films, help the actors in their work?
I like first to observe what they do normally in life and I remind them of it when we shoot so that their acting is natural, comes from real-life experience.

Do you often oversee the camerawork?
I like to look in the viewfinder because I am very precise about the frame that I want. During the shooting of *Two Friends,* the crew under the director of photography felt some resentment towards me because they weren't used to a director who deals with things like that. My director of photography didn't understand what I wanted very well and I had to be very obstinate to impose my views. On the other hand, with Sally Bongers, a friend who studied with me and who shot *Peel* and *A Girl's Own Story,* I had a very good relationship. For *Two Friends,* by contrast. I had to use the television crew. They were very competent, but we very simply had different methods of shooting.

Do you do a lot of takes?
No. For *Two Friends* for example we decided on a visual style. We knew that there would not be close-ups, and as soon as the actors played the scene with the right tone we went on to the next shot. I didn't thus "cover" myself. It was a very economical shoot on the whole.

Do you plan to continue to focus in on intimate stories?
I hope that there will always be the same sense of observation in my films since I think that it's a strength, but I'm not sure that my stories will stay intimate. I have a big desire to work on a larger scale with more powerful stories, different materials. I'm presently working on a project that comes close to the spirit and the atmosphere of a Grimm's fairy tale. It's a love story situated in New Zealand around 1850 with a rather dark tone.

Did you choose to portray youth in A Girl's Own Story *and* Two Friends *because it was reassuring for you in your first work to deal with themes that were familiar to you?*

In the case of *A Girl's Own Story,* I had a desire to explore a universe that I knew well. I also like young people very much: I think they're free and generous with themselves. But it's not an obsession on my part! Of course now whenever someone writes a story with young girls in it, they think of me to make a movie out of it. But each generation interests me. In fact I would like to tell all sorts of stories. I'm currently rereading *Treasure Island* and I'm getting a lot of pleasure out of it. I like its force, its audacity, but also its sense of observation. In any case, I always remember to maintain a certain irony.

Sweetie

What have you done in the three years that separate your short films from Sweetie*?*

After the screening of my films at the Cannes Film Festival, I thought about what I was going to take on given that some possibilities opened up for me. The first project that I wanted very much to do was *Sweetie* because it seemed to be based on the most modern and provocative point of view. Moreover, it was financially doable. I also thought that after a more "serious" film it would be difficult to make *Sweetie*! I have a provocative side and I was very happy to take on this subject. I began to develop this story with my co-screenwriter Gerard Lee, the friend who had already written *Passionless Moments* with me and who is someone who is very intelligent. It was a topic that he was very familiar with, that belonged to both of us, and we were on the same wavelength. It took me three years to make *Sweetie* because during that period I also developed other projects. One was *The Piano,* a very romantic story in the tone of the Brontë sisters that I would like to make later. I also worked on *Janet Frame* which will be my next film. This will be a portrait of a New Zealand author who wrote various autobiographical volumes which revolve around what it means to grow up and what it means to create. I love the style of her autobiographical trilogy: *To the Island,* which concerns her childhood, is full of freshness and is the most seductive of the three. *An Angel at My Table* and *An Envoy to Mirror City* include many events that take place in Europe. It's for that that I recently made some trips to your continent to scout locations. I will shoot it for television in three one-hour parts with the possibility of making a film version.

Did you have difficulty in financing Sweetie?
Finding money to write these three projects was not difficult. As for the production of *Sweetie,* it was done without too many problems since the film was very cheap, less than a million dollars. The screenplay was written with this in mind. It had been inspired by people and events that I was familiar with. I always work like that. It gives me more confidence to write and even if I then stray from these experiences, I always have a base which I can go back to. The character of *Sweetie* was inspired by a man, but for family reasons we changed gender. That was disappointing to me at the beginning, but I respected the feelings of my co-screenwriter. What I loved about *Sweetie* was all the potential there was in her and the way in which it crumbled. That happens to all of us. One day we explore what we could be, then that day passes and it's too late. It's a poignant character with hope.

In one sense Kay is the central character. The others join in the story progressively, first Louis, then Sweetie, *then her parents.*
We called the film *Sweetie* because it was a pretty title, not because she's the heroine of the story. Kay evolves, she feels more courageous. I also believe that you cannot love without having a real base; otherwise you only love an illusion and that doesn't work. But most of us somehow create illusions around what we do. We have an idea in our head of what our partner is like and the fact that they are different from this idea is hard to accept.

Did you always have the idea of beginning with the voice over what's going on in Kay's head?
No. In the beginning I thought I would start with some shots of trees. They were beautiful shots but I thought that that would disorientate the audience, that they had too many elements to put together. At the same time, when I make movies, I have the impression that I can do anything, that I am completely free as long as it contributes to the story, as long as it makes sense. I like things to be fresh and surprising. With Kay's voice-over, we wanted to indicate from the start that we weren't only interested in what the characters do but also in what they think and feel.

In what part of Australia does the action take place?
Essentially in Willoughby, a suburb north of Sydney. The scenes where they go to visit their mother were shot in Warren in the north-west of

South Wales, a fantastic city, a cotton-growing and sheep-raising center. I loved shooting there. We trampled the earth to give it the arid, desert-like look of certain regions of Australia where we didn't have the means to shoot.

In Kafka's The Metamorphoses, *all is seen from the point of view of the "abnormal" son. Here it's more the view of the family who are faced with* Sweetie*'s otherness.*

I thought however that from time to time I would be good to hear what Sweetie thinks or feels, like the moment when the family leaves to go west and where, by her reaction, you understand what a baby she is. Her father is a traitor and a bastard who creates hope in vain. He knows that if he takes Sweetie away he can never bring his wife back. I remember that the actor who played the part of Gordon had the same reactions as his character: he really felt in a fix at that time!

Did you study psychiatric cases, read books on the subject?

No, not really. We had living examples around us. And we talked with a lot of people that we knew who had gone mad. We also sent Geneviève Lemon to a reeducation center to observe the patients. We wanted her to feel the menace. She had a hard time dealing with the experience: there was one patient in particular who threatened her continuously with a razor blade. I can't say that we researched thoroughly, but on the other hand we borrowed a lot from personal experiences. It's a subject I thought about for about a year. I didn't want us to feel obliged to use the usual narratives: we deal rather more with mental states or emotions. I wanted to speak about the difficulty of loving while subtly introducing darker currents. It's then that I had the idea of superstition. I also wanted to use metaphors because I think that people think in metaphors a lot more often than one imagines and you don't often see that on the screen. That gave an additional dimension to the film.

Then I thought about what kind of story we wanted to tell. It was then that Gerard and I got a little money together, went to a beach house for fifteen days, and discussed it all while both acting out the different roles. What seemed important to us was finding the tone of each scene, the way in which the people were going to speak. The development of the screenplay was organic. I didn't know that Sweetie was going to eat ceramic horses until I got to that part of the story; then I asked myself what she would do. We never knew what the next step would be before getting there. It's really true that we had a hard time reorganizing the story: it was like a chain whose links cannot be moved out of place.

Did you work on dialogue with the actors?
Everything was written but we rehearsed a lot which was especially useful to get to know them and help them gain confidence in me, so that we learned also how to support each other. It was also an opportunity to explore all the possibilities of their roles. Each actor is different and I worked with their differences. Genevieve likes to be told everything she should do. I had to trick her, put her in situations where she discovered by herself what we needed. Karen Colston on the other hand knows exactly at every moment who she is and what she needs. My method with her was to ask her opinion about what Kay would do and think at this or that moment. In general she got it right every time. What's interesting is that in life Genevieve is a very strong and intelligent woman.

The subject could have given rise to a film of sordid reality. But you film ugliness and vulgarity by stylizing them.
The director deliberately created drab and ugly sets. We thought about interiors by considering the fact that people bring their furniture to apartments they move into while keeping objects that belonged to former tenants so that there is a mix of styles. What is ugly can also be viewed with elegance by lighting or framing. It's a mark of sympathy. It's more poignant for me than a "pretty" set that offers many fewer possible contrasts.

Your frames are stunning. Are they pre-planned or are you inspired by the filming?
I had nothing to lose, it was a small budget and we could be audacious, take some risks. We were shooting for our own pleasure. Many things were spelled out ahead of time. Sally Bongers, my cinematographer, thinks like me. We talk a lot, drink tea, laugh, imagine shots, look around us to borrow things. We are both very visually oriented and our esthetic senses are very close. Sally also has a lot of good sense regarding scenes: she frames to highlight the dramatic situation and the emotions involved but she's also careful not to attract too much of the audience's attention to the

photography. We made some mistakes of this kind. In certain scenes you don't feel as if the characters are speaking to each other since they were on opposite sides of the frame! We had to re-shoot them. I am good friends with Sally Bongers which doesn't prevent us from arguing because of the control that each of us wants to exert. She is very stubborn, very strong and sometimes wants certain things. And since I resemble her, and I sometimes have opposing ideas, conflict is inevitable! They aren't really disagreements, but the result of the pressures that filming produce.

As for the lighting, Sally was essentially responsible and she was very intuitive. But we discussed it ahead of time and we wanted soft light on the faces since that's what we felt towards the characters. In the beginning I was afraid that the shots would seem pretentious, but I no longer have that horrible feeling. What I wanted was to cross the line that allows a shot to create the emotional aspect of a situation, as in photography, which is a much more adventurous art than film from this point of view. There is a sensibility, a sophistication in photography that I often don't find in film and I would like to be able to continue to tackle this visual research and story development.

Were nature scenes like the swimming scene or the scene of dancing in the night in the country planned as you filmed them?
I set up a storyboard that helps me see what I need but we often modify it according to what happens. For example, the shot where the two cowboys teach each other to dance comes from what I observed between two actors, one showing the other a dance step. I thought it was charming and I decided to put it in the film. You have to be on the alert to seize such details that give a sense of reality but, of course, the big obstacle is time. We had a lot of other ideas but we couldn't shoot them in the forty days of filming. Eight weeks is not very short according to the usual criteria, but it's rather constraining for our way of filming.

The scene with the clairvoyant whose son is retarded announces the appearance of Sweetie.
Except that he's really daft. I liked the idea that this older woman accepted so readily her son's state. You often find that in clairvoyants: contrary to what one thinks, they are very down-to-earth. Sweetie's parents behave very differently.

Was the scene in the cemetery at the end, with the tree in the wind, the tracking shot along the very even hedges, then the shot of the tomb with the plant that had grown in the interior of the hole entirely conceived of at the beginning?
It was different in the screenplay. But when I saw the cemetery, I loved the formal character of the place and I wanted to emphasize it. I also noticed a tree that seemed to breathe. But it was actually in the editing that its living aspect emerged. I spend a lot of time editing, twelve hours by day, six days a week. I love editing, it's a stage where you can still bring a lot, where original ideas appear. The first cut was two and a half hours but I always intended the film to be no longer than an hour and a half.

Where does the music come from?
It's an Australian group of thirty singers, Cafe at the Gates of Salvation, which is not religious. The songs are original compositions that come from the tradition of *White Gospel*. They are very down-to-earth singers who have a great sense of orchestration, meet for the pleasure of being together, and don't work for money. They are getting stronger and stronger and to be in a room with them and listen to them sing is a very intense experience. The last song is not theirs, it comes from a book of Jewish prayers. We were afraid these songs would seem religious but once we put one of them [in a scene] while the characters make love in a parking lot our worries evaporated! I'm not automatically in favor of music in cinema but there are moments when it really makes a difference. For example, in that parking lot sequence between Kay and Louis it allows us to establish our ironic point of view of the two characters at a particular moment.

The danger in this type of film is that it could be condescending.
I thought that the characters, who were very vulnerable and very exposed, would end up earning the audience's sympathy. I wanted the audience to end up identifying with them. In life I think that people are both funny and tragic and I don't mind laughing when people are in absurd situations. Sometimes they're grateful to you because you let them see that there are two sides to every coin. We take our lives too seriously; there should be a limit to that. It's just because of a certain way of thinking that we consider certain events tragic. I'm not overcome with respect when faced with the unhappiness of others, but at the same time I'm very sensi-

tive to it. I myself have the tendency to complain a lot about what happens to me and other people can't help laughing!

Are you conscious of a difference between your short films and Sweetie*?*
Not really. Except that *Sweetie* is the best and the strongest film I've done. It's a film that I controlled the least, which brought me where I didn't really know I was going, and in this sense it was a great adventure. In this sense I was very satisfied.

Are there films where you felt a sensibility similar to yours, a desire to describe mental states?
It's a current trend in literature and I don't see why one wouldn't do it in cinema. You just have to want it, desire to do it like David Lynch. You don't discover the truth just by developing a plot, but by exploring many levels. I don't want to only look at behaviors, but to discover thoughts and emotions as happens in certain novels of Duras or Flannery O'Connor. I find the latter exquisite, merciless, and honest at the same time. *The Violent Bear It Away* is an extraordinary book, both hilarious and horrible. I feel completely naive in relation to these types of stories! I really liked the adaptation that John Huston did of *Wise Blood.* Anyway I like John Huston's films in general.

I think that people understand the world in terms of symbols. Things are rarely what they seem. They are metaphors of what is or what could be. And that also goes for our interior torments. One day a friend came to live at my house because she was very troubled. She didn't know how to choose between two men. I remember that the whole world became a metaphor for her personal problem. When we went shopping together and she noticed some expensive shoes, that meant for her that she wanted to live with the most adventurous man or alternatively that her own adventurous spirit needed the man that was the more stable. When we were driving and she saw a license plate beginning with J that meant that she was supposed to live with John. We all do that more or less.

Are you familiar with the poetry of Emily Dickinson, with her mixture of metaphysics and concreteness?
No, but I like the mixture!

In your films, there is a cosmic sentiment that starts with small physical details—a tree root, for example, and you suggest a relationship between the mind and the exterior world.
That's how I feel things. I think that my generation is drawn to the spiritual and desires less to participate in the ways of the world. I myself have meditated for five years. It helps me to moderate myself. I'm more conscious too of my inner feelings. Often we are led to do things out of pure excitement when they don't correspond to our profound selves.

Your characters are all very solitary.
Not Sweetie. She communicates a lot in her own way and even dishonestly sometimes! She immediately befriends the neighbors, takes Louis to the beach. No-one understands the danger that Sweetie represents except Kay who is the most exposed to it. It's difficult to know to what point Sweetie is mentally retarded. In my opinion she is normal, or at least was normal. Since her childhood, she has been pushed by her environment little by little and ends up by losing her equilibrium and her sense of responsibility. In other circumstances she could have been different.

Was Sweetie*'s barking inspired by a case that you observed?*
No, that was totally my invention. There were a lot of rehearsals for that scene. Genevieve needed courage to be able to frighten everybody. It was a decisive moment for her performance. She really became the character when she felt her power over others and that she was able to scare them.

Why did you dedicate the film to your sister?
Because I was moved by her behavior. While we were shooting, my mother was very sick, dying in fact, and I had to decide to stop, let another director finish the film, or to continue. My sister who was in England came back to New Zealand to take care of her and permitted me to continue.

Sugar with the *Sweetie*

CARLA HALL/1990

SWEETIE IS YOUR NIGHTMARE of a sibling. She's a mess—she's fat, belligerent and bawdy. Emotionally unstable, she ricochets from violent overgrown child to lovable unschooled ham, obsessed with the idea that one day she will be a rock singer. When she lumbers back into the life of her long-suffering and introverted sister, Kay, Sweetie turns it upside down.

"You hear people say, 'Is the character sympathetic enough?' " muses Australian filmmaker Jane Campion about the title character of her first feature, *Sweetie,* now playing in Washington. "I think all the characters have areas of sympathy, but the film isn't based on those concerns. I think everybody in the end, in life, is sympathetic. I've rarely met a person whom I don't feel for in some way or another, no matter how grotesquely they present themselves."

Campion's dark and lyrical tale of a whole family throttled by the difficult daughter has won her impressive reviews, confessions from moviegoers of their own family horror stories, and comparisons to the innovative David Lynch, director of *Blue Velvet* and *Eraserhead.*

"I feel sorry for David," says Campion, 35, with a typical self-deprecating laugh. "I think he's an extraordinary filmmaker. I certainly don't think I've made as bold films as he's made. But we've both got art school background and were both obviously enchanted by the power of the subconscious."

From *The Washington Post,* 4 March 1990. Reprinted by permission of the author.

For the Los Angeles stop of her first American publicity tour, Campion has settled into the Chateau Marmont, which on this rainy night seems even mustier and romantically gloomier than usual. A soft pink light fills the room where she has been receiving visitors, ordering numerous pots of coffee that arrived one each interview.

"I'm not so jaded that it's a pain for me," she says cheerfully. "People bring stuff to the interview and I think, 'Oh, yeah, I never thought of that.' "

But this is the last one of the day, and she's got the newspaper open to the movie listings, thinking of seeing *Born on the Fourth of July.* "I just feel so behind in movies," she laments. She lives in a house—"it's not the same as here, though—mine looks like a little cottage"—in a suburb of Sydney without virtue (or vice) of television and VCR, because those electronic staples were repeatedly stolen, she says.

She's traveling with her boyfriend, William MacKinnon, who is also the co-producer of *Sweetie.* He arrives partway through the interview. He's dark-haired and lanky and handsome and comes in from the rain with books he's just bought. Campion is blond and fair-skinned, and wears bright red lipstick and jeans.

They seem like a fairly low-key Australian couple on holiday in California, bemused but undaunted by $50 cab rides from Santa Monica and the rhythms of American speech.

"We can't understand what Americans say," MacKinnon explains matter-of-factly. When he ordered a hamburger at a restaurant, he recalls, "the waitress said, 'You want jack-or-cheddar?' I said, 'Yes.' "

Of course, they are equally impossible to understand for the first half hour or so—their swallowed twangs sounding just as foreign to an American ear.

Not that Campion, who was born and raised in New Zealand, dreams of Americanizing herself and settling into Hollywood. She has no interest in entering the mainstream.

"I've felt a big disenchantment with movies that were supposedly dominating the cinema—major American movies," she says. "I felt they just didn't represent my life. I felt really alienated from the characters—everyone is so nice and they didn't seem to have any problems. What I wanted to do was offer a series of alternatives. I don't mind vegging out at the movies—I'm not a strict Jesuit about it. I can easily lose an hour and a half of my life to the cinema too, but the films that have really resonated for me have become part of my life."

She counts among her favorite films those of Buñuel, Polanski's *Repulsion,* Antonioni's *L'Avventura* and Bertolucci's *The Conformist.*

"And I suppose because I so admired them," she says, "there's part of me that would like to do that too."

Sweetie was her opportunity to contribute to that genre of filmmaking she defines as "non-stupid cinema."

"It's not that I don't mind an occasional stupid movie," she says. "I just don't want to make them."

Besides directing *Sweetie,* Campion co-wrote the script and cast it herself. The last was a cost-cutting measure, she says.

"I felt really bad about putting people through those auditions," she frets. "I got so close to each of the contenders for Sweetie. And I tried to make an environment where I wanted each of them to succeed. You know, people claim parts. I wanted to see who was going to claim it."

The part of Sweetie was claimed by Australian stage actress Genevieve Lemon. Among other demands of the role, Lemon has a daylong tantrum in a treehouse, completely naked. "I said to Genevieve, 'Oh, you know, if you really want to wear some clothes I'm not going to make a big fuss about it.' She said, 'Jane, *plllease,* can I tell you one thing? I have no problems about being in the nude.' She was in a play called *Steaming* where she spent the entire play in the nude."

Despite the gravity of the family crisis in *Sweetie,* there is an undercurrent of gentleness and humor in the film—perhaps true to Campion's desire to be compassionate to everyone. Her characters are more quirky than tragic.

"What I'd like people to take away from the film," she says, "I'm not even sure I know it's takable. I'd like them to feel a sense of sadness and exhilaration, that life doesn't come in one neat way or another . . . that the family can be a very fertile home for a sort of virus of delusion as well as a place of great support and love. Nobody avoids family in some way or another, you know?"

MacKinnon, who's been quietly reading in a corner, is asked how he likes the film.

"I'm really pleased with it," he says.

"We never believe each other," Campion says. "You're just saying that."

"Well, here are a few things I think are bad with it . . . ," he ventures.

"You bastard!" she laughs giddily.

Campion doesn't expect her film to be very popular. "I sort of really love comfy sofas," she says a bit apologetically, "not hardback chairs. I sort of feel guilty when people say, 'I felt uncomfortable.' "

But it's not really the comfy sofa set she's targeted, and she talks in surprisingly commercial terms about taking the temperature of the "non-stupid" audience. "I'm hoping to be a hit and anticipate public taste," she says. "I think it's part of what you have to do. There's no point in making what people wanted to see 10 years ago."

She entered film school in 1981. But before film school there was art school in London, and Campion was miserable. "I had an obsessional love of films. When I was so lonely I would go to movies all the time in London," she says. "I had to hide my personality. I was too much for them. Well," she sniffs dryly of the Brits, "almost anything was."

Soon she discovered film festivals, where "you could see heaps of films." Eventually she finished up art school in Sydney, but by that time she was tinkering with the notion of being a filmmaker. She had already been exposed to the theatrical world. Her father, Richard, is a director, and her mother, Edith, is an actress who has a part in her daughter's upcoming Australian television series on New Zealand writer Janet Frame.

However, Campion knew little about the movie business. "When you're in your own bedroom trying to work out how to be a filmmaker, there's nothing more pathetic," she says. "You don't know a single other soul who knows how to make films."

So she enrolled in the Australian Film and Television School. To get there she submitted a super-8 short that had been the hilarious hit of art school—*Tissues,* about how tissues figured in a family's life.

"In fact, it was the only movie I took 100 percent pleasure in making," she says affectionately. "It was the last time I had that innocent thrill of 'this is mine, I made it.' "

After that, technique took over. "It was like someone came to me and said, 'Yeah it's funny, Jane, but you know there are not enough wide shots.' " She opens her eyes wide in bewilderment. "I went, 'Wide shots?' It just hadn't occurred to me that there were different types of shots."

There were "years of preoccupation" with the language and craft of cinema. "At the beginning," she says, "it's like learning to ski—you've got to remember to bend your knees and turn and do all these things at the same time, so there ain't too much that's elegant about it."

But the grappling paid off. During her three years at film school she made three short films that were all shown at the Cannes Film Festival in 1986. One of them, *Peel,* won the Palme d'Or for best short film. A 1985 television movie, *2 Friends,* made the rounds of Australian film festivals, and by 1988, when Campion decided to try the offbeat, feature-length *Sweetie,* her producers were able to raise a modest 1.3 million Australian dollars—around $1 million U.S.—from an Australian film distributor and the Australian Film Commission.

"Having spoken to some people here," she says, "I know that for people to get their first film made and to have any creative control over it—and I had 100 percent—is just, like, weird. It doesn't happen. They either have to sort of make films of hundreds of naked women rolling around and about for days or they have to make blood and guts movies."

Nonetheless, the wherewithal to make her film was a little frightening. "I hyperventilated for a week when I heard I got the money," Campion says. "The hardest thing for me was just keeping up my own belief in myself. I doubt things. It's part of the process for me. I have a constant discussion about whether this is good enough or whether I'm good enough—'Why did I do this in the first place? What have I got to say? Why did I ever think I could make a movie?'"

She laughs as she retells her inner dialogue of insecurity.

"The other hard thing was not worrying about other people's opinions of me. I worked so hard to try to get everyone to like me—from the caterer to the director of photography. Since then I'm quite happy for people not to like me. If I seem demanding or anything else it's only because I care. . . .

"It's a big thing to learn in life," she says. "If you want to be in a position to have your own opinion, you have got to value the integrity it gives you to weather a bit of disliking—because it will earn you that, but it's worthwhile."

A Director Strikes an Intimate Chord

CARRIE RICKEY/1990

ROBUST, BROAD-BONED AND radiantly horsey, Jane Campion resembles a jillaroo, which is Australian for "cowgirl."

But even jillaroos get the blues, as Campion could have told you last May at the Cannes Film Festival, where her debut feature, *Sweetie,* instantly polarized the audience.

Midway into the premiere of Campion's imagistic movie about the friction between two sisters, one as reedy and introverted as the other is elephantine and extroverted, half the audience had sped for the doors. Those who remained proclaimed the New Zealand-born director the most unique artist since Diane Arbus.

"Some of the critics found it an abomination, felt that *Sweetie* shouldn't have been in competition with movies like *Do the Right Thing* and *sex, lies, and videotape,"* Campion observed at the time. "But you know what you get at Cannes," said the filmmaker, who won Cannes' Golden Palm in 1986 for her short *Peel.* "You get a lot of people who never see 'art' cinema."

Nearly a year later, *Sweetie* is being released in the States to unanimously positive reviews (it opened at the Ritz Five last week).

Reached at her parents' home in Wellington, New Zealand, where she is vacationing, Campion, 35, notes that in Australia, where *Sweetie* was made, the film critics society voted it the best film of 1989 and named her best director.

From *The Philadelphia Inquirer,* 29 April 1990. Reprinted by permission of *The Philadelphia Inquirer.*

The director thinks she understands what put off some critics: "*Sweetie* issues a personal invitation to people. . . . It has a way of getting intimate with you, chummy with humor, and then showing you the serious consequences of intimacy." Death is one of the consequences in Campion's black comedy.

"My movie doesn't tell you what to think; it's relatively oblique," she says. This distinguishes *Sweetie* from most American movies, which signal the audience how to feel.

Campion develops her themes visually, and one of *Sweetie*'s recurrent (and insistent) images is that of trees. Ominously, some grow roots so deep that they threaten to strangle the landscape. Some get uprooted. Yet others are friendly places in which to build treehouses. In *Sweetie,* no matter what they might explicitly represent, trees implicitly refer to the family tree that connects Sweetie (Genevieve Lemon) with her sister Kay (Karen Colston).

"There actually was a tree in my life," says Campion, laughing lightly. "While we were in film school, my then-boyfriend and I planted three trees in the back yard and he accused me of being self-involved and neglectful of them. Two of them died. The third tree was left, and I used to watch it outside the kitchen window. I had this anxious relationship with it, I thought if it died, so would the love between my boyfriend and I." She saucily adds, "It turned out that the tree outlasted our affair."

In some ways Campion is a spiritual sister of film director David Lynch. Like him, she's an art-school graduate obsessed with above-ground symbols for subterranean phenomena. Also like Lynch, Campion is interested in what's below the surface psychologically. Trees were a handy correlative.

"Trees were fascinating for me to use as a visual reference because there is as much of the tree underneath . . . as there is above. The other thing about trees is that their growth is subtle. . . . You can't actually see them grow but you discern their growth over time. Thinking of growth in tree terms helped me develop the characters in *Sweetie,*" Campion says.

Jane Campion, the daughter of a theater-director father and actress mother, is the younger of two sisters. She dedicated the movie to her sibling, something that shocks some viewers because of the prickly relations between Sweetie and Kay. "My sister, Anna, lives in London and is a filmmaker, too. She just finished her degree at the Royal College of Art and won a BBC drama award for her graduation film. She's the most intuitively inspired in my family," Campion confides.

Like Lynch and Alfred Hitchcock, both Campion sisters are painters-turned-filmmakers. "Art school was where all the learning I did took place," says Campion. At Sydney College of Art, she was inspired by the work of German sculptor Joseph Beuys and Mexican surrealist Frida Kahlo. "I did narrative paintings annotated with dialogue," Campion recalls. "I realized I was trying to storytell, and perhaps I should do the storytelling more directly."

Which is why she enrolled at the Australian Film and Television School. "Everyone was so conservative," she remembers of her first day there, where her pink-and-white striped pants looked Martian amid the khaki and flannel. "Then I saw this girl in spotted pants and we immediately became friends," Campion recalls of her first meeting with cinematographer Sally Bongers, who would shoot Campion's four shorts, two telefilms and *Sweetie.*

Initially, the art-trained punkettes met with resistance from their teachers and fellow students. "Nobody took anything we did with any seriousness because we weren't making what they thought the Australian Broadcasting Co. would want." The Campion-Bongers short films *Peel* and *A Girl's Own Story* got them invited to Cannes and earned them the belated respect of their peers.

"I think most of the students in film school were interested in finding a place in the industry. Sally and I were there because we were interested in finding our own voices. What I was surprised to learn later was that television—at least in Australia—doesn't want the work it already has. It wants the kind of work it's never seen before," says Campion. Which is why, on the strength of her shorts, in 1986 the Australian Broadcasting Co. (ABC) invited her to direct *Two Friends,* about two teenage girls.

"I was hired at ABC by a woman, Jan Chapman. I think women are more supportive of women, and was lucky to have Jan's encouragement," says Campion, who has just completed the three-hour telefilm *An Angel at My Table,* about New Zealand writer Janet Frame, for the network.

Campion also feels lucky to be making movies in Australia, which has supported women directors such as Gillian Armstrong (*High Tide*), Ann Turner (*Celia*) and herself. "I don't know enough of what happens in America, but there's something not happening there that is happening in Australia."

"To deny women directors, as I suspect is happening in the States, is to deny the feminine vision," says Campion, who is being courted by American producers.

"One of the things we learn in movies directed by men is what the 'fantasy woman' is. What we learn in movies directed by women is what real women are about. I don't think that men see things wrong and women right, just that we do see things differently."

Can Campion identify the difference between man-made and woman-made films? "Apart from one or two very special women, women don't seem to want to direct adventures or thrillers.

"I'm bored with those genres. I don't think about cops, robbers, killings, car chases. I think a lot more about relationships, landscapes and food," Campion says with a laugh.

"I don't think men actually think a lot about car chases, but they seem to make movies about them more frequently, eh?" Here's to more films about relationships and food.

The Sweet Smell of Success

DONNA YUZWALK/1990

JANE CAMPION'S DEBUT FEATURE film, *Sweetie,* was—according to where you sat—roundly booed or rapturously applauded at its Cannes screening last year. What polarized the audience is a weirdly comic film set in kitschly suburban Australia where the inactivity of the characters is heightened by the pain of people helplessly out of step with each other.

Sweetie is Kay's story. Emotionally mute, unwilling to sleep with her boyfriend Louis and afraid of trees, her barren landscape is invaded when her sister Dawn (aka Sweetie) comes to stay, punk boyfriend in tow. Overweight in the fertile manner of a Roseanne Barr or Marianne Sagebracht, Sweetie is the polar opposite of her sister and her arrival changes the family for ever.

Sweetie earned Campion comparison with such cult directors as Jim Jarmusch and David Lynch. Yet Campion is far from the inscrutable auteur. At 35, she is shy, almost diffident. Although she has lived in Australia for the past 10 years and speaks with full-blown Aussie vowels, the low-key New Zealander within is still intact.

But Campion obviously possesses an inner spur that her "loosely autobiographical" lead character Kay lacks. Talking about her film career, she once said, "I never considered myself in the front line of anything. I thought it would be wonderful to meet someone really clever and support him. But after awhile I thought 'I'd better take responsibility for myself.

Maybe I'm not doing anything fabulous at the moment, but what if I really tried? After that, everything changed incredibly fast."

It's Kay's lack of galvanizing instinct, however, that endears her to her creator. "I like the fact that she can't erase her anxieties," says Campion. "Basically she's sensitive enough to have them. She doesn't have theories or a university education or religion: she has to create her own. A character like that allows you to explore the way people read meaning into their lives. Some have a more exploring psyche than others and haven't had the chance to develop it. I'm not beyond some of her worries."

Among them, Kay has trouble loving her boyfriend. While Sweetie and her man are going at it hammer and tongs in their bedroom, Kay and Louis perch on the end of their bed. Finally Kay knocks on the door. "Dawn, can you finish?" she asks peevishly. "We want to go to the bathroom."

"I think I was trying to say she only had the power and energy to seduce Louis in the first place because the clairvoyant told her she could and so gave her that power," explains Campion. "But in the day-to-day business of loving she gets lost like a lot of us do. We are skilled at meeting people and having a romantic time to start with but not so good at sustaining a relationship."

After studying painting and anthropology in New Zealand, Campion crossed the Tasmania to attend the Australian Film School. She went on to make four highly acclaimed shorts, collecting a 1988 Palme d'Or at Cannes in the process. The idea for *Sweetie* has been brewing for years. "It was something I really wanted to do but I thought it might not be good enough. I go on like that all the time, entertaining enthusiasms and doubts. I think it will be constantly with me. I try not to make it too debilitating; I accept that I'm learning all the time. I felt *Sweetie* was a really appropriate low budget film for me to make with my own style of humour and spirituality."

Campion is taking this year out—catching up with friends, buying a new car, moving house, reading biographies, walking in the bush, listening to music. Singing; she says, is a liberation. "If I could sing I think I'd be a free person," she adds with typical candour.

She had just completed a three-part television series based on the autobiographies of eminent New Zealand author Janet Frame. Called *An Angel at my Table,* it will be shown on Channel 4 later this year.

Not moving far from *Sweetie*'s territory of deeply sensitive women with membrane-fine psyches, Campion is keen to create a period drama based on her love of the Brönte sisters' and the romantic tradition. But that, she admits, would be "very much in the future."

She is also writing, but concludes, "I'm not nearly as verbal as I am visual. I have very strong visual recall. I get very strong pictures in my head. I managed to develop an aesthetic respecting my own point of view enough to have one to adjust. I could take it into painting if I wanted to, but I do quite enjoy working with people. All film involves collaboration. Film is the art of compromise, and the art of seeing compromise as a challenge. Your bend to your advantage all the time."

Angel with an Eccentric Eye

LYNDEN BARBER/1990

AMID THE USUAL GLITZ and hokum, there was a moment worth remembering in last year's Australian Film Institute (AFI) awards ceremony. Sydney-based director Jane Campion, not able to appear in person to accept the Byron Kennedy Award for "excellence in cinema," appeared in a short thank you film—sitting on the floor surrounded by empty shoes.

These inanimate objects she then proceeded to introduce as the people who had collaborated on her independent debut feature, *Sweetie.*

Affected or charming? Campion didn't seem to care what anyone thought either way. The kind of childlike behaviour anybody else would be too embarrassed to even think of, let alone carry out, all seemed perfectly natural for this 36-year-old.

Campion is widely regarded as the most original talent to have emerged in the Australian film industry in years, and playfulness is to be found in her films in abundance.

"I can't work very well if I get too serious. I find seriousness very inhibiting," she said when we met for an interview just before she was jetting off to Venice, where her new film, *An Angel at My Table,* is one of 20 being entered into competition.

In the clipped vowel sounds of her native New Zealand, she continued: "I don't want to be a child emotionally or in terms of responsibility, but I

From *The Sydney Morning Herald,* 8 September 1990. Reprinted by permission of the author.

do think playfulness can be very liberating," adding that none of her friends had any problem with this.

The way Campion peppers her conversation with references to her friends and "supportive environment" says a lot about the way she works.

If the film world is a promiscuous one, a business-like environment where people drive a hard deal and then move on, Campion's work practices are almost homely. She prefers to surround herself with people she likes and trusts, such as Gerard Lee, the writer and ex-boyfriend who co-scripted *Sweetie,* and New Zealand-born producer Bridget Ikin.

What she hates about going on film shoots is having to leave her personal network behind, she said, teasingly comparing herself with a cat.

The result is that Campion makes films unlike any other. Like her AFI awards acceptance clip, she takes risks seemingly without a second thought, in the search for a more natural, personal mode of expression.

Sweetie, for example, changed its protagonist half-way through, so that from an offbeat story about a withdrawn girl it suddenly switched attention to her eccentric sister and her overly doting father. Yet the most startling thing about the film was the way it looked: aided by lurid colours and deliberately skewed camera angles, the kitsch normality of Australian suburbia suddenly looked mind-bogglingly weird.

Sweetie was the stuff of controversy. It was a box office success in Sydney, Melbourne, New York and London, with many critics praising its director's original vision, yet it failed to be nominated for Best Film at the AFI awards.

She seems more shy than I'd imagined from her press photos, which have tended to portray her wearing the bubbly grin of the natural extrovert. She also makes admissions of vulnerability of the kind rarely on display in the film industry, while her habit of crinkling her nose betrays a slight nervousness, broken by frequent bursts of laughter.

Campion is still sensitive to criticism, admitting to having been "hurt" by the ambivalent tone of the *Herald* review of *Sweetie* (she had wanted to be fully embraced in her home town), and seems to have not quite recovered from the film's first major public screening at the Cannes Film Festival, where sections of the audience walked out or booed.

Based on the autobiographies of writer Janet Frame, *An Angel at My Table* has taken her back to her native land, and offers further evidence that all the praise heaped upon her is yet to go to her head. At Campion's request, this trilogy of 50-minute films made for New Zealand television nearly didn't make it on to cinema screens at all.

The reason is quite incredible: "I was scared I would create at a standard that wasn't up to the standard of cinema, and it would make me and the people in the movie look bad."

Indeed, so bad did it make her look that at this year's Sydney Film Festival the audiences gave it a standing ovation, then voted it their favourite film at the end of the two-week season. Bowled over by the enthusiasm, she relented.

After Venice, the film appears at festivals in Toronto, New York, London, Seattle and Cork, and opens commercially in Sydney on September 20.

Campion puts her apparent modesty down to perfectionism. "I think if you have high standards, you're just aware of what's possible.

"I'm keen to keep trying to achieve. What happens is that your abilities get better but your critical facilities get better too, so that no matter what you're achieving, you're always saying, 'It could have been better.' You could drive yourself crazy with it. So you say, this is the best I could do at this time."

Angel is an extraordinarily striking piece: more naturalistic and less elliptical than *Sweetie,* it's still instantly recognisable as Campion—economical, feminine and full of shots that set the eyes whirring.

New Zealand writer Janet Frame was an unnaturally shy but otherwise normal child whose lack of confidence led to eight years in a psychiatric hospital, where she was misdiagnosed as a schizophrenic; only her writing saved her from a leucotomy.

The three parts of *Angel* cover Frame's rural childhood, her period in hospital, and her European sojourn, when she visited Spain, met other writers, and experienced her first affair.

For Campion, the film is the result of a fascination that began when she read Frame's *Owls Do Cry* at the age of 13. "It really introduced me to the idea that some ideas in the world can't exist in tough storytelling, they have to exist in a more poetic form, and the whole book seemed really moving," she said.

"When I heard that Janet Frame had spent a lot of time in mental hospital, she became somebody I'd think about when we'd drive past the mental hospitals in New Zealand, wondering if Janet was really there.

"She grew to have a mythic proportion to me, her life seemed to sum up the tragic/sad artist. When her autobiographies came out, I was incredibly eager to find out what the story really was, and I was shocked to find out how normal she was, and how much my childhood felt like hers. I thought it was like the unravelling of a myth. I found it very moving, and felt like I would really like to share that experience, and introduce people to Janet."

She approached Sydney-based scriptwriter Laura Jones, best known for *High Tide,* directed by Gillian Armstrong, and found a similar enthusiasm for Frame's work. Jones spent a year writing the script, meeting Campion every so often to discuss progress.

One of the chief motivations behind the film was the desire to find a new way of representing the workings of the memory. The first section, in particular, acts as a kind of mental photograph album. In this, *Angel* is often breathtakingly successful: for example, the opening shot—a child's vision of a mother silhouetted against the sky—hits the viewer like something dredged up from deep within the subconscious.

"The very first memories are just like flashes, not stories at all, just a scene," she said. "Then as you get older you find you can remember little stories, then they get longer until you start to see your life as a whole long story.

"That was kind of how we thought of developing through the three books. Because by the time you get to the second book, it's very much a drama about a woman who's struggling for her life."

Frame co-operated with the filmmakers, giving them virtual carte blanche. "It seems the higher calibre of people you work with, the more generous they are creatively."

As for the subject's opinion of the film: "She said it was delightful, but I wouldn't really know. Maybe she has a lot of different feelings about it. She's not angry, that's for sure."

Campion certainly isn't wanting for qualifications. After completing a degree in anthropology in Wellington, New Zealand, she spent a year at London's Chelsea School of Art before moving to Sydney about 11 years ago, where she did another BA at the Sydney College of the Arts and signed on at the Film Television and Radio School.

Her cinematic talent first surfaced in brilliant short films, including *Peel,* which won the Cannes Palme d'Or for best short film in 1986, even though it had been made before she had graduated from film school.

But like British painter-turned-film-director Peter Greenaway, it's her art background that gives her work much of its intensity.

"I work really hard at it. It's not natural," she said of her visual sense, adding, "Well, it is and it isn't. You work hard at what you have naturally, because if you force things, it looks forced."

At art school she became aware of ideas like economy of vision. Minimalism was an initial influence, although she started developing her ideas in a more personal direction.

"At art school, everything is really pondered and thought about. You're just talking about one shot or one image usually, so it's a very thorough examination."

Yet the film world may not be able to hold Campion forever. She wants to spend more time writing fiction—so far she has written a couple of short stories—and is even toying with the idea of training to become a psychotherapist. "It could be a really interesting way to develop into your older years."

On second thoughts, she joked, "Sometimes when you listen to people's problems, I get really bored with it."

The suggestion may be odd coming from anyone else, but given her two feature films about characters considered by society to be either mad or on the fringes of normality, it's hardly shocking.

Campion admits to being confused by what people consider to be normality. "I think it's just a kind of consensus, an agreed opinion, that we don't mention all our problems."

The Red Wigs of Autobiography: Interview with Jane Campion

MICHEL CIMENT/1990

What did Janet Frame represent for you before you thought about adapting her book?

I remember when I was thirteen years old I read her books lying on my bed and the impact that they had on me. There are a lot of poetic passages in *Owls Do Cry,* her novel, like "Daphne in the tranquil room," which had a particular quality of sadness and which evoked the world of insanity. Her family had known many tragedies. In *Owls Do Cry,* the sister falls into a pile of burning trash and dies. In the autobiography, she drowns, but that provokes the same feeling of fright. When you're very young, at thirteen, you're very impressionable and particularly touched by what reproduces interior life poetically. I must have been strongly influenced, because when I wrote stories at school, I called a character Daphne. I also remember what I read about Janet Frame, explanations that people gave about her manner of writing that tied into her schizophrenia. There was a lot of gossip, a whole mythology around her, and whenever I passed a psychiatric clinic, I asked myself a lot of questions about Janet Frame, as she herself did about the identity of the people she described. That's why, when I heard that she had written her own story, I had a very strong desire to read it. I discovered the first volume of her autobiography, *To the Island,* around the age of twenty-eight when I was at film school. Then my curiosity

---

Interview: Venice, 14 September 1990. From *Positif,* April 1991. Translated by Michele Curley. Reprinted by permission of *Positif* and the author.

about knowing what really happened in her life was transformed into the pleasure of discovering the freshness of her narration and the richness of her detail. It awakened my own memories of my childhood; her book really seemed to me to be an essay on childhood in New Zealand. I loved it; it was very emotional, and I wanted to share this experience with a large number of people.

The set of her autobiographies (three volumes of two hundred and fifty pages each) forced you to condense a substantial amount of material.
It was in effect an enormous effort. When I originally had the idea of this project, I spoke to Bridget Ikin who was at the time John Maynard's production manager. I was visiting a set where they were shooting a film, and I spoke to her about this autobiography that she admitted she had also loved. I proposed that we do it together. It was rather cheeky and ambitious on my part because at the time I had not done much, perhaps *Peel,* my first short film.

Did you envision it for cinema or for television at the start?
I always thought it would be a film for the small screen. I never thought that anyone would like to see that story at the movie theater. My conception of what a film should be was certainly clichéd, but I thought movies needed a lot of action or panoramic scenery while this was a very intimate story. I thought that it would be very difficult to convince producers that this story could interest a lot of people and it's true that we had problems since many of the people we spoke with didn't think Janet Frame was very nice, not the way she appeared in the book! It's difficult to believe today since she seems so intensely nice in the film! It was in any case in that way that Laura Jones, the screenwriter, Jan Chapman and I who collaborated on the script, saw her. Everything that had a relationship with her was placed under the sign of delicacy, of softness. The shooting was harmonious—unlike *Sweetie's* which had sometimes been dramatic—and the whole production seemed to be bathed in the relaxed atmosphere that Janet Frame knows how to create.

I didn't censor myself because I was working for television. The subject didn't lend itself to an experimental style like *Sweetie.* On the contrary. For me, the story as told by Janet Frame imposes the square format of the TV screen. Sometimes you lose the substance of a film when it's on television but not in this case. There are a lot of close-ups for example, but they are suitable to the story which is of an intimate nature.

The problem with films made for the little screen is that often they are not as carefully made because the shooting is too rapid. For *An Angel at My Table,* we worked in conditions near those of filmmaking: twelve weeks of shooting of which two in Europe. It was hard; the conditions were not completely as good as for a film, but it was all right. The real problem was the number of new actors that it was necessary to meet each day since there were so many characters! It was like serial interviews! They all arrived rather anxious, desirous to do the best possible, but knowing that most often there wasn't but one day of shooting. The only character who truly occupies the screen is Janet Frame, but there are very few people with which she has a prolonged relationship. Thus, for me the primary task was to prepare the actors very quickly.

Your mother plays a role in the film.
Yes, she is the teacher who reads Tennyson's poem *Excalibur.* My mother was a very good actor and you can see the particular intensity that she expresses in this scene. She is like that in life. She no longer acts very much but she is a perfectionist to an almost neurotic degree. When I told her that she had been very good, she shrugged her shoulders, having found herself horrible. I'm like her: when I receive compliments, I have the tendency to reject them. I told my mother that she should feel satisfaction for what she had done and she replied that that was impossible since she knows that she could have done a lot better. In her opinion, if she could be happy with herself, she would become lazy!

After Two Friends, *it's the second of your films where you don't sign the screenplay. Is it for you a big difference when shooting?*
Not really, to the extent that I nevertheless collaborated closely on the writing of *An Angel at My Table.* That makes the task seem easier while shooting since you know the material more intimately. I talked a lot with Laura Jones to reach a true community of views, then she wrote and then I made one or two changes. In any case, we always had the book as a mediator between us, which made our communion of minds still easier. I have never done an adaptation alone and I don't think that that tempts me.

Frankly, I had more pleasure in sharing. It was a simple story and we thought that anyone could understand it. In this sense it was a good subject for television and there was no reason to obscure the intention unnecessarily. All that we did was to read the book many times, set it down after each reading and put down on paper all that we liked the most. Then we compared our lists, which were rather close by the way. We then studied the way in which the things that we had retained could be combined together. And Laura wrote the continuity. When I work on a screenplay, I don't think about images, that comes later. In the same way when I shoot, I have to be totally immersed in the text to be able to think only about the visual, and it's for that I collaborate so closely with the screenplay when I am not the author. Moreover I directed *Sweetie* when Laura wrote *An Angel at My Table,* which excluded me from taking on the task. This film was not an experimental or intellectual challenge for me. I had to be the most simple and the most honest possible in relation to the story.

From this point of view, there are real differences of approach between *Sweetie* and *An Angel at My Table*. I like *Sweetie* a lot, I like that tragedy a lot. I think that it's a film that has depth, that possesses dark and difficult zones, that the emotions there are more complicated, less accessible and that it's a film that stays with you a long time. On the other hand, *An Angel at My Table* establishes an strong relationship with the audience by speaking the language of the heart. From a human point of view, it's all that I desire; from cinematography point of view, it's less exciting for me than *Sweetie*. But for my next film people have to prepare themselves for a shock since I will be much less well-mannered than with *An Angel at My Table*!

What there is in common with Sweetie *is your sense of ellipsis. On one hand you have a fluid development of narration, and on the other you practice brutal ruptures.* That has a lot to do with the way in which the screenplay is written. And also because I invent a lot of things during rehearsals. I had an enormous amount of material at the end of shooting. I imagined different beginnings and endings for scenes, and I liked making editing cuts in the middle of sequences very much. Thus the abrupt, elliptic side of certain passages.

One of the most remarkable aspects of the film is the continuity that you established between the three actors who interpret Janet at different stages of her life, Alexia Keogh, Karen Fergusson and Kerry Fox.

The red hair helped us a lot in the resemblance! When the little Alexia Keogh put on her wig for the first time, she started crying. She was so horrified to have that color hair! It was funny to see all three of them with their wigs at lunch time. It was certainly one of the most complex problems to resolve. I remember that we discussed a lot after having seen Bertolucci's *The Last Emperor,* of the way in which they passed from one age to another. What pleased me the most was the actor who played the emperor in the intermediary stage. He expressed his feeling of having privileges very well. I became very attached to him and I had trouble passing to the following [actor] because of the link that I had created with the character. I feared that the same thing would happen with the little Janet in *An Angel at My Table* and that the spectator would regret leaving her. We thought a lot about these transitions as much at the screenplay stage as at the moment of casting and then at that of shooting. Finally, while editing, Veronika Haussler showed me that it was necessary to shoot some supplementary shots to assure a better fluidity. I thought she was right and I filmed the shot of the second Janet reading her poems in a diary on the hillside so that the audience could be alone with her for a moment. In fact each of the three Janets has a moment of this nature: the youngest when she comes towards us on the road and the third when she reads a poem near the railroad tracks. The transition from the second Janet, Karen Fergusson, to the third, Kerry Fox, was difficult since children and adolescents are so honest and innocent that it's hard for an actor to live up to the absolute charm that the very young possess. We had to work hard with Kerry to choose the best moment when she would appear so that she wouldn't seem bleak. It was necessary for the audience to like her immediately, for there not to be any problems. Karen Fergusson who preceded Kerry Fox on the screen is an incredibly timid and very intelligent woman. We chose her in a class where she recited Keats's *Ode to a Nightingale* with some classmates. She was the only one who knew it by heart after two readings and she had an incredible ability to cry. She was the adolescent the most capable of empathy that I had ever met. I loved her. She was fourteen during shooting, the same age as Melina Bernecker who played Myrtle, her friend. Melina, like her character, was very sexy, very orientated towards boys, and Karen was on the contrary like Janet Frame, very reserved, dressed with a little cardigan and a very ordinary skirt. There was something fascinating about seeing these three Janets who were playing the same character sitting together, the youngest adoring to be pampered by the two older ones.

Was Janet Frame in contact with you during the elaboration of the film?
She read the screenplay which she liked a lot and she came to visit us on the set. We were very anxious to know how she would react to our adaptation. But she is a very mature woman who knows that this story of her life is also fiction. She even had the generosity of telling Laura Jones that her screenplay was better than her book. Making herself available to us was for her, who almost never travels, a big deal. She came by train with my godmother who is one of her best friends. They were a curious couple, and Janet, who is curious about everything, didn't give my godmother a moment of rest during the trip, didn't cease in calling to her attention everything that happened. At the beginning on the set, she was very shy, but by the end of the week she had gotten a lot closer to us. Sometimes she made comments on what her father said in the film and offered us modifications.

The film is faithful to her autobiography but it also ties in with the themes and the preoccupation of your other films, without mentioning the events of your own life like your discovery of Europe during your youth.
Everyone in New Zealand goes to the Old Continent one day! But it is true that I'm interested in general in characters that are neglected, abandoned, in whom one is not very interested. And I appreciated Janet because of that. I'm not conscious of my choices. I suppose that it's like falling in love. You don't ask questions, you just do it! And you're grateful to be able to love something or someone. In the beginning I wanted to be of service to Janet Frame and to her vision with this film. There is certainly more of me in the final result than I was conscious of when I started. My goal was to bring to the screen the emotions I had felt while reading the book. I don't know to what extent you find me in *An Angel at My Table.* I'm a little like an actor who chooses projects and has fun doing different things. And you are certainly better placed than I to comment on what I do!

Did you have a palette of colors? Did Janet's red hair determine the color range of the film?
I always thought of green and red for *An Angel at My Table.* Green is the color of New Zealand and red that of Janet's hair. They were primary colors.

By starting with red hair, I could play with a group of soft muffled tones, or on the contrary, give more luminosity to the film by making the red clash with bright colors like green, and that's the solution that I adopted. If you go to New Zealand, you realize the difference of light. The first European painters—English or Dutch—who brought back paintings of their voyages to New Zealand, met with incredulity by their compatriots. Everyone thought that the colors were exaggerated; they didn't believe them, since the light in northern Europe is softer and more diffused. There is also a lot of wind in New Zealand and it sweeps everything. The air is transparent and from Wellington you can see mountains at four hundred kilometers distance. Because of that, the shadows are so black that you cannot see anything. This intensity captivates me and the contrasts are so strong that it's difficult to shoot. For certain sequences of the childhood, we had to put on filters to obtain yellow colors or golden brown ones.

In which part of New Zealand did you shoot?
It's a lie as far as the autobiography goes because we shot around Auckland while Janet Frame grew up in a completely different region near Oamaru. I found nevertheless equivalent scenery. It's not the same type of nature but the sentiment expressed is the same.

How did you approach the scenes in Europe? Weren't you afraid of exoticism by filming in Ibiza, London and Paris?
I was aware of the danger of tourist clichés since I didn't know Europe intimately like my country or Australia. However I had lived for some time in London. Paris was a problem because we only stayed there a half-day and I shot as a tourist for that reason. Paris was totally exotic for me. As for Ibiza, we didn't go there because the place did not resemble at all what it had been in the fifties. We found the equivalent in Cadaquès and in Costa Brava. My director of photography and I tried to find different and bizarre places, a mix of old and new to avoid the clichés. What I prefer in the European sequences, is the scene where Janet walks while reading one of Shelley's poems.

For the hospital scenes you didn't adopt a naturalist style but rather attempted a sort of stylization while emphasizing the cruelty of psychiatric treatment.

I think it's rather traumatizing as it is! Adding to it would not have rendered the scenes more convincing. I wanted to show her progressive decline, passing from a normal state to a beginning of a form of insanity at the end. In her autobiography she doesn't describe her stay in the mental institution at all. She speaks about it, on the other hand, in one of her novels, *A Face in the Water,* from which we drew our inspiration. There was fascinating material in this book that Janet Frame was not willing to let us use at first. Then she ended up accepting.

You never explain in words her progressive plunge into depression tied to the death of her sister, to the crises of epilepsy of her brother, etc. There are suggestions, evocations, rather than a doctor's discourse for example, like in many films, that make the audience understand her evolution.
I don't like to be explicit. What I wanted was to create a feeling of intimacy with Janet's state rather than give reasons for that state. All explication destroys the dramatic essence of a story for me, but obviously the danger is that the spectator no longer understands what is happening very well! As a spectator, I don't like to be told a lesson. I expect a filmmaker to find a more subtle solution to lead me to discover the keys to a behavior.

One of the problems that films about artists pose is showing them in the process of creating. It's almost undoable.
Towards the end of shooting I was very embarrassed to have made a film about a writer who you never saw write! I thus filmed some shots of typewriters. But it's true that this absence troubled me. On the other hand, how do you film the act of writing? There are of course the physical details: Janet Frame has an almost neurotic fear of noise while she's writing. It is believed that Kipling wanted the blackest ink possible and loved the smell of orange peels. Others drink very strong coffee. Each one needs a type of conditioning and comfort that permits the subconscious to take orders. I have recently read a lot of literary autobiographies, but it still seems as difficult to visually express the process of writing.

You also express very strongly the fundamental solitude of the artist. Whether she's in school, with her family or with friends, Janet Frame is nevertheless profoundly alone.

Janet was afraid upon reading the screenplay that people would feel sorry for her. She told me that she didn't feel alone, that the sky, nature were living presences for her, that she felt in intimate relations with them. I took care to show that she wasn't unhappy in spite of everything. On the other hand, I don't think that Janet could have had a sustained relationship with anyone. It was too complicated for her. But I don't think it's as serious as that, and in any case, it's equally too complicated for most of us!

Jane's Film Career Takes Wing

KATHERINE TULICH/1990

WHEN JANE CAMPION MADE her movie debut with a film called *Sweetie* it was like a bolt of lightning had hit the international film industry. *Sweetie* was screened at the Cannes Film Festival and received unanimous rave reviews. Jane Campion found herself suddenly sought after, feted even.

It's supposed to be passé in the 90s to talk about *women* succeeding at this and that, after all, wasn't equality achieved with liberty, not to mention fraternity? Mmmm, well, not always. There are still industries where when a woman succeeds it is news and Jane Campion has won the quinella success in the film industry, where women in powerful positions are still rarities, and where even the most successful operators find it difficult to bring a winner.

Now, Campion, New Zealand-born, out based in Sydney, is following the success of *Sweetie* with another critically acclaimed effort. Her latest film, *An Angel at My Table,* is walking away with a slew of awards from film festivals all over the world. At the Sydney Film Festival it was voted best film and at the noted Venice Film Festival this week it won eight awards. Not bad for a film that was actually made for television as a mini-series.

"I never really thought about it as a feature film originally," said Campion. "But at the Cannes Film Festival this year we had a video cassette of it and people were flocking to see it, asking if they could get it for

---

From *The Daily Telegraph* (Sydney), 23 September 1990. Reprinted by permission of the author.

the cinema. I began to realize that the film was more powerful than I thought."

An Angel at My Table tells the story of one of New Zealand's most distinguished writers, Janet Frame. The film is based on three volumes of autobiography Frame wrote in the the early 80s—*To the Island, An Angel at My Table,* and *The Envoy From Mirror City*—books that were described by *The Sunday Times* in London as "one of the greatest autobiographies written in this century."

Frame's story is more riveting than any concocted plot. She was born into a poor rural family in the South Island of New Zealand in 1924. As a child she was a plump girl with an embarrassing mop of ginger frizz on her head. Feeling like an outcast at school she found solace in writing poetry. As she grew her painful shyness became more intense and with a half hearted suicide attempt she was advised to "rest" in a mental institute where she was diagnosed as schizophrenic. She remained there for eight harrowing years, enduring more than 200 shock treatments, as she said. "Each one the equivalent in fear to an execution."

Frame was literally saved from a lobotomy when her first book of published short stories received a literary prize. Released from the mental institute she finally fulfilled her romantic visions by traveling to Europe on a literary grant.

"I discovered her writing in my teenage years," Campion said. "When I read her first novel, *Owls Do Cry,* I was stunned by the vulnerability and poetry of it. It was well known in New Zealand that she had spent time in a hospital, and the rumors were that she was mad—that used to send shudders down me. But when her autobiographical books came out, they explained all the myths about her life."

While she was still in film school, Campion boldly approached the author (who leads a solitary existence in the New Zealand countryside) with the idea of a film, Campion said. "It was ages before I had made *Sweetie,* so she was very trusting to let me do it."

Campion admires the author as a very strong woman. "Her shyness makes you feel bold next to her, but you can really misinterpret it. It doesn't mean she's naive, and she's certainly aware of her place in world literature."

With an eye to meticulous detail, Campion was determined to make every aspect of the film perfect, even though it was a logistic nightmare.

She had to cast 140 speaking parts and find three different actresses to play Janet Frame from childhood to adult. Casting the child (played in the film by Alexia Keogh) was particularly hard. "We were looking for shy children, so they weren't the ones you'd find in school plays because they'd be too extroverted," she said. "We had to go searching in the playground and the classrooms."

The adult Janet is played by New Zealand actress Kerry Fox, a newcomer making her film debut. A lot of actresses wanted the part but when Kerry walked in it was one of those moments, said Campion. "I think people really cast themselves. They somehow claim the part and you know they're right for it."

Campion found that going back to New Zealand to make the film also became a journey into her own past.

"Going there made me realize what an influence the country had on me," she said. "Although I was a different generation to Janet it still brought back memories of my childhood."

"It's quite a Presbyterian work ethic country. Thinking that you're better than anyone is a cardinal sin," she said.

"New Zealanders believe in modesty at all times and we all thought Australians were vulgar and course. But I enjoy the way Australians are. I moved to Sydney 12 years ago and really developed myself creatively here. I wouldn't have had the same freedom in New Zealand," she said.

With all the international praise Campion's work is gathering, it's no surprise that Hollywood has come courting. What is surprising is that Campion is not interested.

"The privilege I have at the moment is to pursue the kind of ideas that wouldn't happen in America. They wouldn't happen unless I took it into my head to do it," she said.

"It's important to broaden the scope of the cinema appetite. If you go and do the American thing, then you're not really doing what your real freedom is."

Jane Campion Interviewed

HUNTER CORDAIY/1990

You have said elsewhere of An Angel at My Table *that "It's the story of her [Janet Frame's] life but it could have been my life." Was that the starting point of the film for you?*
I said that because one of the things that really inspires me about the autobiographies is that I feel I can really see myself in her story. That makes it attractive and personal for me. I feel other people will see a part of themselves that they hadn't valued before, because what Janet suggests is all the vulnerability and shyness that exists in people. Many people haven't suffered to the degree that she has, and I found it very liberating.

Is there a particular sort of personality that you want to make films about?
It is not something I consciously think about. But there is always something that has attracted me to telling anti-hero stories, and seeing the heroic aspect of them. I'm a lover of the perverse.

Where does that originate?
Maybe coming from New Zealand where you say "small is beautiful," because everything in New Zealand is small compared to the rest of the world. Maybe in that way you learn a kind of respect and regard for the backward, the shy, the countrified.

From *Cinema Papers,* December 1990. Reprinted by permission of MTV Publishing, Ltd. and the author.

And the perverse?
That may be my own little domain.

In Sweetie, *you explored the personality of a troubled artist. Janet Frame is also a troubled personality.*
Yes, I think that's true. What's exciting about troubled people is that they're in action with life; they're not sitting back and contemplating their success but trying to work something out. I find something incredibly endearing about that human effort, a sincere and not cynical effort to try and understand this life we've been given.

I'm reading *War and Peace* at the moment and Tolstoy is grappling with the same questions all the time: Why are we here? What are we here for? And when you see characters or people really struggling with those ideas and not just resigned to getting a mortgage and a job, I think they carry with them the whole meaning of human existence in that struggle, that attempt, to make some sense.

Sweetie *shows how creativity isn't understood; if someone is creative, they have to be troubled so we won't try and understand them. Is that a universal problem?*
Yes, a lot of creative people are misunderstood. But I've also heard a very funny situation where someone was describing their father, who was obviously a drunken pig and liked intimidating everyone, and the umbrella she put him under was to say he was "very creative." So, there are all sorts of ways it can be used and abused.

There is also the idea that if we don't understand someone we can call them mad.
Or creative.

An Angel at My Table *was essentially made for television. How was that decision arrived at?*
Obviously with some degree of error at times! I always felt that this was a project that had an unreasonable length to it. I couldn't imagine it any shorter than three hours, and Janet thought at one stage it would be nice to have a feature film of each of the books. That wasn't a project I wanted to do, but I could imagine it as a sensational three-part series for television, treating it as a medium that deserved respect. That was the idea.

At first, I couldn't see how you could release three one-hour episodes for cinema. But a number of things have turned that around. For one thing, the surprising success of *Sweetie* all over the world, apart from Germany, has meant there are distributors keen for something else. People have seen theatrical opportunities with *An Angel* that we as filmmakers were intimidated by. If I had made it for cinema, I would have wanted a budget like that on *Lawrence of Arabia,* and more time to do a more cinematic response to the work.

You said you wanted to treat television with respect. Is it not usually treated that way?
People have an abominable attitude towards the television audience. They think they're total cretins. My argument is that every human being is really struggling with the big questions, such as "Why am I here in my life?" And while a lot of us go sleepy on it, that's the way I want to address people. I find that every time you speak to a person in that manner, they respond.

Do you think different stories deserve different size screens? Are there some more destined for cinema or television?
I don't know; I'm so confused now! I feel I have it wrong and right. But whatever you do, if you treat it with care, love and respect, it's an unknown how far it can travel. If you only do it as "good enough for television," you can be sure that's all you'll get from it. I didn't behave with *An Angel at My Table* like that; I was just trying to honour the books, which I love. I brought as much quality to them as I could.

How different did you find directing for television?
I thought my love was the big screen, but when you address any problem, in its specifics, it becomes interesting. Television is basically a square, which is great for faces, and it's so nice to know that when it's put on video the integrity of the frame will be intact. I get nightmares about people watching *Sweetie* on tape without the letterbox masking—it's horrible. So, it's really great to know you've taken one of the major considerations of the world in hand and that *An Angel at My Table* will look great on tape. That's one of the good things.

One of the major breakdowns for me was that there's a tradition that television is shot faster than film and we had a 12-week shoot which included overseas travel. We were averaging about 3 minutes a day, which isn't very high for television. Really, we made two feature-length films in 6 weeks each. Some features are made in that time, but usually not very good ones. Six weeks isn't very generous, so we couldn't expect too much and some shortcuts had to be taken. But the pre-production was really hard to fit into the time we had, and I think a project's success is almost entirely equatable to the quality of the pre-production.

I'm a bit of a perfectionist so I wouldn't have been happy if someone had said we're releasing these as features as well. What a bargain: two features back to back in 12 weeks.

In your introductory remarks at the Sydney Film Festival screening, you mentioned there was a moment when you thought Frame's books might be unadaptable. Can you describe that process of adaptation?
My vision on this has been really opened up through this experience. It wasn't *my* feeling that the autobiographies were unadaptable, but that of a lot of other people. I had such a strong love and feeling for them that I was just convinced there was a way to do it. In a lot of ways, I think it's that sort of attitude that makes adaptation possible. Someone has a total belief that they can see it on the screen, and they create the belief and the energy to make it happen. Episode One is basically an essay on childhood and people thought that would be extremely hard to adapt.

You have done several films where there are special moments from childhood, put them together in a sequence and built up a story. Your films give a sense that what's important are the little moments in people's big lives.
It's nice of you to say that, because one of the aims in the first episode was the idea of how your memory develops. I wanted the first bits to be like little slides, visual impressions. If you look back to your very first memory, you can't even put a story together: it's just a picture. So I wanted Episode One to build up the storytelling with very short scenes that get longer and longer, as would a memory. By Episode Two, it's normal storytelling. That was one of the challenges for me, and probably why I like it best.

Did you consider the finished script a rigid text?
No, I see it as a kind of architectural blueprint and you're a fool not to relate to the 'building' that's going up. Things are happening there that you can't see on the paper, and the intentions, the feelings, are in those bits of paper, but you have to put them aside and understand its spirit and feel, rather than the literalness of it. Laura [Jones] has a great trust and it's nice to have that from a [script] writer.

How closely did you work with Jones? What was your contact with the script as it developed?
Long conversations and friendship. Then she just did the entire work. It didn't surprise me ever, because I think Laura is a very clever and subtle writer, except that it was always much better than I was hoping for.

I think I got more courage as I went on, especially with the third episode. I had some worries about it being interesting and exciting, and finally I think that worry and fixation probably made a difference. I don't think it's in any way the fault of Laura or Janet that Episode Three feels less strong; it's just that the middle episode with its extremely strong material made the third a bit harder. Also, Janet was saying good bye to her audience in the third book and I didn't want to do the same thing. I wanted to keep the audience with her to the end.

One of the problems with adaptation is that people say cinema cheapens literature, and films can never give the power, depth and consideration of a book.
I agree with them. I love novels. I get more enjoyment out of novels than I do out of cinema now.

Is that because you didn't before?
I used to love cinema more but now I think that too many films are too cheap, and they're kind of censored by an expectation of a stupid audience. They're not the challenge or the excitement that you can get in books.

Do you mean recent novels?
Not contemporary particularly. I'm talking about *The Iliad, War and Peace,* the opportunity to commune with somebody in your mind from history or present time and live with that relationship for a few days or however

long it takes to read a book. I think that's a really exciting experience and I find it inspiring. I'd probably like to write a novel. Then you wouldn't have to do so much collaborative work, which is the plus and the minus of film-making.

Perhaps cinema hasn't cared so much about the precious nature of creativity. It has always trampled on that and, if that is what you care about, then cinema can be very unkind.
You have to have an extraordinary relationship with that ability to work with others, and see each compromise as an opportunity, not a reduction. If you can cultivate that relationship then you can survive in cinema. If you can't, then it's just awful.

In An Angel at My Table, *there is a moment when Janet sits on the stairs at school with a friend who says Karl Marx is the only true rational thinker. On the other side of the steps is another group who are having fun. It seems she either has to be with one group or the other, not both.*
I think Janet wanted to be part of the group of beautiful girls with long silky hair who discussed whose personality was nicest. The notion of developing your personality was something she was probably more drawn to than Karl Marx. But she felt that world was inaccessible to her. She had frizzy hair and she never had any nice clothes, so she couldn't join in that lot. They had a special attraction they might not have had, had she been included.

What she wanted, like all of us, was to be special in some way, to have some special attention. She is really taken by the girl at school, Shirley, whose father has died. She wants to be what the teacher says—"in the poetic world of her imagination," to be a dreamer—but Shirley is so wan and pretty. So the only direction she could find in the end was to be a bit bookish, and poetry seemed to be a way she could be understood. She tried to get Dr. Forrest interested by writing a very provocative personality piece about her overdosing, so she was obviously trying to attract his attention by being a bold and unusual person.

In the asylum, there are scenes from Bedlam, and I imagine it must be very difficult to find ways to show what people are experiencing without it being stereotyped.

Loony scenes can look cheap, too. It's a worry. Scenes were taken from events she discussed in *Faces in the Water,* which is her book about the experience, and I felt pretty confident that those scenes were particular, and weren't made up to show madness but to describe her situation in a particular way.

What I wanted to show was the degeneration of her person during the experience, from the shock treatment down. I wanted to show the mad liberating aspect, the dance, as well as the awfulness of the dirty day room, which is where you got put if you were naughty or created trouble about your shock treatment.

Kerry [Fox, who plays the eldest Janet] does that wonderful thing where she had a copy of Shakespeare, and a bag which she carried—that's the only thing the patients had that identified them—and she brings the strings of her bag together and puts her hand through them as if it's an achievement. In that moment, you realize how far gone she is. I didn't mean to do it just to shock the audience, but to help them sympathize with that experience.

Why do you think she was, as we know now, mistreated? Was it ignorance on the part of those in charge?
I have an opinion on that but I'm not equipped to say. I think diagnosis has an awesome power. Someone says a person is schizophrenic and everything is then interpreted in that light. It's hard to get anybody to decide differently. Everything they do seems part of the schizophrenic framework. And in the environment of a mental hospital, everyone looks mad. The more you protest about it, the madder you look. It's one of those horrible circles that go on and on.

There are several times when doctors say they have a new treatment and it seems to work.
It's not enough to lay the blame at the hands of the psychiatric people at the time or the doctors, because a lot of people suffering from mental conditions were in an immense amount of pain and grossly unhappy. Shock therapy at the time made the handling of patients easier, because before shock therapy patients were running wild; it really was bedlam. The awful thing about shock therapy, which Janet experienced, was that it was without anaesthetic.

Didn't she say each time was like an execution?
Yes, the fear of execution, and that's what I think is unforgivable. When psychiatrists suggest, as they do today, that maybe a course of shock therapy would be helpful for depression, you think, "Have you tried it?" I'd like to see the psychiatrists themselves experience it with the confidence that they prescribe it.

When Janet gets published and goes overseas, it is as if she is joining the world for the first time. She is not a tourist but a stranger in the world. We see her start writing but it seems very difficult to show writing on the screen.
Yes. I regret now that we didn't show her writing more often. I thought it might have been a bit dull, but now I think it's fantastic to see her writing and we used every scrap of it we had.

The film shows Janet's gradually making contact with the world and people. For her this is not 'growing up' but something greater.
Yes, it's strange. At the end, you might think poor Janet, no lover, none of those things most of us think of as part of the elements of happiness. Yet, I don't feel sorry for her at all. At the end you sense that she's had her fulfilment.

A whole person?
Yes, and I think it's great because it validates a lot of people's lives.

Is An Angel at My Table *an Australasian film? Does it matter what you call it?*
I hope people find it just part of humanity. Its origins are obviously New Zealand. It's Australian as much as I consider myself Australian; my home is Sydney. I think it's a human story and they belong to the whole world.

Do you think the Australian film industry is now rebuilt or in transition?
I'm such a hopeless commentator on Australian cinema. But I do think there are enormous opportunities in Australia to work in cinema because they give you a chance in a way that I don't think you'd get in America. For all the talent and cleverness in America, they don't give their young filmmakers a go. That's why they're scrambling after Australians! I think it's totally up to you here how you do your work. You can create an audience for anything if it's well done, and you are passionate about it.

An Angel at My Table was an outrageous proposition to most people when we were looking for the money. It just didn't fit any categories and it really seemed like an impossible desire. They were wrong about that. If you have the vision and you work hard to make it available to people, you can do anything. I think what goes wrong is that people don't realize how hard it is to do good work. That may sound awfully school maamish of me, but you can't just turn up on the day and call yourself a director. The homework is horrendous, and you have to be prepared to compete with world standards.

Interview with Jane Campion: In the Country of the Hypersensitive

YVES ALION/1991

Janet Frame is an author who is known and recognized in our country.
When I read her autobiographical books, I naturally became interested in this destiny which was both banal and out of the ordinary. And then little by little I was equally touched by her writing, though it can seem a bit dry at first glance. The extraordinary thing in her case is that she succeeds in moving us with simple words, sometimes even naïve ones.

In watching your film, one has the impression that this woman is a subtle mixture of a strong personality and an ever-present fragility.
It's exactly that. It's true that she has possessed rather fixed ideas of great sophistication about the world and her surroundings since her early youth. And at the same time she maintains a timidity, an uncommon inhibition.

The period depicted in the film stops in the sixties. How has she evolved since then?
As far as I know she lives a life much more in keeping with what one imagines about a writer. Which does not eliminate, however, I think, her interior demons.

What did she think about the film?
That's not easy for me to answer. It would be better to ask her. I think she appreciated the film. But the personality of Janet Frame is unusual: she

---

From *Revue du cinéma,* April 1991. Translated by Michele Curley. Reprinted by permission of the author.

doesn't really think that it's her that one sees on the screen. In fact she was more upset for her sister who is still living.

What do you think of the way she perceives the world?
It's without a doubt the way she speaks of her childhood that troubled me the most. Through her, I recovered things, moments, sensations from my own childhood. And in some way, that permitted me to look back with a different, more detached point of view on this period.

After Sweetie, An Angel at My Table *is your second film on insanity. Why this fascination?*
You're going to laugh, but I have never thought of making that connection. In fact the two films are very different: in *Sweetie* there is a complexity and an uneasiness that you don't find in *An Angel at My Table,* at least I don't think so. Rather than insanity, I wanted to speak about hypersensitivity, vulnerability. But it's necessary to put things in context: if Janet had not been so alone, without a doubt she would have been able to speak about her anguish with someone, and the most troubling symptoms of her illness would have been eased.

Seeing your films, one feels that insanity is a social disease that is provoked by the difficulty one encounters in the process of looking for his/her place in the social game.
It's clearly not simple. A personal side of insanity or rather disturbances of human beings also exists. But it's true that each society operates in a certain way. Often the person is only buried, too fragile to react. It's frightening to think that Janet Frame almost underwent an experimental lobotomy because someone had diagnosed a schizophrenia that only existed in her imagination!

Janet seems to hold herself endlessly on the brink of mental breakdown, such that it would take nothing for her to fall to the wrong side and sink. And at the same time they say that it could happen to anyone.
That's right. I'm under the impression that we come into contact more and more often with people who seem to act irrationally and who are on the brink of more serious disturbances.

Do you think that art is a means of finding some sort of equilibrium, whether it's poetry or... cinema?
There is not a rule. It's evident that Janet would not have come out of it as she did had her writing not constituted this pole of attraction. Which does not mean that her so-called schizophrenia was her source of inspiration. Moreover, in certain cases, an artistic activity can turn out to be destabilizing. The life of those who live off their art is not always a model of equilibrium.

Who are your favorite directors?
There are many. I like people like Luis Buñuel, David Lynch and Spike Lee. But that doesn't prevent me from also treating myself by watching *Mad Max*.

There is a question asked of all English speaking directors, that is the relationship that they have with Hollywood. You who have a personal vision of the world, could you, if need be, work in the Hollywood mold?
Why not? I have nothing against the idea of having a comfortable budget at my disposition to make my films with, and I believe that the system does not necessarily erase your personality. That said, I'm not there and I don't run after American producers. My next film will be made with Australian funds.

Is the New Zealand setting too narrow?
I currently live in Sydney. I left New Zealand many years ago. It's a country that is really too provincial, where it's not easy for a director to work, first because the structures of production are truly insufficient; and also because the New Zealand mentality is still a bit cramped. If you say you want to make movies, they say to you: "But who do you think you are? Why you?" It's true in effect, why me?

How Women Live Their Lives

HEIKE-MELBA FENDEL/1991

The autobiography An Angel at My Table *by Janet Frame already impressed you very much as a young girl. Before the shootings you got acquainted with the author. Was it stressful for you to want to do justice to a real person with your film?*
Oh yes, it was peculiar, it demands a lot of respect. To be respectful is not one of my greatest strengths.

Did you get Janet Frame involved in the project?
Janet Frame is very reserved. I accepted that. That I have the rights to her book does not mean that I also have the rights to her as a person. Her situation is that she has literally written off these parts of her life. This past exists for her as fiction. I am not interested in the real Janet Frame but only in the literary character which she made of herself. The latter is what I had to do justice to. Therefore it was only important for the clarification of details—for instance what kind of songs she listened to at the time—that I got to know the author. I think it was much to her interest that I approached her work as an independent artist, not as a slave. She knew that I would add my view and my interpretation.

In your last film Sweetie *you showed two women who could not cope with the world around them. That was in the nature of that character. In this film you pick up that confusion once more by means of Janet Frame's characters. Here, however, it becomes an inevitable part of an artistic existence.*

From *EPD Film,* April 1991. Translated by Andrea Riemann. Reprinted by permission of the author.

I am certainly more interested in people who do not have an easy time functioning in society. In the first place, though, the quality of the literary model convinced me. It is determined by a deeply felt humaneness. *Sweetie* is totally different, much grimmer and darker.

Janet Frame was said to be schizophrenic because her "being different from the others" could not be explained in any other way—neither to her surrounding nor to herself. Are being lost and an outsider driving powers for artistic expression?
I think that if one does not belong, if one has a feeling for one's own inner wounds, one tries to build a bridge. One tries to find oneself in what one expresses. And mostly one finds out, in the end, that this initial motivation does not necessarily have anything to do with the accomplished work per se. It becomes an independent whole and one can confront it as if it were from a completely different person. I think that people who keep in pace with life, who function as they are required to, do not need explanations. Still, there are certainly many people who need that explanation but do nevertheless not have the power to find it on their own.

A great number of artistic biographies have been adapted for the cinema. At the very least, Janet Frame is not a typical film heroine, the way you portray her. Nor are the sisters in Sweetie*—to return to the similarity between the two films.*
It is the greatest present for me if people open up, if they show vulnerability and their character traits that are not very glamorous. I believe that once one can accept these character traits in oneself, one has come a little closer to freedom. In this desire to present the characters in their wholeness the two films resemble each other, I agree.

You also concentrate exclusively on female characters in the work you do for television, that is, on the representation of all sorts of women. Therefore, one could call you a feminist director, even though this does not seem to fit.
I have to admit that I no longer know what this means or expresses. I think that feminist culture arose as a reaction to stereotypical representations, to male dominated perspectives. A lot had to be clarified which, I think, has been clarified by now: my stance towards filming is not defined just by this challenge. This whole discussion is too limited. I am interested in life as a whole. Even if my representation of female characters has a feminist structure, this is nevertheless only one aspect of my approach.

Would a male protagonist also appeal to you?
I am a woman. So it seems totally natural that I have female protagonists. I want to understand as well as possible what life is all about. Consequently I want to inquire into how other women live their lives, what particularities their lives are composed of. I think this is the main reason why men tell predominantly stories about men. I can't imagine telling the story of a man. I don't know why I should, either. Although I am curious about their world I still prefer to be in the center of my imaginary world myself. The same is true for love fantasies, in which I do not take on the male perspective, either.

How much do you share your heroines' feeling of being crazy?
I am certainly very neurotic but not unstable. My sense for the possible is highly developed, especially my sense of possible disasters. I imagine all kinds of things. I think the most banal things through to their extreme. With regard to my own films, I also assume every possible position, I admire it and I consider it totally stupid. Life is not an easy matter for me.

Judging from your films, I get the impression you have an infallible control of form.
I think one has to be self confident to be able to be insecure. That is to say, to have the form of insecurity that leads one to question everything. I find it suffocating to feel secure. I attempt to materialize a vision. My questions, my doubts help me develop a vision with which I can be happy. I mean there is the screenplay, that is one thing. Then there is maybe this odd feeling from which I have to develop everything. That means that I try to scoop the atmosphere out of the material, everything that the process of filming can add. To say what can only be said with the film medium. Regarding *An Angel at My Table* this means to keep it simple, to keep up a close and intimate relationship with Janet Frame. I did not want to create any metaphors.

Because metaphors mean a detour?
My characters and their feelings are no substitutes for anything but themselves. I do not want to prove anything that they can't prove on their own.

In Cannes, where Sweetie *was competing two years ago, some reactions were very negative.*
We were all very excited about participating in the competition. It was my first feature film, a minor film. So we were all the more surprised by the ensuing clamor. We found it totally stupid to consider this film shocking. We were staying in these incredibly expensive hotel suites. We were crying and asking ourselves why we were here among these bastards. They hated us and we hated them.

In Venice you were celebrated in the following year with An Angel at My Table.
I understood that just as little. One has to consider, though, that it ended fairly well with *Sweetie,* after all. It won its audience all over the world and it created a certain prestige for me, especially among those who haven't seen the film.

Do you intend to remain in Australia?
Preferably, yes. Though I also feel attracted to certain ideas that can only be realized elsewhere. I will shoot my next film in New Zealand again. Then I am planning a film about Christopher Isherwood. That will be in Hollywood.

I like Australia. It's warm, the people are relaxed and quite informal. I like this renunciation of formalities. There is a general openness to cultural things because nobody knows exactly where the next good thing will be coming from.

Was it the dream of your life to direct films?
No, I did not plan explicitly to become a director of films. I simply had a few ideas that I wanted to adapt to the screen after I had previously been involved in painting and theater. I had always been fascinated with film. However, I had thought for the longest time that I would not be able to do this because it is so difficult. I am well aware that I was no genius. Finally, I just started without even consciously noticing it. I started filming and I was entirely happy because all the pictures were mine. It took me a while to realize that not everything is great just because I made it myself. Then I really wanted to master the medium and so I started to approach it analytically. The process of becoming conscious led to a great disappointment.

The more I got involved in it, the more I was worried and the more it seemed impossible for me to make my own films.

I think this is a perfectly normal sequence of stages. At first, one has the ignorance and the energy of the beginner and just does it. Then one grasps the true dimension of the thing, feels fear and doubt and either one gets stuck in them or one wins a true security.

Yes, it is like skiing, to give a stupid example. At the beginning one thinks of everything at once, one is tense and all the movements seem so unnatural until the technical basics become part of oneself. Then there is a comfortable lightness. I think I have reached this point. The learning process certainly never stops but the cramps are gone.

Structure is Essential/Absolutely Crucial/ One of the Most Important Things

ANDREAS FURLER/1993

Your film recalls novels of the 19th century in its classical structure. Are those your inspiration?
I love the literature of the 19th century. The story has indeed that flavor and atmosphere.

What exactly do you like about those novels?
Firstly, I like novels in general. As a whole, they satisfy me much more than most films, since they illuminate things much more patiently and deeply. However, I especially like romanticism and, in particular, the Brontë sisters. I had read *Wuthering Heights* already as a child. On a second reading as an adult, I was stunned how mercilessly and precisely the book observes human nature and how extraordinarily inventive it is at the same time. It is incredible, after all, that such a story came out of this small woman, who had hardly seen anything of the world. Emily Brontë spoke barely a word when she went out, and she left her hometown Howarth very rarely. She also writes about the bareness of these marshy areas. I can well imagine that feeling in the New Zealand landscapes. There is the same feeling of isolation—after all we are practically at the end of the world. *The Piano,* is one of those at-the-end-of-the-world stories, where unusual things can happen.

The untamed New Zealand landscape plays a central role in your film. Did you grow up in a rural region yourself?

From *Filmbulletin,* February 1993. Translated by Andrea Riemann. Reprinted by permission of *Filmbulletin* and the author.

We lived in a bush-cabin [she laughs]. No, seriously, I couldn't have done it. I was much too scared of rats and such things. Still, you can't grow up in New Zealand without becoming conscious of the landscape. Even in the capital, you see the bush on the outskirts in place of the industry belt in Europe; and one feels the vastness of nature. As a child, I often went to visit farmer acquaintances of ours, who lived in the bush. I used to love to be there. It was a kind of fairy country for me and it kindled my imagination.

The Piano *has an ingenious, nearly classical structure. Something like that must take time to write.*
Of course I feel flattered if you say that because I love classical structure. A solid structure is one of the most important things. The structuring was hard work for me. I normally tend to get distracted and thus I never really reach my goal. The actual writing of the screen-play took about six months. The whole development, however, lasted from 1984 until 1991. The second draft, which I wrote in 1990 in a two-and-a-half-month period of concentration, was of central importance. Because the first draft had been done years earlier, I could consider it quite coolly. "Well, this is wrong and that is wrong." Of course my writer and my producer, who were very patient and helpful, were also extremely important. A screenplay is a kind of puzzle: One has to solve things in the way in which one started. *The Piano* is not an action thriller but a psychological story. Thus it has to have a psychological or rather lyrical resolution.

The film's resolution was a pleasant surprise for me. From the middle of the film onwards, I expected that the triangle between your heroine and the two men would end in catastrophe, in bloodshed or something like that.
At the beginning we had just such a violent, action-oriented ending. We thought that we couldn't start so much trouble without having a showdown. It seemed very predictable and we were thinking: "How about if someone died at the end?" That was the decisive turning-point in the second draft of the screenplay. At this point, a note was added to the finale that was much more interesting for me and allowed me to investigate the psychology of the characters much better. In other genres I find it all right if everyone kills each other at the end.

Geneviève Lemon as Dawn (a.k.a. Sweetie), *Sweetie*, 1989

Jon Darling as Gordon and Karen Colston as Kay, *Sweetie*, 1989

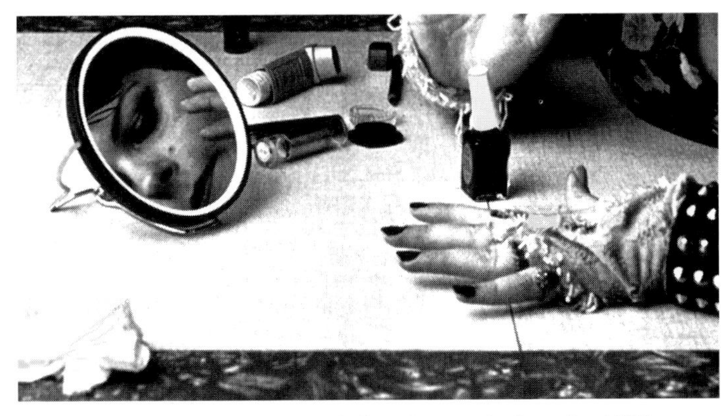

Geneviève Lemon as Dawn (a.k.a. Sweetie), *Sweetie*, 1989

Alexia Keogh as the young Janet Frame, *An Angel at My Table*, 1990

Alexia Keogh as the young Janet Frame, *An Angel at My Table*, 1990

Kerry Fox as Janet Frame, *An Angel at My Table*, 1990

Holly Hunter as Ada and Harvey Keitel as Baines, *The Piano*, 1993

Anna Paquin as Flora and Sam Neill as Stewart, *The Piano*, 1993

The Piano, 1993

Holly Hunter as Ada, *The Piano*, 1993

The Piano, 1993

Nicole Kidman as Isabel Archer, *Portrait of a Lady,* 1996

Portrait of a Lady, 1996

Nicole Kidman as Isabel Archer, *Portrait of a Lady*, 1996

John Malkovich as Gilbert Osmond, *Portrait of a Lady*, 1996

Portrait of a Lady, 1996

Portrait of a Lady, 1996

Nicole Kidman as Isabel Archer and John Malkovich as Gilbert Osmond, *Portrait of a Lady*, 1996

The Piano makes a leap in your career to international production . . .
. . . in the sense that it is financed 100% by the French "CiBy 2000." The wonderful thing about it is that this production company presently lets its directors have complete creative control over the production until the final editing. There was no obligation to employ French actors, either. We could barely believe it at the beginning. There is presently nothing comparable in the world.

You have an international cast.
Holly Hunter and Harvey Keitel are Americans; Sam Neill is internationally known, but he is from New Zealand. However, I created the roles without thinking about the cast. Needless to say, I became confused by the multitude of possibilities. So I had to reconsider the two essential questions: How much do we want certain actors, how much do they want us? That helped a little.

Your two last films featured highly impressive performances by children. How do you work with them?
I think my greatest advantage is that I love children and that they probably know that. I actually don't do anything special with them.

Do you have children yourself?
[Pointing at her belly] That will be my first one. Besides, I'm a bit of a child myself. It seems that children trust me. That is actually all. I didn't discover the girl in *The Piano* myself. I simply had to recognize her talent in the rehearsal, which was easy because she is outstanding. She has this concentration and an infallible instinct for story-telling—I would say a natural talent. I could trust her with the endless passage, in which she is telling an invented story about her father. I never thought I could find a child who was capable of doing that. On top of that, she is not yet aware of her talent. She was totally indifferent toward it. She simply loved to perform.

In the role of the daughter, the girl witnesses how her mother gets a finger chopped off. To what extent does one inform a child about such a violent scene?
That was the scene the girl's parents were most worried about. They obviously had not seen the whole screenplay since it involves more than they

needed to understand. Fortunately, it's in the nature of film making that even a highly dramatic scene is not very dramatic when one is filming it. One laughs, one cracks jokes. There is a sense in which one does not really know the force of the effects until one sees it on screen. In this case, the child had seen the artificial finger that we were using and liked it, just as she did all the gruesome things—but more as a curiosity than as something horrifying.

Yet, she had to be brought into that totally confused state in which she finds herself at the end of the film.
We simply told her that she should shout as loudly as she could. Much more horrible for her was the scene in which her father is chasing her through the forest so as to find out what she knows about the double life of her mother. There is no way to protect children entirely from such scenes. One can only try to make them aware of the fact that everything is only acted. In order to show her this, we let her act the role of her father: She was allowed to grab and shake someone so as to frighten him. The other actors in turn explained our goal to her once more very precisely. The only thing that she was interested in afterwards, by the way, was how the finger was chopped off. We obviously didn't show it to her and she was totally upset during the rushes. She merely heard on the sound track how the ax came down and said: "I didn't even hear how it cut through the bone."

The theme music was composed by Michael Nyman. Were you inspired by the Greenaway films?
Certainly. I was looking for someone who had already been involved in film but who nevertheless had an individual sound. Many composers copy a little bit from here and there and it does not sound all that fresh and original. However I wanted Nyman to sound less emotionally distant than in the Greenaway films and kept asking: "Michael, are you sure you can truly do something with feelings?" That was an interesting challenge for him. He wrote piano pieces for Holly Hunter so that she could play them and he grouped the rest of the scene around them. In this way, the music was anchored, so to speak.

Some of your successful Australian colleagues have emigrated to America after they became successful. Do you have similar plans?

I am indeed going to work with an American producer next. Though not with one from the big studios. The situation will thus be very similar to that in *The Piano*.

Is the film going to be set in the United States?
No, it is not going to be filmed in the United States. Of course it's very tempting to have a large audience. Unfortunately that always entails a great reduction of choices. Personally, I hope that I don't fall into the trap of feeling more appreciated as a director or as a person just because I make a lot of money and attract a large audience. One has to have a good feeling for these situations. One can't make a film for a small audience that costs an enormous sum of money. That is a fact that one has to respect.

Jane Campion: Making Friends by Directing Films

MARLI FELDVOSS/1993

Jane Campion, you spoke about the Piano *project for the first time five years ago, when you made your first feature film* Sweetie. *Although you have made three stylistically very different films,* The Piano *tells a familiar story. What was the greatest challenge in this film project?*
I consider the differences between my films more important than the similarities. Maybe this is because I don't want to see myself as someone who keeps directing the same movies. My main goal is and has always been to tell the story as convincingly as possible. What is entirely new this time is the gothic romantic genre and the significance of the landscapes. There is obviously no architecture at all in this film. Being an urban person to the core, this was hard for me to take. I also think that the characters are more complex than in my earlier films and they exhibit more emotional extremes as well. Then again, maybe not. However, I used a truly experienced cast. This was a challenge to me: to be working with actors who may well have more experience than myself.

What advantages do you have with experienced actors?
I've learned what control means in terms of responsibility. My role as director consists in protecting the story and in doing everything possible to help the actors to perform at their best but at the same time serve the story. I had to find a kind of control that does not trigger dissension or fights but that leads and protects as much as possible. At the end I came to

From *EPD Film,* August 1993. Translated by Andrea Riemann. Reprinted by permission of the author.

this conclusion: It is simply a process of making friends and creating confidence. This may sound very easy but it isn't. One doesn't earn people's confidence by wishing for it; one has to earn it. One has to work in such a way that the points one wants to make are comprehensible, sensible and intelligent. Actors who don't have any experience with film, such as those in my previous films, are much more likely to subordinate themselves to the orders of the director.

Why did The Piano *have to be a costume film?*
Because I like it like that [laughs]. It had to be by all means. Not merely the gothic romantic genre but also the time itself. In New Zealand that was the time of colonization and that is when my story began. That is my inheritance.

The theme "inheritance" seems to have two meanings in this case: on the one hand, it means ancestors and on the other "return to nature." This "return" becomes especially obvious in the character of Baines [Harvey Keitel], who wears the tattoos of the Maori and who, as Ada [Holly Hunter], almost lost his language.
I think that the film approaches this return to nature by means of large confrontations. The nature of this man mirrors, you might say, the beginnings of civilization. The film is set in a time when nature had a much greater influence on people. They lived in the midst of it and tried to tame it, burned down forests to assimilate the environment to that of Europe. But Baines is for me very generally an outsider. He doesn't fit into the nice religious community of the early New Zealand nor is he a Maori—he does not fit anywhere. He's a loner.

Thus Ada and Baines are the ideal couple.
They both have a rebellious quality. Ada, in my opinion, rebels against the extreme suppression of woman in 1850. Baines is from a lower social class than the other settlers. As a consequence, he doesn't feel at ease where he is nor does he respect the settlers. However, it is difficult to describe Baines' rebellion precisely. Men simply have more possibilities to express themselves that do not necessarily entail problematic situations for them.

I find your perspective on Baines very interesting. It is the perspective of a woman toward a man that one does not ordinarily get to see. One normally does not see

a naked man but a naked woman. To me, this naked man was very appealing. He is rather shy, not dominant, and he is learning something. He is learning how to love.
I think he is a kind of female fantasy. He's like the beast in *The Beauty and the Beast.* He's omnipotent but in the presence of a woman he's vulnerable and delicate because he wants to be part of her secret. He wants to know what it is and he realizes that he will only experience it if he gradually wins her confidence. He would never use violence—that would be too simple. I think he's instinctively led by the idea of making this woman, who is so passionately in love with her piano, just as passionately in love with him. He observes the women and he realizes that there's something in their world that he lacks. Of course it's like this with all men. They all feel attracted by the female world and its secrets. Baines, though, spontaneously finds a viable path to this world. He's an honorable beast. He doesn't rape her.

You have never dealt with men at all before.
Not so intimately. This is a study of men and women. I hadn't experienced a close co-operation with male actors before, and it's been a great experience for me. The men are just as important as Ada—everyone is important. It's a film about relationships. And I was burning to know what happens when a woman is directing in such situations, in a women's film.

How was it?
There's a different kind of vulnerability when a woman is directing. It also makes a difference that there are more women on the set than usual. When, for instance, we prepared the love scenes, Holly and I always made suggestions and Harvey kept looking at us shyly. He complained: "You girls are always getting at me." On the whole, however, my men managed the situation quite well. For Sam Neill, there were also quite vulnerable situations, when Ada undresses him, beats him or objectifies him. I hope that nobody felt they were being taken advantage of in any way.

What role does literature play? You made a cinematic adaptation of Janet Frame's autobiography, you refer to Sylvia Plath, now to Emily Brontë and possibly a little bit to D.H. Lawrence.
I owe a lot to literature as well as to poetry. But I can't always remember exactly what. Literature has simply become a part of my whole knowledge.

At any rate, *Wuthering Heights* plays an important role, so do the poems of Emily Dickinson, whose life has also deeply impressed me. I have also reread Tennyson and I know D.H. Lawrence from my girlhood. I'm totally crazy about the novels of the 19th century. This film is like a 19th century novel for me.

What fascinated you most? The sensitivity, which we don't have anymore nowadays because we know too much and because we are prepared for everything, including our sexual lives?
The great advantage in setting the story in 1850 lies in the possibility of developing characters who approach love, sex and eroticism naively, whose first experiences one can observe—there are no more such occasions for us today. I like to imagine what it is like when people experience the power of these things for the first time.

And to this end the bush was perfect.
Definitely, don't you think so?

I remember the way you told me about the bright colors of New Zealand. The palette of colors was completely different in An Angel at My Table.
At that time all of New Zealand was covered by the bush and in the bush it is very dark, hardly any light penetrates. That is why the settlers burned down all the woods, so as not to become claustrophobic. It's claustrophobic, impenetrable, it's like swimming under water. It's a mysterious, beautiful and fairy-like world but it can just as well be unsettling and nightmarish. For me, this landscape is very fascinating.

The landscape is obviously a metaphor, a bearer of signification. Are there any inspirations from landscape painting?
The primitive painter Rousseau, whom I like very much, comes to mind. My mother had a painting by him. I think it's called "The Woman in the Forest." She's wearing a very formal costume in the Edwardian style, in an environment that in complete contrast to it. This has always stayed with me. It seems to be a kind of lingering effect of the unconscious that I've put my woman in such a bush, as well. Civilization versus nature. That constitutes one of the greatest paradoxes of being human. To be cultivated and civilized on the one hand and on the other to have to deal with the worldly appetites and sexual drives and the romantic moments that derive from a completely different corner.

You envisioned for Ada's role an actress of the Frida Kahlo type. Considering her paintings or also her life, Holly Hunter is an absolutely contradictory decision.
That's how it goes with decisions. I am very much attracted by the beauty and power of Frida Kahlo's appearance. The way her eyebrows grow together in the middle, for instance. She is an extraordinary beauty and a strong woman. I made a sharp turn when I got acquainted with Holly Hunter and as a result decided for a totally different kind of 'small' power that I liked about her. She is an excellent actress. I love her eyes. It was really great luck that I could free myself from the ideal that Frida Kahlo had represented for me. This brought me back to reality, and it changed Ada into a more normal figure. Ada had become a myth to me. Holly helped me to let her become real again and also to bring more down-to-earthness and reality into the story.

One part of the tragedy of Frida Kahlo, of her unhappy love-life, has nevertheless remained in the film: the chopped-off finger.
Yes, we have to pay for passions. They have their price. [She laughs] There are diverse kinds of passion. But when one sees passion as a means of escape, one has to pay dearly for it. I'm fantasizing a little bit. Passion can be the path to happiness as well as to folly. For some people it's like a constant danger area in life, like an addiction. I'm interested in this kind of ultimate experience, which some people need.

Is that also part of your own character?
No, but I feel great sympathy and even adoration for people who attack their lives with such acts of violence. They take a risk and at times they don't survive it. I'm certainly not a good champion of senseless passions. That's not my style at all. I think that I create experiences to express in my films things for which I'm much too timid in reality.

Interview with Jane Campion: More Barbarian than Aesthete

THOMAS BOURGUIGNON AND

MICHEL CIMENT/1993

The Piano *is your oldest project; you thought about it even before doing* Sweetie. *What was its starting point?*
After my studies at film school, I thought about the next level which naturally had to be a dramatic film. I had two ideas: *The Piano* and another, *Ebb,* more fantastic, more my sort of thing at the time. *The Piano* seemed more commercial because it was a love story, but it was also a story that needed more maturity. I wrote about half of it, but it seemed that if I was only able to do it on a small scale, I would lack the money to do justice to the scenery. Besides, I didn't have enough experience as a director and I wasn't in a position to really understand all the themes that I wanted to focus on, this archetypal story, the relationships between primitivism and civilization, a whole construction based upon oppositions. I thus decided to let the project rest. In the meantime, I met Pierre Rissient, who showed my shorts at Cannes. This was an important experience because I realized—what I hadn't perceived in Australia—that there was an audience to whom I could make my voice be heard without having to change it. So I returned to Australia to make *Sweetie,* which was a continuation of my film school work and seemed to me to correspond to my state of mind at the time, something more provocative, more rebellious with regard to cinema.

Interview: 23 April 1993. From *Positif,* June 1993. Translated by Michele Curley.

What was the subject of Ebb?
It was an imaginary story about a country where one day the sea leaves to never return, and the way in which the people have to find a spiritual solution to this problem. The natural world had become artificial and unpredictable and the film spoke about faith and doubt. The inhabitants of this country had developed a certain form of spirituality, hearing voices, having visions. At the end, the father of a family central to the story, the man who was the least inclined towards a spiritual adventure, had the most extraordinary experiences. It's for him that the sea returned and his tongue/language began to have a salty taste! He became a sacrificial victim.

What changed in The Piano *since your first idea for the film?*
In the beginning there were very simply piano lessons. But the ending was very traditional, with a violent resolution. After *Sweetie* and *An Angel at my Table,* I came back to this project and I thought that the central idea was too good for such a predictable ending. In speaking with my producer Jan Chapman and with Billy MacKinnon, who helped me write the script, I wondered why we had so much reticence—especially me! Baines killed Stewart; some fingers were even cut off. It was much more violent. So we decided to go deeper into the psychology of the story. The second version of the script had Ada go back to Baines; Stewart saw them together, he fell in love with her and became more vulnerable. The changes were mostly made in the last fifty pages. We introduced the characters of the aunts, and made the main characters less one-dimensional since they were too much like fairy tale characters.

The fairy tale can be found in the story of Bluebeard presented by the shadow theater.
That sequence corresponded to a certain type of experience for the spectator, but I wanted the central story to be as strong, as emotional as possible. The theater scene was always in the script. I had been struck by the photo of a woman from the colonial era whose head appeared between sheets. These amateur theaters have always seemed to me to be remarkably skillful. The scene sums up for me all the power of the invented story: you know it's an imaginary world, yet you believe it. It's the essence of spectacle. People love to be led. When the little girl tells her aunt the story of her

father, she believes it, even though she knows it's a lie. The desire to believe is stronger than anything else.

In Flora's story, there's a shot where you use animation to show the father in flames.
We found a marvelous illustrated book that belonged to a child of that time and we decided that in this story the book would belong to Flora; it was here that we were able to introduce these amazing graphics. Every member of the crew firmly believed the story that Flora told. There was also a practical reason for this animation shot: it permitted us to connect two shots in which Anna Paquin had given the best of herself.

How did you approach the problem of the historical film?
I did a lot of research. I have a good ear for dialogue; I can imitate people very well, and my husband is even better. But for these characters, I had no models, they were not drawn from people I know. It was a real problem: how to give them humanity and use my qualities of observation in the film? I read diaries written by women of the nineteenth century, as well as first-hand accounts of the arrival of Europeans in New Zealand. I tried to recover their voices and their ways of thinking. I also read books of that time. At some point I decided to resolve these problems in my head. I suppose that I needed to feel protected, since this classical story presented a series of obstacles that I couldn't resolve with my narrative technique of diversion, which would really lead nowhere. I wanted to work in a classical tragic form, but at the same time I wasn't equipped for it, and I had to develop new abilities. Each scene posed problems and I couldn't, like in *Sweetie,* go in all directions. I had to follow a path.

Did you do any research on the relationships between the Maori and the Anglo-Saxon colonists?
I was not able to study these contacts since no-one really knows what happened. But one sees the consequences today. I don't feel particularly expert in this domain and there were things that I wanted to say in this film, but my Maori advisors convinced me that it was nonsense! Of course I spoke with specialists, which was especially important as there is a renaissance of Maori culture. The tendency of certain Maori is to have a heroic vision of their past and that was not what I intended to show. Moreover, the points

of view are often very different. I preferred to look around me and observe how people behaved. For example having a homosexual Maori character in the film was dramatic, created a stir. The Maori's contended that if there had been a homosexual at the time, he would have been killed! But in their community, sexuality is totally out in the open; people talk continuously about their genitals. It's part of their vision of others, and there is nothing prudish as in Protestant culture.

The Maori background is like an objective correlative of what the heroine feels: their culture takes care of the spiritual and the sexual as much as the purely material.
Yes. They highlight the Puritan side of the colonists. They have a much more harmonious and stronger relationship with nature. The Anglo-Saxons have not resolved the relationship between what is animal and sexual in themselves and their rationality. Baines is between the two; he belongs neither to the Whites nor to the Maori. He was probably a whaler, settled there, and his unfinished tattoo shows a will to be integrated that has not been totally accomplished. At the same time he makes an effort to learn their language and serves as an interpreter between the Maori and the Europeans. In fact, Harvey Keitel learned to speak more Maori and knew more of it than most of the extras! He was a very good student, while a lot of the natives didn't speak their language very well.

How did you come to cite the poet Thomas Hood?
In fact, I asked my mother, who reads much more poetry than me, to find me a quotation about the sea. At first it was going to be used for *Ebb,* since *The Piano* originally did not finish with the current sequence. Then I placed it at the end of *The Piano*. The film ended with the concert. Baines arrived, brought Ada out of the theater and escaped with her and her daughter. Stewart discovered their absence and left to look for them. A postscript said that he disappeared in the bush and was not found. There were no scenes where they were seen making love. He was more of a one-dimensional character, jealous and angry. In the final version, he's much more human and vulnerable.

You used slow motion many times.
There's one time when I use it and it's not noticeable: it's a way of observing characters with more intensity. Certain passages were even shot in

slow motion "in" the camera. I could permit myself this license because it was a romantic story that one treats in a higher, more dramatic, more lyric style. Slow motion can seem easy and in bad taste in certain circumstances. In others not. When she comes out of the water, the shots were banal without slow motion, I wanted to translate the shock that that represented for her. I think that it works.

There are many angels in your films: An Angel at My Table, *Flora dressed as an angel, and the remark by Stewart to Ada, when he admits having "clipped her wing."*

I don't believe in angels, but I believe in the hope of being an angel, in the desire of the human being of being saved, of being able to fly away. That goes back to the idea of artists. The artist expresses a dissatisfaction, the desire to escape oppression, a form of hope; I don't propose a solution but I express emotion. The people who count for me are those who give meaning to life: artists, poets who want to understand and ask questions that permit one to know oneself better. I cannot imagine a life without this dimension. And at the same time I'm neither an aesthete nor a cinema buff. I quickly become impatient with films that demand too much of my attention. There is a barbaric side to me! Ada is an artist, but at the same time I don't believe that she cares about having an audience. She plays for herself. We modeled her a bit after the Brontë sisters and the imaginary world that they created for themselves. I'm attracted to romantic literature and I wanted to contribute to the genre. As for novels, I especially think of *Wuthering Heights* and as for poetry, Blake, Tennyson and Bryon. I went to the village where Emily Brontë was brought up, I walked on the moor and I tried to retain the atmosphere. But it very evident that I didn't want to make a transposition of *Wuthering Heights,* because I don't think that that story could be told today: it's a saga that extends over two generations and moreover I'm not English. I belong to a colonial culture and I had to invent my own fiction. I wanted to speak of the relationship between men and women, of the complex character of love and of eroticism, but also of the repression of sexuality. I owe a debt not only to Emily Brontë but also to many women artists. There are some specific feminine qualities in this film. Ada is an extremely feminine character with her sense of secrecy and her relationship with her daughter. I also read a lot of Emily Dickinson's poetry while writing the script.

You didn't use music by such Romantic composers as Schubert or Schumann.
That was never our intention! I wanted a musical identity for the film and not a pastiche of composers from the nineteenth century. I needed a personal voice, musical compositions that Ada could have written. Michael Nyman decided to use Scottish airs, pieces which Ada could have heard in her country and which go well with her personality. I don't know much about music and I asked for advice in choosing a composer. Some friends recommended Michael Nyman to me. Nyman's work for Peter Greenaway's films and especially for *Draughtsman's Contract,* where he had captured the feeling of the times and at the same time expressed a very personal style, was of course familiar to me. Michael is not simply a composer for films; he's a complete musician. He has his own integrity. That's what I wanted for this film, not someone who would use tricks. I'm happy with what he did, with the violence of his music in particular.

In the sequence on the sea, you also use Maori songs.
I don't know the Maori culture very well, but I can tell you that all that is authentic. We could have inserted more elements from the Maori culture, but they would not have been integral to the story. There are unsettling stories, passionate aspects that we therefore had to do without. We only kept what could fit with our story.

The romantic dimension of the film is clearly reinforced by the use of nature. How did you choose your scenery?
I knew the atmosphere and the power of this scenery, having grown up there. I walked in the bush, spent nights there, which is a custom in New Zealand. I went on long hikes on trails with my father and I loved that. There is such an intensity in certain parts of the bush that you have the impression of being under water. It's a landscape that is unsettling, claustrophobic and mythic all at the same time. In my childhood it reinforced complicated itineraries that we borrowed. We wanted to give sub-marine colors to the bush scenes to tie them to the final sequence. It's scenery that troubled a lot of Europeans when they arrived, and since they didn't like it, they cleared a lot of it so that it looked more like Europe. I thought that this wild landscape was right for my story. Romanticism has been misunderstood in our era, especially in films. It has become something "pretty" or lovable. Its hardness, its dark side has been forgotten. I wanted to create

a feeling of terror in the spectator when faced with the power of natural elements. That's, I think, the essence of Romanticism: this respect for a nature that is considered larger than you, your mind, or even humanity.

How were two American actors chosen for the roles of Ada and Baines?
Mysteriously as it happened. It wasn't my idea to have Americans in this film. New Zealanders either, by the way, since it's an era that practically precedes the creation of New Zealand. At first we thought more about English actors. I even envisioned French actors, but it's curious how your compatriots—at least those I spoke with—are reticent regarding their own actors. I was much more enthusiastic than they were. But I suppose that it's the same everywhere: one appreciates less that which belongs to one's own culture. I met a lot of fabulous French actors, but I was worried about the language problem. In England too, I met a lot of people. But we never did a systematic and methodical search; it was like flirting with everybody around the world! And we were lucky to make good choices because our approach was rather unfocused. In London, for example, I didn't find anyone who had the presence of Harvey Keitel. It seemed bizarre to some that I chose him. Harvey was linked to strong memories of cinema that I had had when I was very young: *Mean Streets, Bad Timing* or *The Duellists*. I thought that he was interested in different things, experimental things. People told me his age could be a problem. So I watched one of his latest films, *The Two Jakes,* and I thought that he was very good, that he seemed young. I sent him the script, which he liked a lot, and with what was happening in his life at that time, he wanted to act in a film that spoke of the relationships between men and women, rather than another story of cops and robbers. He had not often been given the opportunity to express certain qualities of tenderness that he possesses. I think that at the beginning I was intimidated, but the more we got to know each other, the more we spoke together, the more it became a natural and easy friendship. He's a timid and attentive man, far from the macho and brutal figure in his films! He thought I was funny and I respected him, it all went well! I like Holly Hunter very much as an actor, but I didn't immediately think of her, probably because, like everyone else, I had a stereotypical idea of the romantic heroine, tall with exquisite manners. Then I thought that it would be more intense to go against this stereotype. And I was lucky to have Holly Hunter, because even if she has beauty, it's not what she emphasizes; she

has very strong feelings, relationships with others, and not only outward appearance. She also possesses great concentration and is very vulnerable. She's a small woman who unleashes great power.

Does she play the piano herself?
She already played very well before beginning the film. At her house, there is a grand piano; clearly that was an advantage. I think a lot of people were skeptical about my choice, without daring to say it. I think she's great in this film, acting in a discreet style. Moreover we communicated very easily; we were really on the same wavelength. She has a very practical mind, like me, and neither of us has a lot of theories. I was lucky to have such a passionate collaborator because she really had a lot of work: mastering sign language, playing music. It wasn't easy.

For the third character you chose Sam Neill.
I chose him very early on: he's a very handsome man and I thought it was funny that the "bad guy" looked like "a mother's good-looking son," that he didn't have the ruddy face, the physical ugliness that is often given to these characters. All of a sudden, that allows the spectator to discover the real qualities that he possesses and to see him as a human being. Stewart is a man who transforms himself, and it's hard to express. Sam Neill succeeded in showing that [transformation] even though he doesn't have the same technique as actors like Harvey Keitel who studied the Method of the Actor's Studio, or as Holly Hunter. Sam works in his country and comes with the choices that he has made. I like to protect my actors; I respect their personal conception of acting. I also believe that they were seduced by this natural environment. After the end of the film, Holly explored the bush for two weeks with her sister. I think that Holly and Harvey have personalities that allow them to work anywhere in the world without feeling the absence of Hollywood. They don't act like stars. Besides that would be impossible in New Zealand where people would immediately have the tendency to take you down. They aren't used to being around stars.

Did it take a long time to edit?
A normal length of time for a film of this type; I didn't do a lot of takes even if I used more film than for my two previous films. We didn't have a lot of money: a budget of 6.5 million dollars. The film looks richer than its

cost; the big advantage was that the American dollar is worth three times more than the New Zealand dollar.

The original title is The Piano.
I wanted *The Piano Lesson,* but it was already the title of an American play and we couldn't obtain the rights. With CiBy 2000, we agreed on the title *The Piano,* but in Europe—where the issue of rights is not a problem—it will be *The Piano Lesson.* I also thought of *The Sleep of Reason,* but it wasn't very commercial!

What you were saying about the character of Stewart could apply to the whole film: unpredictable in its unveiling and continuously varying the perspectives one has of the actions and the people. As when Ada caresses Stewart.
In doing that, she is thinking of Baines, but above all of her own eroticism. The whole process of the piano lessons has eroticized her. It reveals her sexuality even if she thinks she's resisting it. It's the most certain way to seduce someone when he is not aware of a deeper motivation. Of course Ada has a sexuality, but she had repressed it at a certain level. She doesn't realize that she has feelings for Stewart: he is a sexual object for her. She doesn't really know what's she's doing, she acting almost like a sleepwalker. It's a very ambiguous scene and I spoke to Holly and Sam about it. I had written it of course but I still needed to really understand it with them! When she caresses Sam, she's searching for herself. Usually it's the opposite that happens: women often have the impression of being treated as objects by their men. It's perhaps a cliché, but men often want a sexual experience without being involved. The film wants to show however that men are vulnerable, and sexually too. They need to be loved and to feel protected.

Ada's past is rather mysterious.
My opinion about this is simple. My characters meet at a certain time in their lives, like us who don't know the past of others, and that is part of the mystery of being with people. We speak with people and their past is in them, in front of us, even if we don't know what it is. I also have a past, but I'm not sure that I understand it, that I can say how it made me what I am. We know however some things about Ada: she stopped speaking when she was six years old and doesn't know why. I remember reading that

Emily Brontë was not happy in the company of people, that she had a certain disdain for society and didn't like to speak in public. Charlotte took her out with her friends and she didn't say a word. Ada's problem is that she's too stubborn, she's romantic to the point of being so involved in her ideals that she could die for them. In order to live, it's necessary to make compromises with one's ideals. Young people often have very strong convictions. Curiously, growing up is adapting and I don't think it's a bad thing. Pure ideas don't take into consideration that there are complexities in the fact of being alive. Ada, at the end, can live her ideals in her imagination, fantasize about herself and be happy in a concrete life. She can separate art from life. Up until then she had a poetic idea of herself, she was in love with her romantic ideals which ended up dominating her, so much so that she couldn't live.

Do you find a lot of yourself in your heroines: Kay, Sweetie's sister, Janet Frame and Ada who also correspond to different ages in life?
I don't think I project my fantasies in these characters, and in any case I don't know who I am. We are what we do. On the other hand, I have a lot of tenderness for them, even if none of them represent me, though Kay is the closest to what I was. What is a part of me is a certain sense of the absolute and a desire to control things. I always had trouble understanding the separation between myself and the world; the mystery of sexuality, of hate, of passions, has always been a problem.

Sweetie *was dedicated to your sister,* The Piano *to Edith.*
She's my mother. All that has a meaning, no!

At the end you insert the words "kia ora" on the screen.
That means thank you in Maori. It's addressed to the actors and the crew. It's also a way of taking leave.

You have the same director of photography, Stuart Dryburgh, as in An Angel at My Table.
In that film, we restrained ourselves in the photography since it wasn't a "big" story. We didn't want to stifle the autobiographical story of Janet Frame. For *The Piano,* it made sense to have a more flamboyant style, a more cinematographic style.

Certain shots have a fairy tale feel, a quality of strangeness, like the one in which Flora is running in the hills.
I loved those hills and I thought about placing the silhouette of the little girl there. I suppose that it's a way of controlling the scenery, because sometimes it dominated me so much that I wondered how to interpret it in a personal way. But those hills were so lovely that I wanted to have them in the film. Anna Paquin on the crest of the hills seemed so minuscule that she practically disappeared. I had to replace her with someone taller so that we could see her. Anna was furious and humiliated!

In your films death is linked to nature. Sweetie *dies while saving a tree. In* An Angel at My Table, *Janet's sister dies by drowning. Here, Ada almost dies in the sea.*
I've never thought about it, but I want to try to find an answer! Maybe it's the same old story: you think you can control nature and she is stronger than you. To survive, it's necessary to make a truce with her, be humble and accept the part of nature that is in you. Human will can become disproportionate in its relationship with the world. As children we think we're the masters of the world, and we have to learn that we are not, otherwise we'll encounter difficult times.

Ada and Flora have a relationship that resembles more that of two friends than that of mother and daughter.
Their situation is very particular: they have neither husband nor father; it is suggested that Flora is an illegitimate child; Ada doesn't speak and Flora speaks for her, which gives her an importance for her age. She maintains a relationship with the world for both of them. They are almost inseparable. They conspire together, they have a specifically feminine intimacy. When Stewart sees them together, he senses in them a power that he really doesn't understand. In the same way, the relationship between Ada and her piano is a mystery for him.

The Piano *is in a certain sense the synthesis of your first two films. It has the poetic force of* Sweetie *and the narrative sense of* An Angel at My Table.
There is even much more narration in *The Piano*; not only a story but also a plot. You rediscover, I hope, the sense of surprise and the poetry of *Sweetie*. In *An Angel at my Table,* I was faithful to a book that I respected.

The Piano, like *Sweetie,* is more faithful to myself or to certain aspects of my personality. But *An Angel at my Table* was important not because it corresponded to my conception of cinema, because I knew I was making it for the small screen, but because it gave me confidence in myself on location. I was relaxed and I felt capable of improvising. I learned how to be more understanding with the actors, to allow them more space. I think that there are things that I wouldn't have been able to do in *The Piano* if I hadn't had the experience of *An Angel at my Table.*

Do you have any plans?
Two really. The first is the child that I'm going to have in two months; it's a big project and I want to take advantage of it. Then I have two adaptations in sight: the first is *Guru and My Disciple* by Christopher Isherwood, for CiBy 2000, the second *A Portrait of a Lady* based on the Henry James novel, for the American company Propaganda.

The Piano

MIRO BILBROUGH/1993

JANE CAMPION'S *THE PIANO* is the story of Ada (Holly Hunter), a woman who arrives on colonial New Zealand shores to wed Stewart (Sam Neill), a man she has never met. Ada brings to the marriage an obsessive attachment to her piano, a young daughter and an enigmatic silence. When Ada's piano falls into the hands of her neighbour Baines (Harvey Keitel), he uses it as a means of bartering Ada's erotic compliance. In the ensuing triangle, it is not long before love rears its head—a journey through Ada's libido, *The Piano*'s story unravels against a backdrop of Maori ancestral lands at the time they were being diverted into settler hands. Campion, who directed and wrote the story, consulted Maori writer Wassie Shortland on the creation of a Maori backstory whose presence resonates ironically against the main action.

The film was shot over thirteen weeks in the studio and on location in New Zealand in what actor Holly Hunter dubbed an "athletic shoot." Produced by Jan Chapman, *The Piano* is a French-financed, New Zealand-Australia co-production. It is Campion's first film since her award-winning *An Angel at My Table*.

From *Cinema Papers* (Melbourne), May 1993. Reprinted by permission of MTV Publishing, Ltd.

What was the genesis of the script?
The script was written over a long period, almost five years, with gaps because I was working on other projects. Writing the script is almost a fairytale in itself.

There were three distinct stages, and about three or four original inspirations. The first stage, quite simply, was getting the idea together. I had just finished film school [Australian Film Television & Radio School] and I wanted to write a feature I thought would be made. That was a very practical consideration. I also wanted to write a story which was very different to my film school short films, which are very episodic in quality.

I had become intrigued over the years with the photographic section of the Turnbull Library in New Zealand which documents, from the earliest days of photography, the ways in which New Zealand became colonized. I was particularly taken by how the Maori people adapted to European clothes, in combination with their own dress, which became such a graphic metaphor for their understanding of Europeanism—and vice versa, in a way. There they were sitting in these photographs with great dignity, with such a fierce look at the camera. Their sense of themselves was so powerful that it transcended anything that might seem ridiculous with the misappropriation of clothes.

From here, the actual storyline came about through a complicated fashion. The end result was I wanted to tell a story around an object, that object being a piano, which would bring all the characters together and which would become the central mechanism from which the story evolves. I wanted the piano to be important enough to carry a lot of meaning for the characters.

Even though I have never seen it, I was struck by descriptions of Polanski's early short film about some men carrying a wardrobe around [*Dwaj ludzie z szasa* (2 Men and a Wardrobe), 1958]. I thought, "Maybe I'll see where I can get to with this piano."

The last of the powerful influences, which has been a very longterm influence, is my love of 19th-Century literature—in particular Emily Brontë's *Wuthering Heights*. It is such a powerful poem about the romance of the soul and seems to strike a basic and strong chord in so many people. She was relating to the stark landscape of the moors, which I visited quite a few years ago. I took the walk she would have done over to what she used to call Wuthering Heights.

For me, and for many New Zealanders, the relationship with very wild beaches, especially the black sands of the west coast beaches around Auckland and New Plymouth, and the very private, secretive and extraordinary world of the bush, is a kind of colonial equivalent to Emily Brontë's moors.

Other things seemed to click for me, too. For instance, the early and major colonization of New Zealand happened at about the same time as the Brontë sisters were writing. In fact, Mary Taylor, who ran one of the first shops in Wellington, was a good friend of Charlotte Brontë and Charlotte sent her *Wuthering Heights* at the time, saying it was a very weird, strange book. In fact, there was a lot of critical rebuke of *Wuthering Heights* for Emily. She was so taken aback it really stopped her from ever writing again.

Did this give you a sense there must have been an underground stream of consciousness which you could open up in another part of the world?
Yes. I felt very excited about the kind of passion and romantic sensibility writers like Emily were talking about. I thought it would transpose effortlessly to the situation where I was setting my story, in 1850s New Zealand.

I feel I owe a great debt to the spirit of Emily Brontë. And perhaps not only her, but also Emily Dickinson for other reasons.

In a way, Dickinson led such a secret life, and my main character, Ada, does as well. She is secretive not because she closeted herself in a room, but because she won't speak.

I found reading Emily Dickinson's poems incredibly moving, and I'm not someone who reads poetry a lot. There's one poem which is really great:

> Much Madness is divinest Sense—,
> To a discerning Eye—
> Much Sense—the starkest Madness—
> 'Tis the majority
> In this, as All, prevail—
> Assert you are sane—
> Demur—you're straightway dangerous—
> And handled with a Chain—

She's so bold, feminine and yet demure, and I was very excited about the admission of femininity.

Ada is an extraordinary heroine as well. In another Emily Dickinson poem, the narrator meets a snake and the last line is a description of how that makes her feel, "And Zero at the bone—." Ada is in one way "Zero at the bone."

Yes, and another quote which really affected me was "Big my Secret but it's *bandaged*—."

I admire Dickinson and Brontë, the sensibility they bring to their work and to the world. Both were recluses and they held their sensibility at some cost to themselves. In some way, I feel I am a kind of charlatan who can live in the world quite happily because I'm quite sociable. I use and put their labour into a more popular and acceptable form, and sometimes I feel guilty as I think it's a corrupted use of their pure wisdom.

In Ada you have created this phenomenally rebellious, secretive female character in a world unto itself, but who has to make a choice about living in the outer world. There is a huge wall between her desire to be totally beyond the social order and almost beyond life, and her desire to be in the world.
Ada is slightly different for me than both the Emilys. There are lots of different ways of seeing her. I always saw her as someone who had very powerfully removed herself from life. She chose not to speak. It's never quite made clear why, and it appears even she can't remember the reason.

There is no sense of her as a handicapped person, however. It's almost as though she treats the world as if it were handicapped. At the same time, there is a great deal of suffering from this position. It is a retreat from a lot of what the world offers, which I imagine for women at that time would have been very mundane and boring—insufferable, in fact. There is advantage in her retreat, but there's a great disadvantage in it as well.

I saw in Ada and her daughter, Flora, the way women may have dramatized their lives. In a fashion, Ada and Flora are dramatic about themselves. Their identity and sense of honour about that dramatization is so extreme they would die for it, particularly Ada.

Ada is such a perfectionist that when her piano is hit with an axe, or has lost a key, it is rendered an imperfect object. She loses a finger and can't play the piano the way she would have wanted to. She finds it very hard to imagine herself continuing to live in these conditions, and also to have experienced the brutality that she did. It is a really hard decision for her to know if she wants to continue at all.

One thinks of other strong, self-willed, female characters, like those in Thelma & Louise *[Ridley Scott, 1992], who drive off the cliff. In their decision to place themselves outside patriarchy and death there is a sort of insane joy.*
It is a great ending to that film.

But there is a real desire in your film to have a meeting place.
I think there is a strong need for redemption as well. Ada didn't and doesn't have the companionship Thelma and Louise had with each other. But, in respect of their suicide bid or bid for freedom, it could have been Ada who drowned down there.

Was it always clear to you whether Ada would live or die?
No. I didn't know what was going to happen to her. It was quite undetermined. I didn't even know as I got towards the last draft of the film, which was done shortly before I went to Venice for *An Angel at My Table* [in 1990].

Probably the last thing I wrote is the sequence in the canoe. I wrote it in one night at two o'clock in the morning. I just thought, "Well, what the hell, let's see what happens." Sometimes when you have a writing spurt at two in the morning, you get up next day and think, "Oh my God, why did I bother?" With this, I didn't feel that way. I rang Jan [Chapman] and asked what she thought. She said she felt it was a good idea to have the piano falling over and Ada following into the ocean. I thought the scene had a sort of poetic justice to it, and I couldn't think of a better way to finish it.

But more came later?
Yes, while we were making the film. There was always a postscript to the film anyway, an epilogue. But I decided to make it more romantic, to have it clear that it's quite possible to go through a difficult initiation in romance and not to then necessarily drift into a totally mundane life. You can still have passion in your romance.

To have your cake and eat it, too?
Yes. It was just a little romantic cake and an "eat it, too" gesture.

There is a great deal of scepticism about passionate or romantic love. It's generally considered to be illusory, whereas in this film you're saying that's not necessarily the case.
It's a very different sort of thing for me to want to say, because one of my opinions is that you do have to do some solid, hard work for a good relationship. There is also a great deal of courage required in the passionate path, and you can have a tough 'rites of passage.' But you can be very lucky and gain extraordinary insights which last your lifetime. Passion is about taking risks, and that's very important in any life.

Do you feel you have brought a 20th-Century feel to this period in your attitude to these aspects?
If I didn't bring a 20th-Century perspective to it, I wouldn't be bringing anything. I would just be riding on the backs of great women.

It's absolutely essential to try to understand the freedoms of today—not only the freedoms, but the questions that are real for us now; to try to create new insights for people today when we see others in a situation set in the 1850s.

The thing that initially fascinated me was how people, without any education of the nature of romance and attraction, react to the raw situation. What really is the nature of attraction? How does it grow? How does it develop? How does it become eroticized? How does it become sexual? How does it transcend us and become something more spiritual? Also, because we have a triangle situation in this story, there are powerful notions of jealousy for men—and for the woman, perhaps.

It's unusual to have a woman exploring her libido without any kind of romantic attachment or sentimental quality, albeit briefly, as it is in this film.

Holly Hunter has emerged as an incredibly potent force in this film. How was your collaboration with her?
Holly was not my image of Ada at all. But, in fact, I was very much saved from myself by Holly. Originally, I had an almost clichéd, romantic view of this tall, statuesque, black-haired, black-eyed beauty. In many ways, she wasn't a very real human being, and when meeting Holly I was not very willing to see her as Ada. Holly was completely the opposite to my understanding of how Ada should be. However, I liked Holly very much and I started to open up to the idea of using her because she was so interested and willing to do an audition.

It's a hard thing to audition when the character does not speak. But Holly read the opening prologue and I started to tape her. I immediately realized she was doing something for me that I wasn't expecting. I was very excited, and very pleased I had left myself open enough to engage in this idea.

Holly Hunter is an extraordinary actor. She brings a tenderness and a strength to Ada. I found her totally believable.

When I took the tapes back to Jan in Australia, I said, "You're not going to believe this. I really think one of our strongest contenders is Holly

Hunter." Jan went, "Well, okay, let's have a look at it." When looking at the tape, it struck me even more powerfully that, for someone who was not going to be speaking, the eyes were going to be such an important element. Holly has these dark-brown, burning eyes and an intense gaze. I found in her eyes something you could hold onto. You could be with her, identify closely with her, you could trust her. They are very eloquent eyes.

The whole thing for me about casting is that you are always making these big decisions at a stage in the film when you know it least well. They're probably the most important decisions you're going to make and that makes you nervous.

Fate just colludes to create someone as the person. In the end, it is not very hard if you can just shut up and take notice. We just finally noticed she was the person we felt we'd most like to work with as Ada.

Holly is a really smart woman and the type of personality that I can understand really well. The two of us were able to work very closely, very intelligently, in sorting out how to cope with this creature. Neither of us have personalities very close to Ada, but we are both very attracted to some of her mysterious qualities. Basically, neither of us feels very mysterious at all.

Holly was such an enthusiastic and intelligent collaborator, it's hard to praise her enough. Yet, at the same time, we had to earn our relationship. You don't just jump in there and trust each other to such a huge degree. It's a complex business, and the main thing for me is having an instinct that we can be friends and that we can work well together. Even though Holly is talented, I just had this feeling that, if the two of us were able to work together, it would be that much stronger. It's not that I was going to do anything for her really; it was more that I would know she was going to be there.

You have said elsewhere that you really wanted to be thrown into a different arena with these actors. What became your role as a director with such actors as Harvey Keitel, Holly Hunter and Sam Neill?
I really did have to re-invent my practice as a director to work with these three successfully. I understood this from the beginning. Sam Neill, Harvey Keitel and Holly Hunter are all very experienced actors who have done a lot of work in the industry and whom I admire greatly. I did feel a little precarious in the sense of, "What have I to offer these three?"

Then I thought they must feel the same thing, which made me anxious and nervous. So, I practised with my husband Colin [Englert], talking to people in an unbossy way in order to gain their co-operation and also the best of their ideas. If I'd been threatened by them and just given them a completely open hand to do whatever they liked, I don't think it would have worked. They still have to be in the same film together.

I came to some particular agreements with Harvey about what he liked, for instance. I remember ringing him up and saying, "One of my concerns, Harvey, is that you've had so much more experience than me. It's a great thing and I'm really thrilled about it, but the only thing that scares me is that, even though you've had all this experience, I still want to be able to direct you. What do you think?" And he said, "Well, Jane, let me tell you something. All actors are very scared, very anxious. All we want to really do is please the director. So why don't we do this: you allow me to do a thing the way I want to do it first of all, and then I'll promise you I will try anything you ask me." I wrote it down! I thought that sounded absolutely fine and a really good thing because that way the film would get the best of both of us. I'd get to see what he was going to create without any prompting from me.

So a lot was happening on the set?
Sometimes yes. Harvey always gave you the idea that something wild was going to happen that you couldn't possibly contain on camera. But I think that was a kind of fabrication of his own. He just tried to give himself room.

Harvey also had some notion that he wasn't able to repeat things, which didn't actually appear to be true. He was able to recreate and repeat with new and interesting nuances quite easily. But I can understand actors feeling, "I really want this captured because it may not come again."

All the actors have very different personalities and I did my hardest to work with them in the way that suited them best. I think Holly and I were like sisters in the end. That was the way we collaborated. We'd just chat about the scenes, what we thought we could get out of it, whether we thought a hand gesture was appropriate or whether we should use face grimaces, how dignified Ada's signature would be, her walk, everything. We keep discussing things through the entire filming.

Sam, who comes from a different background in acting to Harvey and Holly—he hasn't had the same formal training—has his own private methods that work extremely well for him. What seemed to work best for us is to just have friendly conversations. If he got stuck, which wasn't very often, he would say, "What do you think we could try here?"

The actors did take a big responsibility for their own performances. I encouraged them to do that and I think it's great. I would just be there in the way that Jan is for me.

Do you feel that as a producer-director team, you and Jan Chapman have an unusually close collaboration?

Yes, we are very special, good friends. Jan Chapman and I have known each other for many years and we like each other immensely. The stresses and the challenges of the shoot brought a new dimension into the friendship which made it even stronger. We became very direct with each other about what we needed and how we were going to get it. We both came to like that even more. There was nothing wrong with the friendship before; we just hadn't gone through those challenges.

One of the things I really enjoyed about the shoot is how challenging it was and how well people rose to the occasion on every single front: the production designer, the costumer designer, cinematographer, producer and my Maori collaborator. I think for anyone present, there was a really great atmosphere for wanting things to be as good as they could possibly be. I've always had my doubts about collaboration until this project, thinking it was a kind of game you pretend to play. But I have never felt so much support. One of the biggest supports for me was Mark Turnbull, who was my first assistant. And Colin gave me continual and essential feedback as well as doing second unit and the film's trailer.

Now I totally believe in collaboration because there is no way I could possibly have created this work on my own. The film really is the combination of everybody's efforts. I didn't even see me in it when I looked at the work; I saw the film.

How do you feel about the film when you look at it now?

That's a difficult question for me. I never have a very easy relationship with my finished work. I have a kind of natural rejection. Maybe it is a way of moving on. I love it when I'm working on it, and, even though there are some problems, I always think things can be improved, and I still enjoy it. But once I start to look at it as a finished thing, I have a sense of revulsion to do with everything about myself.

By the time I get to be revolted by a film, it's about time it's finished. Then in a few months' time I really look forward to a screening with people, to soak in the atmosphere and their freshness towards the film in order to re-enjoy it.

I remember when I first came into the cutting room after working on the set, I loved every image. This is unusual for me. Usually, there's a stage where you wish you weren't there. But I never felt that about *The Piano.* I just love the work we did.

Instinctively, I know it's my best piece of work, but I don't actually feel that. What I feel is a whole lot of stuff about myself and the need to move on. I felt that about *Angel,* I felt that about *Sweetie,* and I felt that about my short films as well.

Do you feel changed by the experience of The Piano*? You have moved into a more international arena.*
One positive change is that I'm not as intimidated by experienced actors; I'm excited by them.

In terms of material as a writer, I don't think *The Piano* will necessarily lead me down more romantic pathways. In fact, it feels like I've put it to rest for the time being. What it has opened, though, is a desire to work on more sophisticated material. Dialogue in this story is quite basic, because of the nature of the piece. I'd quite like to deal with more subtle dialogue.

The Piano is also the first time I've had the opportunity to use a lot of the filmmaking enhancing equipment. This has made me feel a lot more confident with my ability to use cinema language. I can be as cinematic as I want, and be playful with my own style when I want to be. That is fun.

The particular challenge of this film was to try a way to photograph a story that has epic qualities without seeming like a clone of David Lean—to still have my identity, but also have a feminine epic quality and to recreate it so that the epicness didn't feel like it relates back to other big-look movies. A slightly different language was used for the film than your normal epic movie.

And you achieve this through sly, quite grounding humour?
Humour is for me something instinctive, anyway. I don't even think about humour really. Perhaps it's just opportunities that emerge at the most serious moments.

The humour is sly perhaps because it was added when I felt dissatisfied with the serious stillness of the first draft of the story. I'm really pleased I made those changes; I felt like I reclaimed the story to my personality. Things like the dog licking Stuart's hand when he is peeping at Ada undressing, just appealed to me. I can't really explain it. The best thing is that the characters seem to understand it and enjoy it, too.

Why have you dedicated this film to your mother?
For a long time she has been a very strong advocate for this type of story. She always held up to my sister and myself the role of the martyr. She believes in love and its redemptive power. She is extremely romantic, which is something that both of us recoiled against, but her flame is still there.

I also think she has had a powerful struggle with life and death all through her later life and the courage with which she has encountered this, and the depth it has drawn from me and the rest of the family, I am grateful for. It is not always comfortable, but that depth has been expanding and I guess I love her very much and I'm proud to dedicate the film to her.

The Piano: Interview with Jane Campion

VINCENT OSTRIA AND

THIERRY JOUSSE/1993

Why a period film?

I liked the idea of making a period film for many reasons. For me, whatever the period that you choose, the most exciting part is to create a totally new world. If you make a film situated in the present, you always have to invent a particular world. When you make a film like Kubrick's *2001: Space Odyssey,* you have to imagine a convincing future world. It's the same thing for the past: in spite of photos or paintings no-one knows exactly how things were in 1850. You are thus free to express your personality while recreating a credible past. I was personally fascinated by the clothes of the period. I like the fact that people wore many layers of clothes. The story takes place at the time of the first arrivals of Europeans in New Zealand during the 1850s. For me who comes from New Zealand, it was the moment when my ancestors began to arrive. They thus discovered the Maori culture. That seemed to me an interesting thing to explore.

Do you consider The Piano *a Victorian film?*

The morals of the time were Victorian. The conventions and the period are a given in the film, but when you were on the other end of the world, you could behave differently from when you were at home. You didn't have the same sense of freedom. It's necessary to understand that the Victorian conception of relationships between men and women and that of sexual-

---

From *Cahiers du Cinéma,* May 1993. Translated by Michele Curley.

ity were diametrically opposed to those of the Maori which were much more relaxed. In the film you see the two conceptions.

In addition to the images of vegetation and scenery, what's interesting in the film from an ethnographic point of view is the intrusion of women in crinolines into a primitive universe.
Yes, the primitive and the civilized. I really wanted to show that in a very striking visual manner. There are symbolic signs of European civilization, especially the piano which is a civilized instrument, that intrude on a world that is much more elementary and primitive. All of a sudden the things that happen to the characters are also much more elementary and primitive. The sexual attraction between them is representative of what had been repressed in their own world.

The film seems to me to be close to silent films to the degree that there is not a lot of dialogue and at the same time you seem to have been very inspired by Victorian literature. What novels did you feel close to in making the film? You have mentioned the Brontë sisters.
I am a big admirer of the novelists of the nineteenth century, from George Eliot to Charlotte Brontë. And especially Emily Brontë, who inspired me for this film. These women are models for me to the degree that they knew how to write about life and love in a very romantic way, but at the same time with a lot of authenticity and a certain austerity. I don't think that I would have been able to make this film if their books had not existed. My goal was to contribute my point of view on the nineteenth century, because there are things that I could treat that these writers couldn't speak about so openly. I had the idea of doing an adaptation of *Wuthering Heights,* but upon reading it I thought that it wouldn't work. There are certain aspects that are dated, that work in the book, but that would have been difficult to translate on film in a vivid manner.

A relationship between the film and pre-Raphaelite painting is also apparent.
That's what I thought at the beginning. When I was in London, I went to see the pre-Raphaelite paintings at the Tate Gallery, but I didn't like them at all. I found them too romantic, too idealized. They lacked firmness. That painting style made me think too much about fairy tales. My film is

closer to *Wuthering Heights* which is more austere. I was influenced more by a photographer, Julia Margaret Cameron.

How did you work on the screenplay? In one sense, the plot is very simple and there is very important work on atmosphere and on visual conception. Was it already present in the screenplay?
I must say that I don't agree with you: I think that the plot is rather complicated, perhaps even too much. There are many plot reversals. But to get back to the descriptions, there are effectively a lot of them. Since there is not a lot of dialogue, there are thus many more descriptive passages than in a typical screenplay. It's necessary for a film in which the visual dimension is important. You don't shoot on just any beach, you don't film in just any place in the bush. You need to have a particular atmosphere. During the preparation of the film, my main worry was to find the scenery that could correspond to what I had described at random in the screenplay. It's easy to speak about a beach with black sand and immense cliffs but not so easy to find in reality and near a town. Of course, I knew some of these places, but it's one thing to describe them and another to film there in practice.

Where did you film?
On North Island in New Zealand. Our headquarters were in Auckland. We stayed sometimes for a week or two on location to film the outdoor shots. There were two different places: one near New Plymouth, in the center of North Island, near the sea, which is very humid and where there is a lot of moss on the trees, which I liked a lot; the other, which was more exotic, had palm trees.

I missed one thing, the place where Ada, the heroine, leaves from at the beginning of the film?
She is coming from Scotland. You probably noticed the accents of the characters. You make me think that I probably should have had the name of the country appear at the beginning.

When I say the plot is simple, it's because it's a story between three characters, the classic triangle; it's a sort of "behind closed doors" in the middle of nature.
You must not forget the piano, which is one of the principal characters, and the little girl.

Is plot a priority for you?
There were two important things for me: atmosphere and story. It was necessary to find a way to make them work together. By nature, I am perhaps more interested by atmospheres than by stories. But at the same time, a story gives an idea of the time that passes and advances things. In any case, I think that you have to really respect the power of a plot; if the story doesn't work, the atmosphere has little interest. Thus, for me, the first thing is to emphasize the story with force. The atmosphere has to have a reason for existing, otherwise it doesn't work. A structure is needed to hold it all together. My first concern is to tell a story, especially because my greatest weakness is to have the tendency of forgetting the plot and devoting too much of myself to the details.

In concrete terms, what was the starting point of the screenplay?
First there was the desire to show the New Zealand of the 1850s. And then I wanted to make a love story with few characters, who would bring into play an object like the piano which would be actively involved. There was the desire to see what could happen beginning with that. For me, it was already a challenge to tell a story, because I had mostly done disjointed things up to then. Before I didn't worry about having a strong plot, a plot that gradually grows in size and finishes with a climax. I must say that I had a hard time writing it. It's more difficult to write alone, but at the same time, it was a very personal subject and I wouldn't have had an idea about how to write it with someone else. It was difficult because I needed more discipline that usual: I had to hold myself to the story and I couldn't integrate all the ideas that came spontaneously to mind.

There's a strange passage in the film, which is very short, where the young girl tells about the death of an imaginary father: you used a very brief animated shot where you see the father catch fire. Why in that precise moment of the film?
Oh, I felt like it, very simply. It illustrates the imagination of the young girl, in the form of a child's drawing. It's the only place in the film where this technique appears and I wondered if it wouldn't be more coherent if it appeared in other moments. We thought of other passages where we could have used animation, but it didn't seem as if it would have a lot of force. There wasn't really any reason. It's something you can accept or reject.

Perhaps that would have made the young girl (Anna Paquin) too present.
The young girl was so good during the shooting, she was a young actress so unusually strong, that we were effectively a bit afraid that sometimes her character had too much force in relation to the other actors. But at the end, it's the story that resolves this problem.

Did you direct the actors differently in this film than in your other films? It's the first time that you worked with well-known actors, two of whom were Americans, Harvey Keitel and Holly Hunter.
I've very good memories of the actresses with whom I've worked in the past. We learned together, in a very friendly environment, in confidence. For this film, I needed actors who had a lot of experience and whom I didn't have to prepare. I wanted them to bring things that surprise me. At the same time, I was afraid because I knew that it would be necessary for me to know better than usual how to communicate my vision of things. There was the risk that the actors would do things that I don't like at all and that I wouldn't be able to convince them to try something else, because they have more weight and more experience. That worried me a little. I realized that I shouldn't lose sight of my conceptions and at the same time give them the possibility of being creative. It was necessary to find a place of understanding. We got to know each other in rehearsals. At the beginning, there was a little tension, but it's like with friends, you learn to trust. They have to accept your suggestions. A person doesn't give you his trust straight-away, you have to earn it. I was not directive at all with them, we discussed. Harvey Keitel and I were in agreement from the start. He asked me to let him make suggestions and told me that if I wasn't satisfied, he would do anything I asked.

It's a bit like the deal that his character makes with the heroine in the film.
[*Laughs*] Yes, but our deal did not have such consequences! We had a very good relationship. I had seen Harvey in roles of macho cops, rather frightening and aggressive men who upset everything in their paths. I was a bit afraid that he would be like that in real life, that he would be disturbed. But he wasn't at all like that. He's someone who probably works better with a woman than other actors. He is very respectful, funny and nice. He and Sam Neill are men I get along very well with. I was lucky. Holly

Hunter has even become a friend, like a sister. The choice of Holly was probably the most surprising. I wanted to meet her because she's a fabulous actor. Her beauty is not evident at first glance, but I believed in her as a character. Moreover she plays the piano very well. She really plays the piano pieces in the film.

I spoke a little while ago about silent films. Do you think that your film has some points in common with silent films?
It's simply because there is much less dialogue than in most films. I think that the silence is one of the strengths of the film and one of its risks. Once you accept the idea that Ada doesn't speak, you adapt to the situation. There are some passages where Baines [Harvey Keitel] doesn't do anything but monologues in front of her. In one sense it's interesting because people are obliged to express themselves more. When you talk to a mute, you don't say the same things as when you dialogue. There are all sorts of interesting things in this context. You have the impression that if you confide in a mute, she will keep your secret. Thus, you can trust in her more. In a sense mutes are rather close to animals, you have a more instinctive and animal relationship with them. But Ada doesn't grunt like an animal; she is very sophisticated. At the same time, she pushes us to ask ourselves questions about language and non-verbal communication, which is probably as essential for us as verbal communication. I think it's the most important aspect of the film, that you can link to the issues of sex and love. It works rather well in this sense.

Do you think there is a relationship between the main characters of your three films?
Yes, there is one, but it bothers me. When you think about these characters, you can say that Sweetie was rather bizarre, that Janet Frame also had her problems, and that Ada is another unbalanced character. I don't know why that bothers me. When I write, I don't think I'm creating an unbalanced character; I think I'm inventing a character who is mysterious and interesting. What's very important is that all of these characters are women. It's not very common. There are not a lot of films where the heroes are women. And I think I know things about women that men cannot express. The case of the Victorian woman is a particularly critical one.

She had enormous constraints. During the 1850s, a strong woman had a much more tumultuous and dangerous life than today. If I had lived during that time, I would have been very frustrated.

One has the impression that the film is a description of the mental universe of a woman. Men are only objects of her desire.
I think that the film is very feminine on the whole. It's the feminine description of a mythic love story. In the story, men are seen as objects: it's a bit a role reversal. I think it's amusing because more often you see women who are looking for an emotional relationship with men, while men think only about sex. Here, Ada is the one who has an erotic temperament, which is interesting. She thinks she's only interested in the sexual aspects of things and is not looking to establish an affective relationship with her husband. This man feels vulnerable and perturbed when his wife doesn't want to kiss him but simply prefers to touch him. It's something that women have lived with for a very long time. I think it's interesting to see men in that situation.

There's a reference to Bluebeard *in the film. Is this fairy tale a symbol of sexual repression for you?*
[*Laughs*]. Oh I wouldn't go that far! The idea for *Bluebeard* came to me when I saw a very old photo with women's heads lying on a sheet; an image appropriated in the theatrical representation of *Bluebeard* in the film. It coincided precisely with the episode of the ax and the mutilation in the film. I had almost finished the screenplay when I finally decided to read the story of *Bluebeard*. I found it went very well with the subject of the film. But I think you shouldn't burden a film with too many metaphors. You can look for meanings if you want to.

How did you work with the Maori? Did they participate in the screenplay?
Yes, they helped me with the Maori part of the screenplay. They thought that my first description of the Maori in the screenplay was bad. They spoke frankly about it and offered to fix it. I worked with Waihoroi Shortland who wrote the Maori dialogues. He wanted to help me represent the Maori universe in a convincing way. In his mind, it was the occasion to make them better known. But I explained to him that I didn't want to approach the question from a political angle. I wanted to find the reality

and authenticity of Maori behavior, of their way of speaking, without trying to impose a political point of view. Waihoroi understood fully that if he wanted to make a political work it was up to him to make it. I'm not Maori and I don't have a Maori mentality. The role of Waihoroi was to help me and to help the Maori who were in the film. Most of them didn't speak Maori, unlike him who speaks it as a native tongue. He is very cultivated; he has mastered English as well. The Maori have a patriarchal system and in all of the important situations of their lives, they need the presence of an elder in their community. The actors were reassured that Wasi was present, that he knew perfectly the Maori language and traditions. With them everything is ritualized. He prayed before shooting a scene, or at daybreak. They did a sort of ceremony before the start of shooting. The Maori of the region blessed us. All the members of the crew had to rub noses with them. It was very intimate. We did like this [*Jane Campion demonstrates nose rubbing with Thierry Jousse*]. It's a very special way of getting to know people.

Music plays an essential role in the film. How did you conceive it?
With some difficulty, because I'm not a musician. I began taking piano lessons when I was writing the screenplay to understand what that would be like for the actor. I first looked for a composer for the music. I liked very much what Michael Nyman had done for *Draughtsman's Contract*: I liked the aspect of the music that was modern and old at the same time. So I called him. He was the first person to work on the film. Our collaboration was easy and fruitful. We decided that Ada had invented her own music and that she had adapted pieces in her own way. Just like the Brontë sisters had invented a world of their own—they had newspapers, a gallery of characters. Michael decided to compose something in the spirit of the great musicians of the nineteenth century, like Chopin. His best invention was to also look for inspiration in Scottish songs. And then, seeing that Holly Hunter could do that with the piano—while looking at her hands—, Michael composed emotional pieces that corresponded to her better than rhythmic pieces. Although the originality of Michael's music is of a rhythmic order, I explained to him that I preferred that he try something very different from what he had done in the past. Something more feminine, more romantic, with more feeling. Here the music transcends language; it speaks more directly to the emotions.

Let's speak about the future: in New York I met a writer, Philip Lopate, who told me that he was working on a screenplay for you. Can you talk to us about it?
Philip is working on an adaptation of *My Guru and his Disciple* by Christopher Isherwood: the story takes place from the 40s to the 70s in Hollywood. It's about the friendship between Christopher Isherwood and his guru Prava Vananda. But I have another project which I think I'll make first; it's *Portrait of a Lady,* based on the novel by Henry James, which is perhaps my favorite book. In theory, I'll start shooting in Italy and England in November. I would prefer not to throw myself in another period film right away, but I have the possibility of making this movie and I really want to do it because I love the book. It's a great story.

You're not afraid of shooting outside of New Zealand and Australia—although you did shoot some scenes of An Angel at My Table *in Europe?*
No, not really. I think it's amusing to shoot elsewhere. And then, for the moment, I've felt I have exhausted New Zealand subjects. I will make another film later in Australia with my sister. But I don't have the time to write it. Maybe after *Portrait of a Lady* and *My Guru and his Disciple,* I'll take the time to write a contemporary subject. I don't know. At this time I have so many offers that I could work nonstop. [*We should mention that at the time of the interview Jane Campion was pregnant, which didn't seem to hinder her capacity to work very much*]. You wonder how to get out of such a situation; you wonder if you're always doing what you love. I think I'll end up taking a year off to reflect peacefully on what I really feel like doing. Maybe one of my films will be a big failure, so then I'll have time. [*Laughs*].

At Cannes, A Fade-in On Women

SHARON WAXMAN/1993

WITH HER GREAT, ROUND belly clad in black washable silk, Jane Campion—eight months pregnant—is looking very much like the Mother of All Directors. She's certainly the queen of Cannes.

For the Australian filmmaker, this is one of those few shining moments in life: Her film *The Piano* premiered at the festival this week to universal euphoria and is the favorite for the Golden Palm. Her cast describes her as, among other things, a "goddess." She leads an unprecedented pack of female directors in Cannes this year. She's about to become a mother. And she's really, thoroughly nice.

"I'm very grounded by the fact that I'm going to become a mother—it's such an important time in my life," says Campion, 39, her voice rhythmic and relaxed. "It's important to me not to be swept up in all this—for good or bad. I don't want to be addicted to being loved and favored."

While Campion appreciated the wild cheering after the screening of *The Piano,* she also remembers the boos when her film *Sweetie* premiered in Cannes in 1989—she counted about six hoots. "I remember me and the actors just lying on our beds and crying our eyes out, and then saying, 'Oh, bugger them.' So now I think I've got a little more protection," she says. *Sweetie* later won awards, and Campion subsequently made *An Angel at My Table,* a critically acclaimed film that told the tragic life story of writer Janet Frame.

From *The Washington Post,* 20 May 1993. Reprinted by permission of the author.

With blond wavy hair and clear blue eyes, the director-writer has a broad face that openly registers her emotions—surprise, fatigue, delight. She's had to do umpteen interviews over the past three days. That's the joy of Cannes: repeating the same 15 minutes' worth of information 50 times in a row.

"This morning I got up and said, 'I just can't say another word about this movie.' It just gets worse and worse," she groaned. "I mean, I know it's not *that* good. I love my films at the time I'm working on them. But once it's done, all that I can see is what I can't fix."

There's not much worth fixing, according to most who've seen it. Written by Campion, *The Piano* stars Holly Hunter, Harvey Keitel and Sam Neill, and tells the story of Ada, a 19th-century woman who arrives with her 9-year-old daughter in the New Zealand bush for an arranged marriage. The story of Ada's psychological and emotional journey, the film takes as its starting point her relationship to her piano—because she is mute, she best expresses herself through her music—and slowly weaves in the relationship that develops with Keitel, an illiterate neighbor, and her uncomprehending husband, Neill. The three-way—or perhaps four-way—relationship leads to conflict and suffering.

Campion's movies are not at all about sexual politics, but it seems clear that she makes films for and about women. Even as a Victorian woman sold into wedlock, Campion's Ada is a remarkably strong, complete person, the sort of female role that too rarely seems to come from Hollywood.

"It's true," says Campion, "I felt so desperate for American women when I went there [to interview actresses]. I met 10 or 12, and they were all so desperate to have a chance to do something that would include their acting skills, to use what they were in this business to offer. On those occasions I really feel, 'Oh, I just won't do any stories with men in them.'"

Holly Hunter does not hide the fact that she would have done anything to get the part. She brought Campion a tape of her piano playing; her agent faxed the director on her talent hunt around the world, reminding her that Hunter was available wherever, whenever. The persistence paid off.

"All this talk about women directors at the festival," says Campion, "and there's—what—*three* women directors in the official competition.

Of 23 films. In the big, grown-up section." The other two are the Australian Laurie McInnes and her *Broken Highway* and South African director Elaine Proctor and *Friends*.

This is true, but there are also seven female directors—none American—in the prestigious "A Certain Regard" series screened at the Palais de Festival, and several more in other official screenings. So it does seem to be a sort of turning point.

"I'm so glad not to be out there alone with my job anymore," said Allison Anders, an American director (*Gas Food Lodging*), whose film *Mi Vida Loca* was chosen for the Director's Fortnight series. The film chronicles the life of young Hispanic women in the Los Angeles barrio, starring young Hispanic women from the Los Angeles barrio.

"When I wanted to become a filmmaker there was nobody for me to look up to," said Anders. "For me the most exciting thing is that Jane Campion is a woman we can all really look up to. She doesn't have the body of work that some other directors do—no woman director does—but her work is so consistently original, wonderful, masterful."

Campion says: "I'm completely thrilled that there will be more feminine perspectives. I'm not saying they should be grouped together—there are some quite nice and poufy men directors who are sensitive, and there are some girls who are not skilled enough. I can only say that the 19th century benefited so much from the fabulous contribution of women writers. It seems to me instinctively obvious that it would be really nice to have women's stories with strong protagonists."

Some of the inspiration for *Piano* came from Campion's passion for 19th-century female writers. Born in Wellington, New Zealand, the director studied anthropology and painting at university. Her painting led her to consider cinema, and after getting the rudimentary skills in a film school, she began making short films in the early 1980s.

Her early ignorance was blissful. "My best film was my first film, called *Tissues,*" she says. "I couldn't find a fault in it. It was my last pure experience of happiness and joy. You know, someone would say, 'There's not enough wide shots.' I'd say, 'Wide shots?' "

Campion says she's had no particular "aggravation" in working as a woman, but that the attitude is still different. "I never really experienced"—she pauses, and starts again—"no more than little insults, patronage, you know, like you're not really a director, you're a *woman* director. Like the Olympics, you're in a different category."

But with *The Piano,* that attitude seems destined to become part of the past, and indeed its definitive passage might be marked here in Cannes. Campion is basking in the unique sort of acclaim that this festival can bring, and preparing for the July 1 arrival of a son—Shelley, Johnny, Jasper, Arthur or maybe Merlin—with her husband, Colin Englert.

And it couldn't happen to a nicer girl.

Me Jane

JIM SCHEMBRI/1993

When Jane Campion faced the Melbourne audience after the premiere screening of her acclaimed film *The Piano* on Wednesday night she looked like a schoolgirl with a bad case of show'n'tell.

After a severe attack of feedback, Campion—not a natural when it comes to public speaking—groped for words. Humbled by the applause and squinting in the glare of the spotlight, she thanked everyone, said how glad she was that one of her films was showing in such a big cinema, and made a graceful retreat.

One-on-one, Campion is a much more relaxed, spontaneous soul. She is a little flighty and very frank. The previous night *The Piano* screened in Sydney, her home town for about the last 14 years. She didn't see it.

"I've seen it so many times I couldn't bear to!" she quips. "I've seen the film between 50 and 100 times. We just went off and had something to eat. If my mum was there [to whom the film is dedicated] I'd sit next to her and watch her watch it. That situation would have been fun for me."

You can tell Campion is in good humor. Laughter bursts through the remnants of her clipped New Zealand accent like mortar fire. When she laughs—sometimes at something you say, mostly at something she's said herself—her lips drape back over her pearly white teeth and bounce the sunlight like a reflecting board.

The reason for her high spirits has been jamming the fax machine since mid-May when word got out about her film *The Piano,* a beautifully crafted

---

From *The Age,* 8 July 1993. Reprinted by permission of *The Age* and the author.

period piece about sexual repression finding expression in the dank landscape of a blustery New Zealand coast. The film recently shared the coveted Palme d'Or award at the Cannes film festival.

The flywheel effect of her growing reputation in Europe has already made *The Piano* a hit in Italy and Belgium, and helped secure financing for the film. A French company, CiBy 2000, was happy to supply the $9-million-plus budget, and give Campion final cut.

But Campion has greeted her swelling reputation—which has been building since her short film *Peel* won the Palme d'Or in 1986, and *Sweetie* (1989) and *Angel at My Table* (1990) were hits—with level-headed nonchalance.

"If it happens it happens, but it's not something you can control," she says. "From a personal perspective I don't really think about it. I think about what my opportunities are workwise, what I'm going to do next, what story I'm interested in next, who I'm going to work with and how funding's going to come together. Once I work that out I don't really think about the rest very much."

She is aware of the danger of becoming overrated, and of letting her ego and reputation get ahead of themselves.

"It's the way these things work," she says. "There is a public perception of someone having had enough attention or too much attention, and a sense that the public has to help them by putting them in their place!" She barks a laugh. "That's the truth and I think it's wise to watch the amount of exposure you get."

Which helps explain why her interview roster for *The Piano* was so limited.

"I'm not really trying to sell myself, I'm trying to let people know that the film's on and a little about what it's about. I'm not selling myself. I don't need to sell myself, I've got work. There's not a lot of interest for me personally in doing profiles. I really don't want to be famous."

Campion had her cinema education in Australia and is currently our industry's darling. But try telling her that, and her wry humor spurts forth, almost in defiance of the remark being serious. She jokes about plotting her "darling" rating when she gets up each morning, then laughs like a banshee. But seriously: "It's a perspective I really don't participate in, you know? My life is just with my friends and family and the success part of it, or the 'darling' part of it, doesn't really figure at all."

Australian money could have paid for *The Piano,* but that may have taken too long, she says. Is that a weakness of the local industry? "I don't think it's a weakness," she says. "You've got to remember that one of the concepts of the Australian industry is to encourage investment overseas. I mean, why use Australian money when we can use French money? Put it that way!" She laughs.

The French financing led to nasty rumors. Would *The Piano* have won in Cannes if it hadn't have been made with francs? "They paid a lot of money in order to get the Palme d'Or, and I think they should have got it," Campion says, deadly serious. Then, again with the laugh: "Campion exposes fraud in Cannes!"

In fact, Campion explains how the press screening for *The Piano* and interviews she did about it was what got people excited. Indeed, she feared the pre-Cannes hype may have prompted judges to react against the vibe, as happened a few years before when Spike Lee's *Do the Right Thing* was snubbed.

The success of *The Piano* is especially significant for Campion: it is the first time she has directed a major work from her own script.

"There's always a much bigger measure of vulnerability about what you come up with yourself," she explains.

This probably explains why she is so cool to criticism of *The Piano*. The humor is still there—she jokes about throwing things at the reporter—and she is never less than polite, but she does begin to fidget. A point about how the film's story seems unbalanced, how Campion's direction seems to spend too much time on the build-up and not enough on the pay-off, is politely rebuked while she plays with one of her earrings, which has been removed.

Under fire, she refuses to slip into arrogance. Suggesting that Campion opted for a more conventional shooting style in *The Piano* compared with her previous films, for instance, draws a duly liberal, if slightly uncomfortable response. "I don't agree with you at all about that. I don't think this is conventional at all.

Campion never allows her humor to leave her. She greets the introduction to a series of critical questions with a mock-indignant "What!." Later she says she welcomes such questions, and, in trying to praise the "critical faculties" behind the questions, comes out with "cracital ficculties."

Campion completely breaks up. If she wasn't on the couch, she'd be on the floor. She repeats her spoonerism to her own uproarious delight, and breaks up again.

The Piano is set in the 19th century, something rare for an original work—and risky. The trade-off, though, was being able to explore 19th century sexuality with what Campion calls "20th century permission."

"I could have characters that were completely naive sexually," she says. "Characters for whom the whole experience (of sex) was innocent. They had to learn on their feet, whereas today we have such a vast social and magazine-type education about romance and sexuality."

Wanting to evoke the classic feel of Emily Brontë and Emily Dickinson, *The Piano* often feels like Thomas Hardy with a mean streak. Ravishingly shot in a style inspired by early color photography, Campion invests the sensuality of her story of a romantic quadrangle with occasional gothic savagery—including one horrific scene that makes the ankle scene in *Misery* look like a cookery lesson.

"I don't really like violence myself," she says, "but there is a gothic element in the story, when people's passions are aroused and frustrated, and jealousy comes into the picture. What we're trying to describe is the full gamut of human possibilities, and one of them is violence. In this case, it is very specific, chillingly specific." Making films, like writing books, can be an unstable way to make a living.

"The one thing I'd really love is a good house, you know? We've got a pretty small apartment." She pauses. "I'm not complaining. It's great to have anything and it really doesn't matter in the long run. It's not where you live, it's how you live and if you're happy. I'm sure a big house won't make a big difference. "But I'd just like to have enough room to have my friends to stay, you know? And have a bit of a haven, have a bit of a garden."

She does have enough room in her life, however, for the kind of big-budget Hollywood formula films her work contrasts with so starkly.

"I like 'em because I couldn't do them," she says with laugh. "I'm a big fan of Clint Eastwood, a big fan of Arnie. We kill ourselves watching his movies. We love them. He's such a hopeless actor. He doesn't even have to be an actor, it's just like a famous person pretending to act."

The Piano is already attracting Oscars talk. If the offer came to do *Jurassic Park 2* would she go to Hollywood? "No. Well, I think it would be hilarious because I would probably do a terrible job and I'd laugh my way through it!" She laughs, then reflects for a second. "I reckon I'm really lucky to be able to just dream up my own ideas, and that someone's prepared to pay for it. If you're enjoying what you're doing right now, then life's really working out. I think I'm extremely lucky. It would be pretty sad for me if I did get really seduced."

She laughs again, with good reason.

Playing It Low-Key

LYNDEN BARBER/1993

THE FIRST TIME JANE Campion realised she might have something special on her hands with her third film, *The Piano,* came in the first week of the rushes, when she thought: "I really love the look of this material; this is better than I've done before; I've surprised myself; that's exciting."

The Sydney-based director's second moment of revelation came in the first few weeks of the editing. "There were really not many scenes that were in trouble or bad," she says with characteristic understatement, adding that after this point in the production she got too close to it to judge. "I get to the stage where you go full circle and you think it's really hopeless."

So hopeless that when people saw the completed film in the run-up to its Cannes screening and French release, "individuals would talk to us about it and they were saying things like, 'I really feel this is the best film I've ever seen.' "

Her reaction? Pride? Arrogance? Campion, with Antipodean self-deprecation, thinks it hilarious. "I'm afraid I'm not very exciting in my reactions to those things!" she laughs. "I guess half of me wonders, Well I wonder what else they've seen! They can't have seen half of the films I've seen!"

While admitting, once the laughter has died down, to also being grateful for the compliment, the New Zealand-born film-maker puts the self-deprecation down to her need for in-built protection. "The next film I might want to do might be a lot less popular, you know, a lot less adored. I don't want to become like I need it [the acclaim]."

From *The Sydney Morning Herald,* 3 August 1993. Reprinted by permission of the author.

The Piano—produced by an Australian (Jan Chapman), filmed in New Zealand and financed by the French company CiBy 2000—went on to win the Cannes Film Festival's top prize, scoring two firsts: the first ever for a woman director and the first ever for an Australian production.

It subsequently became a major hit at both the French and Italian box offices and this week Australian audiences get the chance to see it for themselves.

As was widely reported at the time, the then pregnant Campion was unable to be in Cannes to receive her prize since she had had to fly back to Sydney a few days before the results were announced. Tragically, she lost her son, her first, 12 days after the birth. To be giving even a limited number of interviews for the film's Australian release is admirably brave, even given the expected proviso that no personal questions be asked.

The Piano is her third feature following *Sweetie* and *An Angel At My Table* (which was originally conceived for television), and has a lover's triangle played out against the wild landscapes of 19th-century New Zealand.

This, note, is a far from conventional triangle. The heroine (played by Holly Hunter) is mute. Her non-starter of an arranged marriage to Sam Neill's landowner leads to most unusual "piano lessons" with a neighbour (Harvey Keitel), who has possession of the instrument, which was originally hers. She agrees to trade sexual favours for its return.

The inspiration for the film, Campion explains, "came from a lot of different sources. I wanted to write a love story, a fairly daring one, and set it in a world that I had some particular knowledge of that would be fresh to the rest of the world."

Researching early photography in New Zealand she had come across shots of Maoris "cross-dressing between Victorian clothes and their own clothes" and found it "a really great visual metaphor for colonialism and how it happened in New Zealand."

"And I became more interested in that. Who my ancestors were, how they were, how it must have been for them, a very puritanical society, going to a place like New Zealand, which was so astonishingly different, not only physically from England, but also culturally in the sense of what the Maori culture was like.

"I also read quite a lot of diaries of men and women from the time, and it was obviously incredibly difficult, things that you couldn't imagine. Like, it was very hard to get food; they couldn't grow vegetables to begin with. Also the rats were the size of cats and would drop in their beds at night—we didn't even go the full way because I can't stand rats!"

Reflected in the film is the contrast between Maori and settler attitudes towards the body and sex, also to land and property. "Maori culture is incredibly at ease sexually," says Campion. "Older ladies use a lot of sexual metaphors with pipis and shellfish. They talk about vaginas and penises. There isn't a sense of privacy about it, which is, of course, incredibly different for Europeans from England around that time."

The reason Neill's character lives in a patch of semi-cleared bush awash with mud and tree-stumps is that "we were trying to get this idea that he was trying to burn back everything," she says. "He couldn't cope with the claustrophobia of the bush; he was trying to turn it into pasture. Things definitely had to be transformed for him to accept them."

The film's far-from obvious casting turns out to be perfect, although American Holly Hunter (*Broadcast News, Raising Arizona*) initially struck even the director as "completely inappropriate" for the lead role. She didn't even want to meet the actor (the script originally called for a tall woman—Hunter is short) but eventually bowed to pressure from her agent. After this, Campion was so encouraged she loosened up in her casting for the other roles.

The muteness of Hunter's character, Ada, was conceived as "a device I tried on simply to make the story work better," she says. "What I really wanted was that the piano meant so much more to her than it would to somebody who was able to speak, because that became like her soul, her way of communicating and expressing herself. I wanted it to help Ada in the sense that she would probably do anything to get that back.

"The film is also very much about love and sex . . . her not talking is more animally, you know. It takes you back into a feeling world rather than a thinking world."

Another remarkable piece of casting is Anna Paquin, as Ada's nine-year-old daughter, though Campion says the credit should really go to her Kiwi-based casting director Diana Rowan, and Hunter, who befriended the girl on set.

"I have a kind of conservation theory about how to work with actors. You kind of work out why you love them and what you love about them, and then make sure you don't destroy it.

"With a little girl like Anna, she's just got great instincts; I don't know where it comes from. She's just an example of how some people have that acting spirit." While grateful for the 13 AFI nominations *The Piano* has received, she thinks Paquin's failure to be nominated "was a bit of an oversight. She should have got one too!"

In the meantime Campion has begun work on her next film, an adaptation of Henry James's *Portrait of a Lady,* to star Nicole Kidman, with Laura Jones (*An Angel At My Table*) as scriptwriter and Monty Montgomery, an American associate of David Lynch, producing.

"I just find the book so endlessly fascinating and complex and subtle," Campion says, adding that Kidman is "looking to find something which has a lot more depth than what she's had so far in Hollywood." She would appear to have found it.

Piano's Good Companions

ANDREW L. URBAN/1993

"I FEEL A KINSHIP between the kind of romance that Emily Brontë portrayed in *Wuthering Heights* and this film. Hers is not the notion of romance that we've come to use, it's very harsh and extreme, a gothic exploration of the romantic impulse I wanted to respond to those ideas in my own century."

This is how Jane Campion introduced *The Piano* to the Cannes Film Festival, writing in a beautiful, limited edition booklet on the film, printed on ivory Lanagrain paper. But her exploration was free of the social constraints of Bronte's time, and thus far more sexual; "a lot more investigative of eroticism—which can add another dimension."

In Sydney this week, she spoke at greater length of some of the decisions she made in the process of creating what some film writers at Cannes have referred to as her masterpiece. For example, writing in the influential film trade daily, *Moving Pictures,* at the Festival, Jan Epstein wrote: "Jane Campion has created a masterpiece of startlingly beautiful images and powerful eroticism that satisfies the deepest need of the heart as much as it thrills the eye and satisfies the soul."

Certainly, Campion was delighted that palates as sophisticated and developed as those at Cannes responded to her 'vision'; "We all have our fantasies of recognition, things you keep striving for," she says, "and the acknowledgment is fabulous in a formal sort of way, but the real satisfaction is in the little breakthroughs I make . . . a lot of it in the early stages,

From *The Australian,* 6 August 1993. Reprinted by permission of the author.

often with (producer) Jan Chapman in a little shack somewhere (working on the script) or travelling the world with NO money, trying to work out how to finance the film.

"We started in France and went around the world to the US. We'd say to each other before meetings, 'If they bring up money, let's just say we'll get back to them!' not having worked out the details." Campion is laughing at the memory of it now, the truth of it, the chaotic nature of the film business, and how ironically easy the financing became.

"It was all due to Pierre Rissient (the Cannes Festival scout who comes to Australia each year appraising and previewing films) who suggested we get in touch with CiBy 2000—he'd read the script and was sure CiBy would love it. We didn't believe it . . . it's very unusual." But CiBy 2000 did love it. Offshoot of a French construction company, CiBy 2000 was set up five years ago to develop films and film makers from all over the world. The old construction boss turned patron of the arts, Francois Bouyges who died last week after a long illness, was at least alive to hear of the Palme d'Or success of *The Piano.*

"I feel very grateful to this Medici-like person," says Campion. "CiBy is a sort of showcase company, and they want to help certain independent directors . . . it's unbelievable but they gave us 100 per cent creative control, and 100 per cent of the money—with a generous share of the profits. It's fabulous for filmmakers."

Campion began writing *The Piano* (originally called *The Piano Lesson,* but shortened in deference to an American play of the same name doing the rounds) in 1984, well before her successes with *Sweetie* and *An Angel at My Table.*

"Originally the story was a history of the piano—and its life in New Zealand, then a lot of other characters got involved," Campion recalls. One of these was Ada (Holly Hunter), the arranged wife of Englishman Stewart (Sam Neill), who has not spoken since she was six.

Campion explains how she arrived at the notion of making her central character mute: "I wanted to create a strong relationship with the piano . . . she compromises herself so much for it, it would have to be something really big to make her do that. So I felt if she couldn't speak, the piano would mean so much more to her, it'd be her voice. And it did have useful repurcussions through the movie; for example, her daughter speaks for her, which sets up a secretive communication between the two women, quite true to life . . . and the men feel even less able to understand them. Makes it sexier, too: if you can't talk things out, you have to do it in other ways."

Stewart, a decent if repressed man, "who probably never had sex in his life, he's an auntie's boy," says Campion, "becomes aroused when he spies on Ada and Baines (Harvey Keitel, playing the neighbour) in action. It's passion! Wow! It unlocks something in him . . ."

And eventually leads to a single act of violence "miniscule by Hollywood standards," as Sam Neill puts it, "but it made me sick."

What Campion was trying to investigate was the 19th century colonial world of her native country, New Zealand, and how most white people like Ada and Stewart were completely unprepared for the power of sexual passion; by contrast, the Maoris, who play an important role in *The Piano,* speak freely of penises and vaginas and use sexual symbols in everyday communication.

Stewart's incomprehension of Ada is displayed at the very beginning; they land on the shores of their new homeland and disembark from a long journey, their belongings dragged painfully from boat to beach to homestead. Except the piano. On Stewart's orders, it is left in its crate on the beach, much to Ada's anxiety. When neighbour Baines offers Ada a deal for fetching the piano in return for lessons—with subtle implication of something else—Ada's sense of propriety gives way to her attachment to the piano. As she slowly, slowly entangles herself in a sensuous web with Baines, her untapped emotions erupt, but the affair ignites all of them, and Baines falls painfully in love with her—and out of lust. Stewart is startled out of his composure, and by the end of the film Ada is sufficiently changed to toy with the notion of Stewart becoming her sex slave—in a sort of muted, 19th century fashion.

As Campion says, she could have cast unknown actors in the roles. "There are lots of superb people around . . . But I felt it was a crucial time for me . . . I could either work small, or work in a way to be challenged, with actors of the experience and caliber of Sam and Holly and Harvey. They are all very committed actors, and they bring unique strengths."

Asked to comment on accusations made by a New Zealander that *The Piano* was somehow the result of plagerism, Campion smiles sarcastically. "Yeah, the guy hadn't even seen the film. It's a beat up. You can't make a film like this infringing copyright . . . He was involved in an early draft of a thing called *The River.* Friends of mine own the copyright. Look, it's so inaccurate (the claim) it's not worth commenting on."

Campion speaks now about how "sensible" her progress as a film maker seems to have been, although unplanned. "I started with a seven minute film, but it seemed big to me. Than I did a half hour, then 70 minutes, and then you realise you can do a feature."

And although she thoroughly enjoyed making the film, it was tough. "I loved it actually, more than I had before . . . it used to terrify me. Now it's a big high. But directing is a very hard job. It's a long time commitment, an intense six months of my life. That's a long time to be so intense about something that all your relationships fade into the background."

But there is no sign of Campion settling into some different line of work, with at least two new films to make one after the other (*Portrait of a Lady,* and *My Guru and His Disciple,* both adaptations from novels). "Without doubt I'll make a film less successful (than *The Piano*) but that's all right with me, as long as it's satisfying to make. I just hope I don't get addicted to the salary level."

Jane Campion Directs on Instinct

DAVID STERRITT/1993

HARVEY KEITEL IS BETTER known for bruising pictures like *Taxi Driver* and *Bad Lieutenant* than for international art films like *The Piano,* a top prizewinner at the Cannes Film Festival last May. Yet asked for a one-word description of filmmaker Jane Campion, as she directed him in his new movie, he replies without a pause: "goddess."

Told about Mr. Keitel's remark a few minutes later, Ms. Campion laughs delightedly. "Lately he's changed his tune," she chuckles, explaining that there were moments during the making of her ambitious film when feelings weren't quite so positive.

In any case, the hard work by cast and director has paid off handsomely. *The Piano* won the Golden Palm for best picture at Cannes, sharing the award with *Farewell, My Concubine,* a large-scale Chinese drama. This marked the first time a Chinese director—or a female director from *any* country—had garnered the top prize at the world's most renowned filmfest. (The Chinese government has banned the film.)

Another winner was Holly Hunter, whose performance in *The Piano* earned her the award for best actress. She plays Ada, a 19th-century woman who mysteriously stopped speaking while a child, and expresses her emotions through written words and the music she plays on her beloved piano. Her story begins when she arrives in a remote area of New Zealand, with her young daughter and as many possessions as her boat can carry;

From *The Christian Science Monitor,* 17 August 1993. Reprinted by permission.

for an arranged marriage with a handsome landowner, played by Sam Neill.

When he declares it too expensive to bring her piano to their home—leaving it abandoned on the beach where it was unloaded—she starts to resent him and refuses to consummate their marriage. Instead she develops a complex relationship with an illiterate neighbor who has taken possession of the piano. At first he blackmails her, allowing her to earn the instrument back by indulging his sexual wishes. Later they recognize each other's higher qualities, however, and fall in love. The climax of the film is a horrific confrontation between Ada and her husband. The end is contrastingly gentle and mature.

The Piano has ingredients that often make for commercial success in American theaters, including some harrowing violence and a couple of surprisingly graphic sex scenes. Its intelligent screenplay and resonant images were enthusiastically received by the art-film connoisseurs at Cannes, however, and it promptly became the most talked-about picture of the festival.

This marked a major change from Campion's previous experience at Cannes, when her debut feature—the acerbic comedy *Sweetie,* made five years ago—was booed by many at its initial press screening. Campion still remembers how she and her collaborators "cried our eyes out" shortly after that incident.

The joke, however, was on the people who jeered. *Sweetie* became an international success and was soon followed by *An Angel at My Table,* a film biography of author Janet Frame, directed by Campion with unfailing taste and intelligence. Today she looks back at the booing with a healthy sense of perspective. "What *you* feel about what you've done is the most important thing," she says, adding that her close encounter with film-festival scorn may have helped her avoid becoming "addicted" to nothing but favorable responses.

What inspired her to write and direct *The Piano,* with its challenging mixture of moods, characters, and ideas? One motivation was strictly professional. "I wanted to try and write a proper story with a narrative," she says, noting that "the straightforward three-act kind of narrative" is not a form she automatically feels comfortable with.

Other motivations came from her enjoyment of Victorian gothic novels and her knowledge of history in New Zealand, her native country. "A lot of Victorian women who came to New Zealand brought pianos with them," she says, "and this struck me as an extraordinary instrument to have in that situation." Still another influence was a movie she's never seen, but has often heard about: *Two Men and a Wardrobe,* an early Roman Polanski short about two loners who run into trouble when they travel around a city with a huge piece of furniture in their hands.

In the end, though, Campion says instinct and impulse had as much to do with the development of *The Piano* as any conscious inspirations. "Ideas don't arrive as one whole," she says. "My mind doesn't think in very logical ways all the time."

For this reason, she relies more on the visual training she received as an art student than on the analytical techniques—such as semiology, the study of communication through signs—that are fashionable in intellectual circles today.

"I did my semiotics and everything when I was at university," she says with a rueful smile, "and I decided that didn't help me think of anything creatively, whatsoever. There's a background of that [in my mind] somewhere, but I don't want to bring it to the fore anymore, because I know it doesn't work. To be able to pull [things] apart . . . isn't the same as [knowing] how to put together!"

Although plans for its international release are not yet finalized, *The Piano* has been acquired for United States distribution by Miramax Films and should arrive in American theaters this fall, after more appearances on the film-festival circuit. Others who contributed to the movie's success include cinematographer Stuart Dryburgh, who superbly captures the mixture of realism and surrealism that is a key part of Campion's style, and composer Michael Nyman, whose minimalist piano pieces—smartly played by Ms. Hunter herself—brilliantly enhance the subtly dreamlike aspects of the film.

Campion is now working on two literary adaptations: *My Guru and His Disciple,* from Christopher Isherwood's autobiographical account of his years as a student of Hinduism in Los Angeles, and *Portrait of a Lady,* from Henry James's classic novel. One of these is expected to become Campion's next production, and moviegoers around the world are already waiting for it eagerly.

Jane Campion's Lunatic Women

MARY CANTWELL/1993

THIS OCTOBER, A ROMANTIC epic titled "The Piano," written and directed by a New Zealander named Jane Campion, will be the grand finale of the New York Film Festival at Lincoln Center. In November it will open all over the country. *The Piano,* which is set in 19th-century New Zealand, has already made Campion the first woman to win the Palme d'Or at the Cannes Film Festival, and the reviews so far—but for a cavil about its being too consciously an "art" film—have been ecstatic. Vincent Canby of The New York Times, for instance, described *The Piano* as "a triumph . . . so good, so tough, so moving and, especially, so original." Yet when I asked a friend, like me a great admirer of Campion's work, what she wanted to learn from my interview with the film maker, she replied, "First, I want to know if she's sane."

I had expected curiosity about why Australia, where Campion went to film school and lives, has produced what seems to be an inordinate number of world-class directors: Bruce Beresford and Peter Weir and George Miller among them. Or why, given the hen's tooth scarcity of prominent female directors anywhere in the world, three—Campion, Gillian Armstrong and Jocelyn Moorhouse—emerged from a country associated with a certain cheerful misogyny. But why be curious about Campion's sanity?

"Because," my friend answered, "she's obsessed with lunatic women."

In truth, only the eponymous protagonist of Campion's first feature film, the extraordinary *Sweetie,* is genuinely mad. The New Zealand novelist Janet Frame, whose autobiography, *An Angel at My Table,* became Campion's second film, was only *thought* to be mad. Diagnosed in her early 20's as a schizophrenic and institutionalized, she was within inches of a lobotomy when her doctors decided that a woman who had managed to write and publish distinguished fiction while in the bin was probably not in need of a brain correction. Ada in *The Piano* isn't mad either, but her mulishness approaches sublimity. That Ada doesn't speak, for instance, isn't because she can't but because she will not.

Lunatic women? Except for the simultaneously hilarious and tragic Sweetie, no. But powerful women, which in some minds may add up to the same thing? Yes. Sweetie has a tornado's destructiveness, Janet Frame stayed sane in the midst of madness and Ada's will is iron. What roles!

If artists looked like their creations, the progenitor of *The Piano* would resemble a Brontë sister or George Eliot. Instead, Campion looks like a commercial for Fun and Sun in Australia. Her hair is very fair, her eyes are very blue and her speech—typically antipodean in its narrow vowels and the upward curve of its sentences—is spattered with self-mockery and great bursts of laughter. "Mum" and "Dad" are a big part of her conversation; so are her friends, whom one half-expects her to call, as do most of the residents of her part of the world, "mates."

On a day in mid-June of this year, Campion was a month away from having won the Palme d'Or. She was two weeks away from giving birth to her first child, a son whose presence was already inescapable in the Sydney apartment she shares with her husband, Colin Englert, a television producer and director. The baby's crib was set up in Englert's small office, and Campion lifted her billowy white shirt once to stare at her swollen belly. "Is he kicking?" her visitor asked. "Mmmmm," she answered, lost for a moment in that curious bubble that encloses the pregnant.

Campion was, in brief, at the pinnacle of her particular world, at a place where the professional and the personal were about to meet in blessed convergence. And although she'd done her share of interviews, she wasn't yet weary of the same old questions because she hadn't yet heard them all. Chatty, spontaneous (once, she unexpectedly kissed my cheek), Campion in June of 1993 was, to an interviewer, equivalent to an unplowed field.

Campion was born 39 years ago, to parents whom she describes as having had "a strange life compared to most New Zealanders." They had a strange life compared with almost everybody's.

"My mother was an heiress, but an orphan at the same time, so she was brought up by different people and finally given her inheritance," she said. "She and my father met at university, then went to England to study at the Old Vic. When they came back, they started the first official touring company in New Zealand. It wasn't a financial success at all, and so they just started working in other established theaters. Mother retired when she had the three of us, but Dad's still doing a lot of things, like opera."

At Victoria University, where she majored in anthropology, Campion was interested in acting. "But I felt I had to distinguish myself from the family. You know? Besides, I thought acting quite frivolous. Now I'm grateful that I was raised in an atmosphere which had some sort of gaiety to it. But at the time, I thought that these people were . . . *insincere.*

"After that, the thing was to try and travel and take a look at where I came from, along with the rest of Europe. You know?"

Anyone who has ever run into Australians and New Zealanders on what they usually call "my trip" knows. The trip is their Wanderjahr, and analogous to the lazing-about-Europe-after-graduation done by countless young Americans in the days when a college degree was a guarantee of a job offer. To hear Campion talk about her trip is to be reminded of theirs: of the postcards detailing the wonders of Chartres, the mysteries of the bidet and a whole litany of missed trains and misunderstandings.

"My other aim was to go to art school. The first attempt was to go to one in Venice, but all sorts of complicated issues turned up. This boy I knew was arrested for cocaine trafficking. And I couldn't speak Italian very well. And I was going to the school, but I wasn't really enrolled because no one could work out who I was or what I was supposed to be doing there. And then it was winter, and they had the *agua alta,* the water that comes up over your gum boots. Then, of course, I was under suspicion, too, because I was a friend of his. He told me later that his mother had sent him some potato purée from Hungary and that it had been misinterpreted. But that sounds a little unlikely to me now, you know?"

Eventually Campion left Venice for London and a job assisting someone who made documentaries and commercials. Getting into an art school was still on her mind, but none were interested, mostly because her work was primitive, but partly, she suspects, because she may have looked like a ditz.

"I remember going to one of them, with a copy of Cosmopolitan magazine under my arm, and somebody coming to the door while I was still putting on lipstick. 'Uh, oh,' I thought. 'This isn't the right image.'

"I didn't like England. I couldn't take the look of the place or the style of friendship. I need more intimacy from people than is considered O.K. there, and I felt that my personality and my enthusiasms weren't understood. I had to put a big lid on myself. But I thought: 'You've just got to live with this. This is the rite of passage to being an adult—misery.'

"I have a complicated theory for why I was so depressed—that in the Southern Hemisphere you can use the weather to relate your moods with. If you did that in England, where it's continuously bleak, you'd just die.

"Also, there's a fury I have when I hear an English upper-class voice—that voice that speaks really loudly about its 'dahhhhggs.' Grrrr!"

There was nothing to do but go back: to the sun and the blue, blue skies and a society determined on classlessness. It doesn't quite succeed, but never mind. The accent, so contagious that even the most recent immigrant is speaking "Strine" seemingly within minutes of arrival, is a great leveler.

This time, Campion went to Australia, to Sydney rather than Melbourne, because in the first city she had one friend and in the second, none. There a life that had been hitherto purposeless, if pleasant, finally took on a point.

"The art school I went to had young tutors who were into minimalist and conceptual art. They made everybody rethink their thinking about everything, which sent some people into sort of schizophrenic binges. But it was a brilliantly exciting atmosphere. You could do anything—installations, performance, whatever.

"First I was a bit at sea. Then, suddenly, for the first time in my life I really tried to do something. I'd never had a commitment to my ability: I knew there were people cleverer than me. What I was looking to do was to just learn enough so that I could in some way be supportive of somebody who really *was* gifted.

"There was another thing. About that stage I had a couple of boyfriends, and they both kind of disappeared. Being alone was a shock to me, and a good shock. Because I said: 'O.K., you've got nobody now. You're by yourself. So maybe it's time you had a look at what you can do if you really try to find out what your potential really is.'

"I decided to try and make my artwork directly about the things that I'd rush home to ruminate about. Things like confusions about sex and intimacy, for instance.

"I was painting at the time, crude sexual paintings, I suppose, with some feminist imagery as well.

"There was a lot of performance stuff going on, too, so I used to put on little plays about women and sex—things like that. Pretty weird, really. Next, I decided that instead of being in a play I'd film it.

"So, in my last year, I made this little film called *Tissues,* probably the only one I ever made that I loved. It was a very funny, rather crazy film about a father who'd been arrested for child molestation. The family tried to deal with it, and in every scene a tissue was used. Dum da dum!

"After that, I was just trying to get into the film industry in any way I could, and going through the usual stuff where everybody tells you, 'Yeah, maybe you can write, but you've got no directing skills.' And I thought, 'How on earth am I going to start?' "

By now the possessor of a B.A. in structural anthropology and a diploma in fine arts, Campion started by going back. Once again, she went to school. Her father groaned.

Entering the Australian Film, Television and Radio School, however, is tantamount to becoming a part of the Australian film industry in that it's financed by the Government and gives its students—only 25 are chosen every year—a small stipend. For a prospective film maker, it is also a lot like going to heaven. "You could do any story you wanted to without having to argue for it. You had a chance to see how your ideas would turn out."

From the beginning, Campion's ideas were sui generis: the anthropologist sees coolly and dispassionately; the artist translates the spectacle into images unlike anyone else's.

In *Peel,* for instance, which she made in her second year and which eventually won an award at Cannes, a little boy is ordered by his father to pick up every piece of orange peel he's tossed from a car window. The boy looks like his father, his mother looks like her husband, the sun is merciless and the entire transaction is a ludicrous lesson in discipline. Like *Sweetie, Peel* is curiously mysterious in that Campion offers the viewer no clues as to what to think of it all. Herself averse to being told what to feel, she claims a corresponding reluctance to tell an audience what to feel.

The last of Campion's student films, *A Girl's Own Story,* is an intensely personal oddity about innocence, pubescence and childhood incest and, in a sense, a precursor to *The Piano.* In their frank acknowledgment of the awful power of sex, and, not incidentally, its awful messiness, both carry a disconcerting erotic charge. In *A Girl's Own Story,* a brother and sister embark on intercourse as casually as cats. In *The Piano,* in which petticoats and pantalets seem endless barriers to consummation, a mere half-inch of flesh is enough to tantalize.

After film school, Campion joined the Women's Film Unit, an Australian remedy for the imbalance between the number of men and women in Government-sponsored film programs (about even) and the number in the film industry (not even close). Her first assignment was a film on sexual harassment in the work place, which "I agree is a pain, but I'm so perverse I'm going the other way," she said. "I think everybody should be harassing each other a whole lot more. I'm averse to teaching messages—they're a load of rubbish."

The Women's Film Unit was also a bit of a pain. "Basically, the way film sets work is very undemocratic, whereas the idea behind the unit—the idealism—predisposed its members to expect a lot more say. On a normal set, the priority is the work; in a situation like the Women's Film Unit, the politics were the work.

"All the same, the unit did address a major inequality. Also, there was a radical feminist group, film makers and activists, who had a huge impact on the Australian Film Commission. They were astonishing in their ability to intimidate the bureaucracy into supporting more women. But I think it's quite clear in my work that my orientation isn't political or doesn't come out of modern politics."

There, of course, is the rub. Campion is, to a degree, the beneficiary of a group effort. But what makes her a remarkable director is a truly singular talent, which is why she squirms when asked about being the first woman to win the Palme d'Or. To mention her sex is, however inadvertently, to modify the accomplishment. But if art, as the singer K.D. Lang put it, "transcends the tools you carry," the fact remains that Campion's tools, especially when she is dealing with sexuality, are often splendidly, uniquely female.

It may also be her sex that allows Campion to confess that although she had received development money for *The Piano* from the Australian Film Commission, it was loneliness that drove her to accept the producer Jan Chapman's offer of work on Australian television.

The experience ballooned Campion's confidence to the point where she was bursting to speak with her own voice. But because she believed that neither her understanding nor her skills as a movie maker were yet up to *The Piano,* she chose instead to do "something wilder, a bit younger, a bit more obnoxious. Provocative, you know?" She did *Sweetie.*

Sweetie, which she cowrote with her then-boyfriend, Gerard Lee, is all those things. *Sweetie* is about a young woman whose burning desire to be in show business is predicated on her ability to ride a toppling chair until it (slowly) hits the ground. Sweetie was not supposed to be the star; her younger sister, a kind of walking recessive gene, was. But Sweetie, who is nuts, took over the film as surely as she took over her family.

An Angel at My Table came next. Originally, it was meant for New Zealand television. Had it not been, Laura Jones, who wrote the script, said she would have done it differently: "I might have thought of dealing with a smaller time frame. And one wouldn't normally have such discursive storytelling in a feature film. But it worked, which made me rethink what *does* work."

What works in *Angel* is Campion's eye. Every image is freighted with meaning. A teacher, an insignificant-looking young man bent on bonhomie, stretches himself along his desk. Janet Frame, shy, a virgin and irredeemably isolate, stares fixedly at his trousers' fly. There, under the buttons, is the means to connection. A student-teacher, Frame picks up the chalk. Suddenly, she doesn't know what it is, what it's for. "I write for Jane," Jones said, "in a way I couldn't write for any other director."

Finally, there is *The Piano. Sweetie* cost less than $1 million; *Angel,* very little more. *The Piano,* which had seed money from the Australian Film Commission and major money from its French producers, was big-budget and thus scary.

"I thought: 'I haven't got any excuses. I have enough money to do this film really well,'" Campion said. "But I soon realized the anxiety was stifling, that I had to throw it away and just be naughty.

"*The Piano,* like *A Girl's Own Story,* is my territory—things I know about, that nobody else could easily get access to. I'd become fascinated by early photographs of New Zealand, and especially by portraits of Europeans and married people, and I was dying to do my version of a period film. Also, I've always wanted to tell an erotic story, particularly from a woman's perspective."

The story is simple. Ada, a Scotswoman with an illegitimate child, is married by proxy to a New Zealand settler, Stewart, and shipped to the other side of the world. With her are her small daughter and her piano, which, together, are her voice. When Stewart refuses to transport the piano to his farm, another settler, Baines, buys it and makes a bargain. He will give the piano to Ada if she will give him piano lessons. In truth, he does not want to learn the piano. He wants to learn Ada.

Sam Neill plays Stewart, a more or less predictable piece of casting, since Neill, himself a New Zealander, specializes in projecting a certain innocent, albeit sexy, confusion. But Harvey Keitel, he of the terrier ferocity, is hardly the first person one would think of for a scarcely housebroken, illiterate English settler with a tattooed (Maori-style) nose. Nor does Holly Hunter, who won the best-actress award at Cannes, seem a natural for a 19th-century woman who's constrained not only by custom and corsets but also by her stubborn and seemingly intractable speechlessness. But Campion casts "according to whom I am attracted to, and some people can't understand at first glance why that would be. But if you can see the potential in that person's character, it's really more interesting that others cannot. Because they're going to learn through you."

Asked to describe working with Campion, Keitel said: "Jane Campion is a goddess, and it's difficult for a mere mortal to talk about a goddess. I fear being struck by lightning bolts." The next day he called to clarify. "What's unusual about her," he continued, "has to do with ethereal things. She is at play, like a warm breeze."

Fortunately for someone who prefers to build with concrete, there was Neill. "Jane works in an unusually intimate way with people," he said. "When you're an actor, you're always putting yourself in other people's hands anyway, and she repays the gesture many times over. Jane's interested in complexity, not reductiveness, and very sure of what she's doing. If you have an opinion contrary to hers, she listens with the greatest care and consideration, then does what she had in mind all along."

Genevieve Lemon, who played Sweetie and the silly, love-starved Nessie of *The Piano,* said of Campion: "She digs deep when she's working with an actor, and that can be pretty confronting. She's always saying, 'Strip, strip, give me less acting,' and you try to give her exactly what she wants because her instincts are so sound. Most of the time with a director you think, 'Stop! What's going on here? Where am I going?' But you trust Jane absolutely."

("Gen's method," Campion said, "is impenetrable by somebody else, but that's true of a lot of actors. How they do it is alarming for them. That's why you have to be very careful about interfering with their securities and their methods. I just contribute in however much room they leave for me to contribute.")

The Piano is intensely romantic on several counts. All three of its protagonists are sexual innocents (Stewart may even be a virgin), which is why their introduction to eroticism constitutes an inundation. Ada's music, which was composed by Michael Nyman and played by Hunter herself, is as somber and powerful as Ada is. And New Zealand's bush, albeit a very different landscape, seems as magical as the moors near Wuthering Heights.

Campion's movies don't resemble anyone else's, and neither do they resemble one another. The strange, skewed look of *Sweetie,* for example, was influenced by the work of certain American photographers, Diane Arbus in particular. The look of *Angel,* however, is simple, allusionless: it was Janet Frame's story, after all, and Campion "had to stay out of its way." But for *Piano,* Campion and the director of photography, Stuart Dryburgh, dove right in. Using as their starting point a mutual love of autochromes, an early color process based on potato dyes, they allowed some tints to completely drain scenes and turned the bush into a kind of underwater world.

"Only Stuart and I really liked what we liked," she said. "Everyone else was, 'Mmmmmmmmm.' It's scary, you know? But to get a look you have to stick your foot out. You can't play it safe.

"I had this spooky psychological thing about *The Piano* before it began, which was how everybody was going to go nuts on the set. Because a film tends to set up the way people are going to behave. But then I said to myself, 'O.K., it doesn't actually matter what people do so long as you go through it, as long as you don't pull back, as long as you take responsibility.' In the end, the making of *The Piano* was an enormous pleasure, and it encouraged me to take some risks romantically which paid off very well."

"Getting married, you mean?" her visitor asked.

"Oh, no," Campion said. "I wanted to get married. Colin and I had been best friends for six or seven years. The big emotional risk was in becoming lovers."

Jan Chapman, who produced *The Piano,* works out of two large, airy rooms above a fish restaurant. Campion's apartment, though in a chic part of Sydney, is modest and does not feature an art collection. Laura Jones, upon entering a rather grand hotel for morning coffee, said, "This isn't my usual kind of place," and when asked about Robert Altman's film *The Player,* in which writers "pitch" and producers murder, replied, "Well, with us there's more chatting than pitching."

In June, Jones, Campion and Chapman were chatting about *The Portrait of a Lady,* the Henry James novel for which Jones is writing the adaptation, Campion is directing and Chapman is the script consultant. (Nicole Kidman will play the heroine, Isabel Archer, for whom self-creation and, indeed, self-perfection, is life's purpose.) Unlike Campion's other films, this one is large American dollars all the way—which at this point may make no difference in the final product. But it might have made a difference once. "The Government support here," Chapman said, "has enabled producers and directors to pursue their own talents early on. As soon as you start having big systems trying to simplify ideas you lose that spark." And although she is as reluctant as Campion to discuss sexual politics, she added: "And because of this Government assistance, nothing stopped us. There wasn't a male-based system that, consciously or unconsciously, we had to adapt ourselves to."

Portrait, Campion said, is one of her favorite books, partly because she herself feels "so Isabel Archerish. I think that coming from Australia or New Zealand now makes one more like Americans going to Europe were then than Americans going to Europe are now. They're much more sophisticated, whereas we have more of a colonial attitude about ourselves, a more can-do, anything's-possible attitude. I felt so much like Isabel as a young woman, a sense of having extraordinary potential without knowing what the hell to do with it. Before *Piano,* I wouldn't have had the guts to take on a big classic thing. But now I don't feel frightened at all.

"I seem to have been able to make a career out of doing what I feel like doing, so why not keep doing it? What's corrupting is wanting to be more important. You want to be more arty—you get your identity from that. Or you get your identity out of making more money. I get my pleasure, which is far more important to me, out of trying to follow my instincts."

In tracking those instincts, her film editor Veronika Jenet said, "Jane always surrounds herself with people who are very supportive and give her free range." If sanity lies in knowing your strengths and how to capitalize on them, then Campion is clearly a monument thereto.

By the middle of June, the chatting with Laura Jones and Jan Chapman about Isabel, her aunt Mrs. Touchett, her friend Henrietta Stackpole, the sinuous Madame Merle ("Great parts for women! But, of course, the point about Henry James is that all the parts are good") and Isabel's quartet of swains had more or less ceased. Jane had high blood pressure, and nobody could tell her and Colin precisely what that might mean. Still, they consoled themselves with the thought that, after having had three miscarriages, Jane had only two weeks to go to term. Two weeks to go—it was like being in a marathon and knowing you had only another ten yards to run.

"I was getting a bit sick of myself toward the end of my 30's, thinking, 'Is this all there is to know?' " she said. "Having a baby has completely distracted me from that. Now I have a big stake in the future because his will be part of mine. At the same time, I'll be forced back, because I'll be part of being a child again through him. And as he grows up and has his problems, I'll be part of that, too."

A few days later, Jane Campion's son, Jasper, was delivered by emergency Caesarean section. His parents were told almost immediately that he could not live outside an incubator, and that he would die soon. When, in fact, was up to them. Twelve days after his birth, Jane and Colin took Jasper home, where he died the following dawn.

The day after Jasper's cremation, 35 of his parents' family and friends gathered at Neilson Park, on the cliffs overlooking Sydney Harbor, to honor his brief life. Rugs were spread for the guests to sit upon, food was served and Jane and Colin talked about their baby and what he had meant to them. There were other speakers, and some people read poems they had written.

To hear of that sad, brave ceremony was suddenly to remember Colette's harsh "Who said you should be happy? Do your work." It was also to hope that in special gifts lie special consolations.

The Arts/Film

SANDRA HALL/1993

WHEN JANE CAMPION NEXT goes to work, she will step into the ultra-refined world of Henry James, which is about as far as you can get from the stark, psychological landscape of her current hit, *The Piano*.

She will direct Nicole Kidman in an adaptation of James' *Portrait of a Lady,* a property that has also attracted attention from the team of Ismail Merchant and James Ivory. "We thought we'd do it sooner," says Campion. Hearing of her interest, Kidman made an approach through the office of her husband, Tom Cruise, and Campion and her producer, Jan Chapman, responded.

"We thought if they've got the guts to do it, then we'll have proper creative control instead of doing it through a studio," Campion says.

As usual the 39-year-old writer-director is dressed in art school black, her face carefully made up for the photo. It is a mobile face, with a wide smile; she has a big, noisy laugh and her healthy sense of the ridiculous enlivens every film she has made.

Instinct: "It's a useful thing to have a bit of irony in your life," she says when I admire the way she doesn't make martyrs of her characters. Even *The Piano's* heroine, Ada (played by Holly Hunter), a character thoroughly infused with the spirit of Emily Brontë, has a potent instinct for survival. She lives for the romantic ideal until the script hits her just in time with a

From *The Bulletin* (Sydney), 26 October 1993. Reprinted by permission of *The Bulletin* and the author.

bracing belt of commonsense. Remarkably, Campion manages this touch of earthiness without sacrificing any of the film's poetry.

"Ada is marvellous to me," she says. "She is so dogmatic . . . I could never be like that. I was attracted to her strictness. At the same time, I wanted her to snap out of her over-enlarged sense of her own dramatic life."

Portrait of a Lady will take Campion into new territory. In the films she has made so far, she has used visual imagery brilliantly to express emotional extremes. Dialogue has been a minor part of her artistic equipment. In fact, the heroines of her two most recent films have been famously inarticulate, at least when it comes to conversation. Ada is mute (the piano is her way of communicating feelings) and Janet Frame in Campion's film of the New Zealand writer's autobiography, *An Angel At My Table,* is so shy that long, painful scenes go by while she struggles to complete a sentence.

James, in contrast, was wedded to the complete sentence, the more sinuous the better. "The great thing about him is his dialogue," says Campion. "His ability to turn the tone around in a sentence or a scene or within a series of scenes. And the characters are wonderful. It's a great portrait of a woman with what seems like extraordinary potential. Although it's set in that rarefied world that James often talks about, it resonates for many, many women and for men, too. It's just insightful about human beings."

Laura Jones, who worked with Campion on *An Angel At My Table,* is writing the adaptation and she, Campion and Chapman have already had long script sessions together. It is Campion's favourite part of the process. She is also going to take some "master classes" with the novelist David Malouf on James' ending to the book.

The film is to be made in next year's spring and summer in England, Italy and Turkey. She and Chapman are working in association with US producer Monty Montgomery, whose company, Propaganda, produced David Lynch's *Wild At Heart* and the *Twin Peaks* pilot.

They met in the US after the release of *An Angel At My Table.* Although *The Piano* was seen at the New York Film Festival, it does not open commercially in the US until November 10; a box-office success could pitch her into a much bigger league. "I haven't been courted in the same way as Baz [Luhrmann] and some of the others have. Until *The Piano,* I haven't looked nearly as commercial. There have been no approaches from the studios. I think they and I realise that we wouldn't be a match made in heaven."

Wouldn't the money be nice? The question provokes another burst of laughter. "The million-dollar offer, you mean? No, I'm not in it to get the million-dollar offer."

Spirit: *The Piano* is dedicated to her mother, Edith. She and Campion's father, Richard, were actors and trained at London's Old Vic together. He now directs opera in New Zealand. "My mother carries a very feminine poetic spirit which was an inspiration for this film."

Her sister, Anna, is in London making her first film and Campion hopes that one day they will work together. "We're passionate about each other. We were passionate as children, too, except that it was in the opposite way. We hated each other. It's one of the greatest turnarounds in a relationship that I've ever had."

Family life has been the butt of some very dark humour in her films. Her shorts, *Peel* and *A Girl's Own Story,* and her feature *Sweetie,* all featured bizarre behaviour by both parents and siblings. What was the inspiration?

"Not my family," she says firmly. "If my family was really weird, I think I'd have found it very hard to do stories that reveal what can go wrong with the family unit. Probably, when I began film-making I was more rebellious. It was the age group and everything. It makes you feel there's so much dishonesty about. Those TV series with gorgeous, happy, smiling families. You feel impelled to tell the other side and enjoy the other side, too."

Students: Her collaborators on these early films were novelist and short story writer Gerard Lee (*Troppo Man, True Love and How to Get It*) and cinematographer Sally Bongers. The three met as students at the Australian Film, Television and Radio School. Campion and Lee used to work up their scripts by acting out scenes; she and Bongers developed a distinctive visual humour based on surreal tricks of framing and composition which produced a beguiling conjunction of the mundane and the completely chaotic.

"A lot of people found it irritating." She starts to laugh. "Gerard and I had a screaming match in a car park once—a humorous one. He said, 'You've ruined the movie. It's a mess.' He'd been looking at it without sound. Then when he finally saw it, he really did adore it. When your collaborators really get high on something—when they've entrusted you to direct the film—that's one of the best moments."

The visual style of *The Piano* is more conventional, although there are typical Campion moments. Suppressed agitation is reflected in an overhead shot of tea slopping about in a china cup; an eerie close-up of outstretched hands heralds Ada's arrival in the New World. But now that bigger budgets give Campion access to more equipment, these moments of contemplation are bound to decrease as she learns more about moving the camera around.

Her point of view is changing, too, she thinks. While she is a great admirer of the Spanish director Luis Buñuel, whose taste for perversity was lifelong, she is feeling a bit more compassionate these days. Does she resist unhappy endings? Not consciously. "But I like to get the audience back on their feet. Give them something to get them out of the cinema, so they can walk back home."

Jane Campion, the Classical Romantic

JAY CARR/1993

ONE OF THE MOST striking images you're going to see on any movie screen this year is of Holly Hunter, staring fiercely from beneath the hood of a 19th-century bonnet as the heroine of Jane Campion's film *The Piano,* which opens Friday. Hunter's Ada, a stonily stubborn Scotswoman who refuses to speak except through her keyboard and whose sexuality is awakened after she lands in the New Zealand brush, is the latest in a series of extraordinary women at the center of Campion's three features. They include Genevieve Lemon's fatally primal *Sweetie* and Kerry Fox's portrayal of Janet Frame, who became New Zealand's best-known novelist after narrowly escaping being lobotomized and whose autobiography Campion traced in *Angel at My Table.* Campion, a fair-haired woman whose blue eyes seem no strangers to reverie, sits in a Manhattan hotel suite, smiling at the contrast between Ada and herself.

Ada is a romantic, Campion explains, whereas she, holder of a degree in structural anthropology, possesses an essentially classical temperament. "I've got a good check on the passions," she says. But while Campion carefully storyboards her films, she's quick to add that she is an intuitive filmmaker. "It starts with a feeling that is quite unnameable. And a mood, you know? And then you try to write things that create the mood you are feeling or thinking of. I do think it's intuitive, and the solutions to problems are intuitive. In this case, I was trying to tell a very extreme story in a romantic condition, and I can't describe the mood. The film is the mood.

None of the other films could be described as romantic. This is romantic. It has a climax, it has a narrative and things like that.

"People are run by their emotions and their passions," Campion continues; her face clouds over, perhaps in recollection of her film's leads—Hunter, Sam Neill as the bottled-up husband who sends for Ada and then makes the mistake of leaving her precious piano on the beach, and Harvey Keitel as the rootless neighbor who buys the piano from the opaque husband of the mail-order bride in order to gain access to her. "I'm very romantic about these passions, about passion-driven people.

"Byron, for example. He was a symbol for someone who speaks his mind, a great sex symbol who died—well, actually of a cold—but ostensibly fighting for Greece. There's something in my spirit that wishes that I was more able to take those kinds of risks in living, in living life more dangerously than I am prepared to do. I am actually quite romantic about Ada and the kind of pointless, ridiculous stands that she has taken in her life.

"I am very influenced by *Wuthering Heights,*'" Campion adds, "and by Emily Bronte's way of using the atmosphere and the way the atmosphere was created out of the landscape and the bleakness and the weather. I wanted to write a complex love story, an erotic story, and one from a woman's viewpoint. I did feel that New Zealand, which was particular to my upbringing, had an equivalently exotic—or actually more exotic and equivalently powerful—landscape that was not unfamiliar territory to me, as opposed to the Yorkshire moors. You've got those magnificent beaches in New Zealand, those black-sand beaches. And it does carry a lot of impact, the New Zealand brush. It has a lot of intimacy about it, and at the same time a claustrophobia and a threateningness, and a charm, you know? A kind of enchantment about it. It's kind of fairy-tale-ish, you know, how people go into the woods. It's a rite-of-passage type of landscape. The journey these people take is towards a kind of awakening of their sexual passions."

Campion's imagery can be considered minimalist, but also surrealistic. Image after image seems to exist in a world of its own and come floating off the screen, a fragment of a shared dream. Since *Sweetie,* Campion has favored the use of autochromes, a sometimes primitive-looking color process. Some tints drain scenes, imparting otherworldliness. When we finally see an underwater scene in *The Piano,* we realize its quality of underwaterness has been replicated earlier, on land. Campion's camera angles and framing are original, her images at once lush and grave, instinctive and carefully thought out. So it was with the characters' historical underpinnings, which are both "authentic" and imagined.

"It was a very free thing," Campion says. "In the end, I'm telling a story and that's more important. The authenticity is just an effect as well. I wasn't trying to be historical. Still, we used daguerreotypes quite a lot for hair and makeup ideas. I don't know where people get their ideas from. Some of the old paintings were interesting, but only because they were pretty inaccurate and romanticized. I was really struck by how weird and strange and individual everybody looked in the daguerreotypes. It was just right up my alley. And not at all because of the cliche of the period look—because there is no period look. The period look was invented by Hollywood."

Campion, 39, a New Zealander, lives with her husband, Colin Englert, a TV producer and director, in a flat in Sydney, Australia. She had gained international attention with her previous films but nothing like the acclaim that came when *The Piano* won the Golden Palm at Cannes this summer—it's the festival's equivalent of a best-picture prize, and was split with Chen Kaige's *Farewell, My Concubine*. The joy Campion felt was shattered shortly afterward by the death of her 12-day-old son and first child, Jasper.

Campion thinks of herself as antipodean, she says, but much is made down under of the differences between Australia and New Zealand—even if, as she points out, the biggest differences stem from the indigenous populations of each country. New Zealand had been inhabited by the Maori, a Polynesian people whose propensity for trading allowed them to interact more easily with Europeans than Australia's nomadic, mystical aborigines have. One possible reason for Campion's matter-of-factness about national identity is that her family has been in New Zealand long enough to feel secure about it.

Her great-grandfather was a cobbler who arrived in New Zealand in 1860, profiting from the gold rush there. Her mother and father met while studying acting in England at the Old Vic, married and returned home. "My father was a big director, and my mother was an actress. They still work. Of course, as a young person, I rejected their world. I thought the whole theater world was highly pretentious, and I didn't want to have anything to do with it. I really disliked the theatricality of their social life. Now I sort of think, 'No wonder they were like that.' They were so repressed that they must have sought every theatrical or overly exuberant person out and just included them in their social life. Which is what I wound up doing. The prevailing thing about the New Zealanders and the Australians is not to be theatrical. It's like, 'Don't waste time, and above all, be modest.' Particularly in New Zealand. They have a program that sort of spoofs that temperament. They call it 'That's Fairly Interesting.' "

It took Campion a while to decide that film was to be her calling. She didn't enjoy a stay in England. "Actually, I felt a deep antipathy," she recalls. "I felt enraged every time I heard that toff-y accent. All my egalitarian spirit really sent me into a fury every time I heard those sort of dandy voices with nooooo ability to feel emotional or feel for anybody else. It was only recently that I can hear that kind of voice and suddenly recognize it not so much as my enemy as a sort of weird antiquated cultural design. What's most sad is the resignation amongst English people about their opportunities in life. Where they begin is where they end. We colonials have a different spirit—like anybody can have a go." Campion does not, in short, share the Anglophile views of American novelist Henry James. Which is why she will go to Italy next year to film James' *Portrait of a Lady,* with Australia's Nicole Kidman as the self-transforming Isabelle Archer.

For all the down under flavor of *The Piano,* Campion acknowledges that she raised a few eyebrows when she cast Americans Hunter and Keitel. She met with Hunter reluctantly, she admits, on her way back to Australia from an unsuccessful casting effort in Europe. "I resisted the idea of meeting people outside my own ideas, but then I agreed to meet on the basis of not being so uptight. When she did the audition, I really got what a difference actors could make." So Campion abandoned her idea of a more statuesque Ada. That Hunter could play the piano was a bonus.

"With Harvey, I guess I was looking for someone who could fill the role out because it was underwritten and I realized I'd need help in making that character live. I felt Harvey was too New York, but then I remembered *The Duelist,* when he had a very neutral accent. When I saw him in 'The Two Jakes,' he really looked up for more, so I sent him the script."

The fact that the film is one of the decade's most erotic posed less of a problem than Campion feared, she says. "What you are trying to do is remove all the obstacles for people to enter into some intimate relationship with the story, and trust the story. We rehearsed a lot. Holly and I particularly had a lot of talks about it. Harvey seemed a bit shy about talking about things like that. We didn't worry about it. We just used a sort of pillow to represent him. Luckily, as it turned out, we liked each other, and it became not a problem to discuss it and even laugh about it. Basically, they just wanted to honor the script and do it the right way, and their concerns about nudity and privacy just weren't present. We weren't worried about showing this much or that much. I decided I didn't want to do a lot of shots and panning. I just wanted to try and use their attention on each other."

Campion Takes on Spielberg at His Game

VICKY ROACH/1994

JANE CAMPION WAS ONE of the last people in the film industry to find out her film *The Piano* had won a whopping eight Oscar nominations—because she had her phone off the hook.

At the time, the New Zealand-born film-maker was holed up in a bungalow at the exclusive Kim's resort, a lush getaway on the Central Coast with writer/producer Billy MacKinnon and US producer Laurie Parker.

They were working on the film adaptation of the Christopher Isherwood novel, *My Guru*—one of Campion's upcoming projects—and they didn't want to be distracted. Oscar nominations or not.

As Campion herself readily admits, the show side of the business is not really her style.

"And as a director and writer those are the two things I do. I try to concentrate my efforts on making films as well as I can," she said in a rare interview yesterday.

Nevertheless, Campion said she was excited at the news that her dark and brooding love story had been nominated for eight Academy Awards—including Best Picture, Best Actress and Best Director.

"It's incredibly good fun and a great surprise," she said. "It's not something I've ever thought about. The sort of films I make have always been nowhere near mainstream, so I never expected to be a part of this event."

And despite her usual red carpet reluctance, Campion said she would almost certainly make it to the Oscars night, "though it'll probably be crushingly boring."

From *The Sydney Daily Telegraph*, 17 February 1994.

"I've always enjoyed it when there's an Australian in the Academy Awards—like Judy Davis was last year. It's good fun to see them there representing the industry.

"And we're convinced it's going to be a big turn around. Spielberg's had it too good for too long. The girls are fighting back," she joked.

"We're in there for the fight and the fun."

Campion is only the second woman ever to be nominated for an Oscar for Best Director—Lina Wertmuller was nominated in 1976 for *Seven Beauties.*

"She's a big heroine of mine anyway—I love her work and *Seven Beauties* is an absolute classic," Campion said.

"It's great to be nominated in that regard because I remember feeling so much encouragement when I was at film school, from seeing people like Lina Wertmuller and Gillian Armstrong doing what they did and realising it was possible to be a woman and a director."

The film-maker also pointed out the high representation of women in *The Piano*'s Oscar nominations—Jan Chapman, who as producer would accept the award for Best Film; Holly Hunter, nominated for Best Actress; Anna Paquin, for Best Supporting Actress; Jane Patterson for Costume Design; and Veronika Jenet for Editing—while at the same time paying tribute to the men who collaborated on the film.

"I don't want to trumpet up the girls at the expense of the men," she said. "Harvey Keitel and Sam Niell for instance were just great—a lot of men would have shied away from the roles they had to play. And Michael Nyman. They are really sophisticated, strong men.

The director says that so far she has managed to resist the creative and commercial pressures that have accompanied the phenomenal success of *The Piano.*

"There's a lot of opportunity out there for me at the moment and I think I have to distinguish between what is real opportunity and what is just quick money talking," she said.

A Light on the Dark Secrets of Depression

SUE WILLIAMS/1995

When Oscar winning film-maker Jane Campion was in her teens her mother was affected so badly by depression she offered to help her die. Her mother turned her down, but the experience has had a deep and lasting impact on Campion's life.

"I had to get away, I couldn't breathe, I couldn't see for myself my own optimism any more because it's so seductive," says Campion, who wrote and directed the acclaimed Australian film *The Piano.*

"And her [way of] looking at the world seemed almost contagious to the point that I one time said to her, 'Look mum, if you really would like to die, if you think you would be happier, I'll be with you, I'll help you.'

"And she said to me, 'I don't want to die, I don't want to die, I want to feel good about things,' and that was the real turning point for me. I realised that my job was not to sort of see her in darkness, but say, 'Oh, it's going to be better, you're going to get better.'"

Campion makes her extraordinary revelation in a moving documentary on depression on SBS tonight. In the documentary, from Lina Safro, the award-winning maker of the film about breast cancer, *Agatha's Curse,* Campion joins others such as musician Tim Finn and author William Styron in talking about how depression has affected their lives.

For her, however the experience has been channelled into a positive force. With her mother now much better after ECT treatments—also known as electric shock therapy—Campion has been able to learn from

---

From *The Australian* (Sydney), 2 May 1995. Reprinted by permission of the author.

those dark years and turn them into a state of mind that has helped her in her own career and personal life.

Because many believe depression can be genetic, she has been careful to think through life and make sure she is as prepared as she can be before any major catastrophe.

It was this approach that helped Campion to endure the death of her baby just 12 days after he was born in 1993.

"In the grief that I suffered when Jasper died, it was my spirit that brought me back through," she says. "But if you haven't got your spirit to bring you through it, you know, I don't know what you do. You just wait until things to change, you know.

"When mum is feeling good, it's a precious thing and when good things happen, they feel better. In terms of the work that I do, and when I'm writing, for a short period of time, I enter into that, in the spirit of whatever it is. For instance, when I was writing *The Piano,* it had quite a lot of dark notes in it and dark feelings in it and the way I do it, it's almost like an actor, I spend some time alone, a week or something like that and try to enter right into the mood of the whole story and understand Ada's being, thinking and sometimes I'd cry and totally try to enjoy the whole emotional mood. And I have to spend a few days in it and then once I've got it, I can sort of go out and work more sort of from a nine to five basis."

A Voyage to Discover Herself

MICHEL CIMENT/1996

Two of your films were made from original screenplays, and the other two, written with Laura Jones, were made from literary works. Were the problems posed by the adaptation of Henry James' novel, Portrait of a Lady *different from those that you found in adapting* An Angel at My Table, *Janet Frame's autobiographical work?*
James' book is a masterpiece of fiction and a story structured in a very complex way. He also has many strong characters, while Janet Frame's narratives have, in reality, only one. *An Angel at My Table* follows the course of one life; *Portrait of a Lady* has philosophical implications. It's truly a young girl's voyage towards darkness and underground regions. There is also a mythic dimension, with an awakening at the end. Adapting James' novel for the screen was a difficult task which sometimes even scared me, given the size of the work.

When did you discover it?
I don't remember exactly when it happened, but it was surely when I was around 20, when I devoured that type of fiction. I had thought about making a film out of it for a long time. I remember talking to a friend about it when I joked with her about founding a production company to do screen adaptations of classical novels like this one, or those of Jane Austen whose complex stories provided a change from the boring films that we were see-

---

Interview: 11 September 1996. From *Positif,* December 1996. Translated by Michele Curley. Reprinted by permission of *Positif* and the author.

ing in those days. Obviously, for several years now, many people have had the same idea as us!

Faced with a book of over 600 pages, how did you decide what to cut? The film leaves out large parts, such as the first chapters in New England.
They were obviously difficult choices, and we even wondered in the beginning if it was even possible to do such an adaptation, until the moment I realized, while rereading the novel, that we weren't going to shoot *Portrait of a Lady,* but simply the story of *Portrait of a Lady* interpreted by me, with some of the original dialogue. I love James' subtle psychological analyses, his manner of weaving his web around his characters, but obviously that's not what you can do in film. My aims were to make the situations physical, develop the sexual elements that were only suggested, give Isabel
some fantasies. On the other hand, Laura and I did not have too many problems in sacrificing the first third of the novel, which is a sort of long prologue with conversations about a possible marriage. We began by doing a scene breakdown of it, but it didn't lead anywhere. On the other hand, very early on we had the idea of symmetry with the tree under which Warburton proposes to Isabel in the beginning scene, and the tree, naked, of the last scene in the dead of winter, where everything seems stark and vulnerable like Isabel herself. So many things have happened between the characters and within them that many people don't notice that it's the same tree.

Your last scene is different from the book's because it's more "open." In James' work Henrietta tells Goodwood that Isabel left to reconcile with Osmond, even though James doesn't exclude another future for Isabel either.
I don't think that James wants the reader to really know which path his heroine is going to take either. I think there are contradictory tensions in his book, which explains why the ending is unresolved. On one hand, there's the fairy tale/melodramatic side that he tells, and on the other hand, the burden of reality that he brings to his story since James is a realist, with characters that are described in a strong, intimate and true manner. He tries to meld these two tendencies in the epilogue of his novel. Personally, I didn't want to come to a resolution and preferred the symmetry of the

two trees and Isabel's slow motion run.

Isn't there in you also a conflict between a taste for romantic stories and a desire for a "realist" approach?
I like to enter a story as a member of the audience. I like to feel the reality of the drama that I describe without restraint, because it's one of the big pleasures that all fiction provides. And all my effort is to enable my actors, and then the future spectators, to share in this impression of reality. At the same time I love the "romance"; it's part of my nature because I am very romantic in my life. I don't mean that from a sentimental point of view, but in a larger sense: I am fundamentally an optimist.

Isabel is close to your other heroines. She embarks on a voyage to discover life.
She is courageous and looking for truth; it's what pushes her forward. Personally, I feel in myself, among other things, two principle forces that guide me: the excitement of discovering the truth of things and beings, where it's found, and the desire to be loved. They are two companions that are difficult to reconcile. If, for example, one of my films becomes very popular, I begin to ask myself questions about the degree of truth that it contains, and wonder if that truth isn't too easy to accept!

In Portrait of a Lady, *you made some decisions that were not easy, in particular the one to erase the decorative aspects of the period re-creation that are most often found in this type of adaptation. You concentrate on the passions.*
It was a very conscious decision. We knew that we needed a period background because it was in this context that the story unfolded, but the true subject was the intimacy of the relationships between these characters. It's a very demanding story and it was the story that interested me rather than the splendor of Italy. We also had to show darkness, and that was only possible in winter: the dark face of beautiful Italy, which is like that of Madame Merle and of Osmond, whose sunny disposition is the only thing that she sees at the beginning. I discovered this Italy myself when I was twenty-one and I left to study art in Venice. I passed the winter there profoundly depressed by the cold, the humidity, the imprisonment, and also my terrible loneliness since I didn't know anyone. It was my first existential experience of isolation. That helped me to understand Isabel's feelings

very much, especially since the summer preceding that stay in Venice, I had passed a marvelous summer in Pérouse where everyone loved me, the weather was splendid and I thought I was in paradise. A few months later, I really felt the fragility of my happiness!

Three times in the film, you abandon the "realist" approach of the narrative. First in the opening credits, with the voice-over conversations of the young women.
I thought that it was necessary to suggest to the audience what the romantic hopes of young girls could be. The decision was taken very early on to have that introduction, which serves as a link to our era, and which is like a poem before the journey of a young woman. She begins it with a mythic vision of life, and the process of disenchantment is going to be a very difficult experience. It's then that I had the idea of gathering all the lively, intelligent young women that I had met in Australia during the preparation of the film and asking them to speak off the cuff of their aspirations and their sentimental experiences. Some friends joined them, like Geneviève Lemon who played Sweetie. There were absolutely fascinating conversations of which you only hear fragments and which would make an astonishing radio program, were it only with all the stories of kisses that they tell!

There is also the scene where Isabel makes love with three men in a dream. Did you think about introducing other dream-like moments of this type?
No, not really. The development of the story is so dramatic that I didn't see how I could interrupt it. I did film another sequence of this type, but I didn't include it while editing. At this point in the story, I wanted to show that Isabel was a woman with very strong sexual aspirations, who wants to be loved and who feels frustrated. Even though she speaks of completely different things, of starting a career, etc., at her core, she is looking for passion. A critic of James' novel wrote—and with a lot of justice in my opinion—that Isabel was divided in two. On the one hand, since she didn't know her father, she was looking for a substitute. On the other hand, she was fascinated by images of domination and submission. I think that her attraction for Osmond took her by surprise and that she trusted in him, so strong this experience seemed to her. In fact, she likes the idea that she will no longer have her future in her hands and that she will be able to entrust it to this dominating "genie." In one sense, Osmond is a negative mirror-

image of Isabel's spiritual aspirations. She refuses Warburton, who offers her material security, and Goodwood, with his physical seduction, in favor of Osmond whom she idealizes. She believes that she's looking for light, when she's attracted by shadow, by a somber adventure that's going to swallow her up. When Osmond makes his declaration of love, it's in a place plunged in darkness, with beams of light. The set seems haunted.

The third imaginary scene is that trip to the Orient, shot in black and white like a primitive film.
We came up with a mental diary under the form of a home movie. It's very entertaining, a bit in the spirit of *Sweetie*. The shots where isolated mouths move by themselves are risky, but I thought they're the types of things that work or not, and . . . it's necessary to take risks without asking oneself too many questions about their meaning. The sequence also helps to explain why she falls in love with Osmond, since the spectator tends to see him as a bad choice. The problem is that Isabel is an easy victim, so much does she want to fall in love. During this voyage, she convinces herself to make the fatal decision.

When you chose John Malkovich, you knew, with the cunning devil image that he projects on the screen, that the audience would discover the true nature of his character before Isabel would.
But James, from the onset of his presentation of the character of Osmond, tells you that there is no revelation to wait for and describes him to you such as he is. I like this idea, because it permits the reader to be in on the secret of the strategy concocted by Madame Merle and Osmond to conquer Isabel. I wanted, at the same time, for people to know from the beginning that Osmond is bad. The reader or spectator has the feeling that the author reveals everything to us in advance. Thus her total surprise when she learns that Pansy is the daughter of Osmond and Madame Merle.

You originally thought of asking William Hurt to play Osmond?
Yes, but Hurt would have projected a more subtle image of the "bad guy." He refused my proposal because it bothered him to play an evil character with no redeeming features. You cannot convince an actor to interpret a role that he doesn't want to take on. Hurt's refusal was lucky for me because Malkovich was ready to freely explore the blackest zones of a

human being. In addition, we ourselves can identify with Osmond and Madame Merle when, for example, they talk and criticize the people they know. What is also curious about Osmond is that he always tells the truth even if it's in a crafty manner.

Madame Merle is a more compassionate figure in the novel.
In my opinion, she's a great character. And I agree with James when he says that the great characters of literature are great because they understand their own tragedy. Madame Merle, somewhere in herself, feels love for Isabel, and she is repulsed at a certain stage by what she has undertaken to do in order to protect her daughter.

Nicole Kidman, with her red hair, reminds one of Kerry Fox who played the adult Janet Frame in An Angel at My Table.
It was Nicole's idea to have that curly hair, because she had it that way when she was young and she didn't like herself like that. She especially didn't want her character to be a "beauty." In life, she is. Nicole is a very intelligent woman, who doesn't like to advertise it, even displays a lot of reserve. When Laura Jones, my screenwriter, Janet Patterson, my costume artist, and I talked about Isabel's character, we wondered how she would dress if she were our contemporary. For us, she was the kind of young woman who would wear black hose and men's shoes, who wouldn't dress in a feminine manner and would want to be taken seriously for her ideas. There are such very beautiful women who don't like to be elegant. Isabel doesn't know who she is, and, when she thinks that she's on a voyage to discover truth, in fact she's on a trip to discover herself. At the end, when she confesses her love for Ralph, she is completely naked, simple, sure of her emotions and determined to make her feelings known to him. She has had the revelation of her real self.

You already knew Nicole Kidman before directing her.
We met many times in Australia, but without really being friends. I had thought of her in 1983 for one of my short films, *A Girl's Own Story,* which I had made during my studies at the Australian Film School, but she had to take an exam and wasn't free. Later, I dreamed of having her come back from Hollywood to have her play Isabel in a theatrical production of *Portrait of a Lady* that I wanted to stage in Sydney. At the time I didn't think one

could make a "large-audience" film out of this novel, and I didn't have enough confidence in myself to face its complexity in order to transform it into images. The stage seemed a more appropriate place to me. When I finally decided to make the film, I thought of her because she's a woman who has the feeling that she can aspire to anything, that she can assume she has a right to things, that she possesses intellectual superiority. And at the same time, she has a deep sense of humility and spend a good deal of time blaming herself for things. In a word, she is very brilliant. She can be overly blunt, then regret having wounded you. I needed this type of personality, strong, courageous and intelligent, to portray Isabel. She also has a great capacity to express various emotions very quickly. She's really one of the princesses of our generation. Moreover, she stuck with the project until the end; she was a "fan!"

I have the feeling that New Zealanders and Australians resemble the Americans at the beginning of the century who were less blasé, less superior than today, and who went to discover Europe to gain experience.
Yes, there is a certain innocence in us. Our countries are younger than America. The United States is now very strong and the relationship has been reversed. Now it's Europeans who traverse the Atlantic to discover the power that exists over there. We don't have that power, we lack experience, and our heritage comes from Europe. That also brought me close to James. I remember when I saw Paris and Rome for the first time, I was really taken out of myself, deeply moved.

You brought out the melodramatic aspect of James' art, which is like Balzac, while one can also see the precursor of Proust in him. As in his novels, your film proposes a heightened, "theatrical" reality.
We use this dramatic quality to express ideas about life and people. It's very practical! James understood the public's taste for drama and he used recognized forms to explore human beings. It's what made me think that that could work in film because it's fundamentally a beautiful story. I tried to discover the power of intimate relationships, to make them dynamic, cinematographic, by filming the clashes between the characters. I could have been more sober, told the whole story shot-counter shot of characters seated in armchairs engaged in conversations. That would have been interesting for a handful of persons, but surely not for the majority and maybe

not for me. I really wanted to engage myself violently in this story so that the audience in turn would share these emotions.

You use architecture and background a lot to express these emotions, as in the scene with Henrietta and Isabel in front of the recumbent effigies of the Victoria and Albert Museum in London or the one with Madame Merle and Isabel in front of the statues of the Capitoline in Rome, places which are not depicted in the novel.
I liked the morbid fantastical aspect of these effigies, and it seemed that the frame of this museum, which I like a lot, was appropriate for this conversation between two friends who have come as tourists to London. For the second scene, I chose those Capitoline statues because they have always moved me very much. I don't know why they make such an impression on me. Perhaps because of their size and the fact that they're broken. There's something there like an echo of Isabel's emotional state. In James' book, she walked in the country among the ruins.

Why do you use tilted frames to show the Duomo of Florence and the Coliseum?
In the first case, to be able to show the summit of the cathedral. In the second, in order not to see what shouldn't be seen: cars and other modern details. It doesn't bother me to tilt the camera every once in a while!

How did you approach, with your director of photography Stuart Dryburgh, the chromatic texture of the film?
We made two major decisions. Make our interior shots in Italy as dark as possible and have exterior shots almost overexposed to obtain those incredible contrasts. That corresponded to the reality that I observed in Italy, and also to the emotional reality of the story, with that opposition of shadow and light. We also wanted to avoid glamour in the intimate scenes, be as close as possible to the bodies.

You had never before worked with the musician Wojciech Kilar.
At the beginning, Michael Nyman was supposed to write the music. He decided against it finally, and I think it was better that way because he had a lot of reservations about the novel, which he really didn't like. On the other hand, it caused us problems since it was necessary to find a replacement rather late. I knew a student in Sydney who had been recommended

to me and who was totally obsessed by film music. He is very intelligent and very sensible, works in a CD shop, possesses an incredible collection of soundtracks. He had me listen to a lot of film music by Americans and Europeans, until he got to the Kilar's score of Coppola's *Dracula,* which immediately seduced me. I loved the unsentimental romanticism of it, its sense of mystery and depth. We didn't know anything about him; we called him in Poland. He didn't have any further desire to write music for films, but was willing reconsider his position. He came to Australia, loved the film, found in it a romanticism he could relate to, but he refused nevertheless to work for us. He felt blocked, and since he's a true artist, there was no way to change his mind. A week later, he sent me a fax saying that he thought he had found some solutions to various problems that we had come upon together. Then I went to Poland, and I was blown away by his work and the way in which he had understood the film.

It's a film in which one really feels the passage of time and how the main character changes between the first and last image.
Obviously there is no satisfying end for Isabel. The man she feels the closest to, Ralph, is going to die. The marriage with Osmond is no longer viable. For me, *Portrait of a Lady* speaks of the choices that one has to make in life, and tells us also that we can make sense of our destiny—disastrous as it may be, as is Isabel's—if we approach life with love, with honesty and with a will to self-discovery. That's for me the sense of the voyage that Isabel took. She believed that the voyage would be a battle with the elements, a completely exterior journey, and she realized, at the end, that she had taken this voyage inside of herself in order to find herself.

Jane Campion

RACHEL ABRAMOWITZ/1996

When Jane Campion was casting *The Portrait of a Lady,* she overlooked one woman who would have been perfect for the part of Henry James's headstrong heroine, Isabel Archer: herself. She laughs at the suggestion, but the 41-year-old New Zealander clearly identifies with her protagonist's arrogance, her generosity, and her desire to live life on her own terms. Campion is unpretentious and direct: She starts off lunch in a London restaurant by saying that she doesn't think following up the much-loved *The Piano* with a rendition of James's masterpiece is going to be a very popular choice.

"One in ten thousand people reads the novel, and of those who read it, many don't bother finishing it," she explains. "But I did this for myself. Sometimes in life you read things or see things that make what you're struggling with seem real or reasonable. I think Henry James has the gift of doing that for me. He's grappled with telling stories that are profound and yet . . . human."

In many ways *Portrait* is a darker shadow of *The Piano,* Campion's Oscar winner for original screenplay, about a 19th-century mute who travels to the forests of New Zealand for an arranged marriage and, instead, is liberated by erotic passion. Now Campion focuses her sumptuous visual style on the immaculate estates of upper-crust England and Italy. Like Ada, Isabel (Nicole Kidman) wishes to march to her own drummer; she rebuffs a number of eminent suitors, only to be drawn to Gilbert Osmond, a self-serving dilettante played with brilliant malevolence by John Malkovich.

While some James readers might be surprised by the director's focus on the novel's psychosexual underpinnings, Campion enthusiasts will not. Her very first student film, *Tissues,* featured a tissue in every scene and a man arrested for child molestation. She says the experience of making that little Super-8 left her "mad with the obsession" for filmmaking.

Campion now lives in Sydney with her husband, Colin Englert, a TV director, and their daughter, Alice, age two.

RACHEL ABRAMOWITZ: *At the beginning of* The Portrait of a Lady, *Isabel Archer doesn't seem to care what people think of her.*

JANE CAMPION: This is my interpretation of it: She's a flawed heroine in the sense that she's a truth seeker and she's concerned in a naive way about whatever her destiny means to her. She says, "I don't intend to marry. I don't want to be a mere sheep in the flock." She has that kind of arrogant conviction that she's worth more than most and she's been told so. Henry James talks affectionately about her arrogance in many funny ways. After she's had a major attack of arrogance, she'll have "fits of humiliation," he says, and "these don't last too long." But also she's feeling. She's sensitive. She participates in her fate. She's not just a sad victim to it. She also participates in the decisions that occur through her blindness and her own self-inflation, and also through things deeper than any of us can imagine.

I think it is a really important issue for women today, or men and women today, [to realize] that life is not made up of career choices. One of the most important things is to participate in relationships and friendships and particularly in the mythology of love. I have a deep need for intimacy. Almost every human being has it, and how you reconcile that with everything else in your life is a problem that comes up. Isabel denies its power to such an extent that when it hits her, when it's calculated in the way that Osmond calculates it, she falls for it in a devastating way. I love this quote [*She points to a quote from James scholar Alfred Habeggar that is printed on a European press kit for the movie*]: "Freedom and fatherlessness have split the heroine into two disconnected halves—a partly factitious determination to be her own master, and a dark fascination with images of dominance and submission." The attraction is deeper than you can control.

RA: Portrait *is filled with sexual undertones—most of which aren't so apparent in the book.*

JC: I had a funny discussion with [screenwriter] Laura Jones about that because she didn't see it either. Isabel's sexuality is a lot more repressed [than Osmond's], therefore she can be much more the victim of it. My belief is, anything you know about, you've got some protection from; what you don't know just really knocks you over. Osmond is very clever; he doesn't say, "Will you marry me?" He says, "I'm not a suitable person to marry, but I have to tell you I'm absolutely in love with you," which is so perfectly manipulative. He steals a kiss from her, and it's the kiss of a very experienced lover. It's a great kiss. John Malkovich could really do it. It's not a big, crushing thing. It's very sensitive. It must have eroticized Isabel and probably made her think, I'm in love.

RA: *You seem attracted to these themes of sexual emancipation.*

JC: I have a frank interest in how you reconcile your sexuality with your intellect—and with how leveling sexuality is. It humbles us all. Look at how many politicians have been caught up in it. I don't criticize them or moralize about them, because I accept their humanity.

RA: *Some time after offering Kidman the part of Isabel Archer, you had second thoughts. What happened?*

JC: It's something I'm a little ashamed of because you should think very, very deeply before you get as far as I got with Nicole. I just felt that it was very important to me that we should really get on and that she was prepared to go as far as I needed Isabel to go. I didn't know her work anymore. She hadn't done *To Die For* then. She was really unhappy with the work she'd been able to get in Hollywood. I think they select women for roles in Hollywood on the basis of whom they'd like to have sex with, and then every man will admire them because they have a desirable sex mate in their movie. There's a flattering quality to that, but it ain't very sustaining. She was really reeling from it. She told me that. I suppose I was worried that it had corrupted her talent in the plainest of ways. But it worked out very well for us in the end. We worked together for two days and I was blown away by her courage and honesty and development. So she didn't have to enter rehearsal wondering, Oh, when Jane sees my work, she won't like what I've done. She knew that I'd seen what she could do. That's huge confidence.

RA: *Kidman has to endure a lot of abuse in the movie. How did you help her handle it?*
JC: I had a lot of other things to do, so it was left a lot to her family to keep her together. But I obviously tried as much as possible to be there for her. I've never been so involved with the actors on a movie before. As a young director, I had a very different idea about the whole thing. I was embarrassed by emotion. I'd be snickering.

RA: *Was this during 1989's* Sweetie*?*
JC: No, no, I had grown up enough by then. Just before that, really, I would be giggling because I was embarrassed by the degree of emotion that someone had to get through. I'd watch myself snickering and I'd think, You bitch. You pathetic creature. You have got to stand by these people. They are out there. I realized I was kind of cowardly emotionally. I had to solve that before going any further.

RA: *When you were growing up, did you imagine you'd be a director?*
JC: I could never have dreamed that I would become a director. I wasn't even that interested in movies. I wasn't someone who grew up with a big passion for it.

RA: *I thought your mother took you to Buñuel movies.*
JC: Yeah, but she was arty. She did take me to the movies in Wellington. You can't imagine this town anywhere in the world. Just kind of old-fashioned and conservative. My mother was an actress. She had a Chanel suit and great legs and she'd want to go and see *Belle de Jour.* It is funny to see those movies at an age—I think I was about thirteen or fourteen—when you couldn't possibly grasp the moment. But the sense of adult complications, the mystique of it, has really stayed with me. I loved it. I just thought you had to become a kind of near genius to be able to make movies. I knew I wasn't, so why bother thinking about it? It took me a long time to gain confidence.

RA: *Where did you develop that confidence, in school?*
JC: I first went to university at sixteen. I had never been to a coed school. I was so overcome by just having boys everywhere. I was distracted and incredibly embarrassed by the tensions. I ended up going home to my parents' farm and working in a library for the rest of the year. I went back the following year, when I was seventeen.

RA: *After receiving a bachelors degree in anthropology, you went on to earn a second bachelors degree in painting, and then to attend film school. It seems like you spent most of your twenties . . .*
JC: Studying. There's something great about that period of time in a person's life when you finish school and then you go on to some deeper study—if you get the opportunity to do it. I think it's really something that forms you. I didn't know what else to do anyway. I had no idea what to do with myself. Studying was a way of postponing any decisions.

RA: *How did you finally settle on becoming a director?*
JC: It was never about making movies, it was about expressing myself. I had my Super-8 and my first film, *Tissues,* was an ambitious kind of European-influenced nonsense piece I made at art school. I became obsessed by movies in the process. I worked all the time on it, but it didn't feel like work, it was like the most desirable thing in the world to do.

RA: *Were you surprised by the success of* The Piano*?*
JC: People would say to me, "Oh, it's done so much." And I just said, "Is that good? Or does that mean I get any money?" Fortunately, I know more about the box office now than I knew at that time. What was very touching to me was when people would come up to me at the chemist and say, "I loved your movie." I somewhat expressed myself in that movie, and people got it—it made me feel less lonely. I just didn't think it would be nearly that popular. I thought it would be an art movie somewhere. Don't get me wrong, there's a part of me that wants to be popular too. I haven't existed very long in this business. I want to be loved. I sort of envy John Malkovich because he seemed to be just as happy to be hated. He doesn't give a damn.

RA: Portrait *was, in some respects, a family affair. Your husband, Colin Englert, did the second-unit shots.*
JC: All the beautiful shots are his.

RA: *And your infant daughter, Alice, was on location with you.*
JC: She really gave me a lot of energy. It would have been disastrous if she had gotten sick. That was my great fear. I just couldn't have worked if she had been ill. I think it's really hard for women who work and have babies. I want to do both. My mother gave up her acting and after a while we kind of [saw] that that wasn't a good decision. It didn't help us because she was frustrated, and it didn't help her. My father only did what he wanted to do, and of course, he enjoyed it. So you remember that.

RA: *Your father spent some time on the set of* Portrait *as well, didn't he?*
JC: He was there for only five weeks. He was a theater director. He was extremely helpful not so much in actual ideas, but just because of his level of support. I found that really, really great. It's hard for men or women who go out in the creative world, because somewhere back there you need to have a depth of support so you can risk being out there publicly. There are elements of me that are completely fearless, and I'm sure it's because my parents were in some odd way deeply encouraging. I never worry. I am just excited by the material itself. I don't think about failure.

Portrait of a Director

KENNEDY FRASER/1997

"It's a damn extraordinary book!" says Jane Campion, speaking of *The Portrait of a Lady.* "Embrace it. Offer it everything you've got and take from it everything it can give. It's very big!" For her first film since *The Piano,* the Australian-based director has adapted Henry James's great novel, first published in 1880. She is an attractive woman in her early 40s, with short blonde hair and attentive, periwinkle eyes. Her talk, like her work, is generous, quirky, and stubbornly self-confident. It is punctuated by the occasional good-natured, Down Underish expletive, upward-inflected "y'know?," or hooting laugh. Henry James was such a genius that his turn-of-the-century admirers called him "The Master." Sometimes, in referring to him, Campion calls him "Henry" in a breezily familiar way. But when she speaks of his fictional art—in which he uses the riches of the English language to delineate the most exquisite layers of perception and shades of emotion—she speaks with something approaching reverence. "It's so complex in terms of relationships," she said of *The Portrait* at the start of the four-month-long shooting of the film. "I've got skills that make me feel I can handle it now. I was too intimidated by actors before." She might also have found herself intimidated, as a younger woman, by Henry James.

The novel's protagonist is a lovely young American woman ("the mere slim shade of an intelligent but presumptuous girl") named Isabel Archer. She ranks with Emma Bovary, Jane Eyre, and Anna Karenina as one of the

---

most incandescent fictional heroines of all time. Recently bereaved of a beloved but ne'er-do-well father, she is whisked off first to England and then to Italy by a wealthy aunt. There she is wooed by a succession of suitors before—blinded by the pride, näiveté, and independence of mind that make her endearing to us, on the whole—she falls in love with and marries Gilbert Osmond, an American who lives in Italy. Hers is a generous spirit, and his a narrow one. He is, says Isabel's heartbroken cousin, Ralph Touchett, merely a "sterile dilettante." Osmond is much older than his young wife and bent on manipulating her; he sets out, systematically, to clip her wings. For susceptible readers—especially women, I would guess, but for anyone who has known relationships where a weak partner struggles to control and if need be destroy a freer one—*The Portrait of a Lady* feels archetypal. I know a woman who has read it every few years for decades, alternating it with George Eliot's *Middlemarch.*

Jane Campion loves reading novels and stories of every kind. For her, too, *The Portrait* has been something of a touchstone, and she had read it several times before she immersed herself in it to make the film. Nicole Kidman, who gives the performance of her life as Isabel in the new film, read the book first in her Australian girlhood and again in her 20s, when she was, she says, "blown away" by it. The actress had longed to work with Campion ever since, at fourteen, she was cast in the director's early short *A Girl's Own Story*—a sad, funny story of teenage girls and their sexual experiments, ranging from kissing each other to having intercourse with a brother—but was unable to take part because of school exams. She even auditioned for a role in *Sweetie,* Campion's first feature film, in which a sexually uninhibited, half-mad young woman creates havoc in her family before she dies, naked and paint-daubed, in a fall from a tree house in a suburban backyard.

Campion has said how closely she identifies with Isabel Archer and recognizes the potential of young women's lives to go awry. In youth, like her heroine, she was addicted to romance. "When I was young and falling in love, I did a con job on myself, occasionally with most unsuitable people!" she said in a documentary about the making of *The Portrait.* In fact Campion felt as if she knew Isabel personally, and it was this, she said, that finally gave her "permission to get in there and be involved with James's story playfully, and at the same time very seriously and dangerously." She had wanted to make her *Portrait* for some years but held back until Kidman really nudged her into taking the plunge. "I thought, Well, if she's got the guts, why haven't I?" Campion said when her film was first shown, at the Venice Film Festival. The real inspiration about how to make the movie in her own way came to her when she was at her hairdresser's. She was having her hair color done, so she had plenty of time to think things out.

At first blush—to use a favorite Jamesian phrase—Jane and Henry make an improbable pair. As a girl in 1960s New Zealand (she moved to Australia to get her B.A. in anthropology), Campion needed no boost from the Zeitgeist to challenge authority. In school, she resented being asked to write reports about the British royal family and insisted on subjects like earthquakes and other disasters. "I guess it's always been my nature to be a little perverse," she told me in Venice, with a smile. Henry James, for his part, was a dutiful member of a highminded, intellectual family in nineteenth-century New England. He was the son of one well-known sage (Henry Sr., a follower of Swedenborg and friend of Emerson who wrote copiously, especially on the need to keep women at home and out of the polling booth) and the brother of another (William, the philosopher and psychologist best known for his book *The Varieties of Religious Experience*). Like Isabel and many of his fictional characters, James was an expatriate. He lived mostly in England but traveled often to Paris, Florence, Rome, and Venice—where in a room with a view of gondolas and hunchbacked bridges he worked on bringing Isabel to life. Throughout Europe, he tended to move in a conservative and aristocratic little world. It was around tea tables set out on lawns by butlers and in the buzz of drawing rooms, palazzi, and salons that he found his subjects: genteel people meeting and mating; covertly maneuvering in what feel like life-or-death struggles for money or objects; corruptly combining in Machiavellian alliances to get some innocent (like Isabel) in their power.

Henry James once said that a novelist ought to be "one on whom nothing is lost," and one of the main things not lost on him was that people's behavior was often determined by their sexual lives. "The great relation" was how he described love between men and women, with a delicacy that sometimes tipped toward prudishness. He was as fascinated as any entomologist by his human specimens, but he deplored fiction that spelled out the "convulsions and spasms" going on behind their bedroom doors. In his mind, this failed to reveal the truth at all. James was a lifelong bachelor.

He was much at home in women's company, and must have empathized very closely with them. Every novel he wrote after *The Portrait* was to have a woman or a young girl at its heart. In life, he seems to have had sexual feelings for some men. In the end, like many great artists, he was probably vaguely androgynous. The legend that he was impotent as the result of a youthful injury is now believed to have been a falsehood spread by Ernest Hemingway, in a particularly parricidal mood. Still, there is hot dispute among scholars as to whether James had hands-on sexual experience with anyone at all.

Campion is supremely interested in "the great relation," but unlike The Master she doesn't hold sexuality at arm's length. On the contrary, she realized as a student filmmaker that she had to have something of her own to say, and she staked out as her turf female erotic experience, which she felt the movies had never really conveyed. At one time she even contemplated making pornographic movies for women, as a way of earning a living. *The Piano,* with its love triangle played out among settlers on a New Zealand farm that is literally stuck in the Victorian mud, was notable for an eroticism that felt unusually authentic to many women. Historically, the movie industry has been slow to encourage the visions of women directors; it seems unimaginable that Campion could have found her way without funding from the Australian and New Zealand governments. "The Hollywood scene is very male dominated, and not incredibly intelligently so," Campion told me, looking wry. "A lot of it is about exploring concepts of masculinity and virility, which make men feel strong and proud."

Sexuality is not the only aspect of female physicality accorded her unflinching gaze. James, decorous even by the standards of his era, might be shaken to find himself the posthumous partner of a woman whose camera, in three out of her seven earlier films, has dwelled on the comic and vulnerable prospect of a woman urinating in the open air. With James, we find ourselves staring at physical events that are equally humble but far more polite: the nervous poking of a parasol tip into the ground; the stare of a lovesick suitor into the upturned hat on his lap; the rise of a tint to the cheek or a tear to the eye. Sometimes we recognize these as signs of seismic shifts in the plot. Campion's own eye rests not just on peeing women but on domestic, perfectly proper subjects not unlike those of James—a pair of gloves, a teacup—and like him she lingers until the sight surrenders its secret meaning. Her images are rarely careless. They swell, from time to time, to fill what have been called her "extended moments," which feel inexplicably feminine.

The sets and costumes for *The Portrait* are rich with portent. The piled-up hair and bonnets, the *S*-shaped silhouettes with trains and bustles of the belle epoque—so wearily familiar from a hundred adaptations on *Masterpiece Theatre*—glow with fresh life for the thoroughly modern Campion. As befits a film conceived in a hair salon, the hairstyles in it are unusually intelligent and change with the journey of its heroine. The unmarried girl, "very fond of her liberty" and with a head swarming with ideas, wears a cottage-loaf-style, chestnut-colored chignon that fizzes and tumbles about her head like her undisciplined thoughts. The young wife, whom her husband has done his best to turn into another of the well-chosen objects in his collections, holds her head tragically high under a heavy, disciplined crown of braided hair—a coiffure that adds years to her age and turns her beauty into something dead, like a bronze intaglio of a Roman matron. Isabel's dresses and accessories are also freighted with meaning. Her slight, black-clad silhouette, framed in a massive doorway and graphic as a fashion photograph by Irving Penn, speaks volumes about the spiritual isolation of her life in a gorgeous marital home that is really "a dark, narrow alley with a dead wall at the end." Her chic silk dress over a tightly laced corset (Kidman, who is nearly six feet tall, cinched her waist span down to nineteen inches), her jaunty veiled hat, and her absurdly tiny handbag are a cry, no louder than a bat squeak, for our compassion.

Campion and her screenwriter, Laura Jones, have been broadly faithful to the book, but they have opened up James's famous interior monologues, stripped the veil from his eroticism, and beefed up Osmond's abusiveness. In the whole long novel, there is only a single kiss for Isabel—exchanged briefly and on the next-to-last page with a former suitor whose character is scarcely developed. Even for Henry himself, that must have come to seem a little niggardly, or else he got braver: When he published a new edition of the novel a quarter-century after he wrote it, he expanded the kiss to a whole paragraph. But what would he have made of Campion's addition of a rather dopey scene where Isabel imagines herself having sex with all of her suitors at once? Campion's changes stem partly from the need to keep a movie audience's attention and partly from her creative temperament: close to the world of dreams, yet also robustly rooted in the earth. "Sometimes I'm having a really inspired time, I'm really feeling like I'm penetrating some ideas, I'm working and working," she says. "Then I get hungry or tired, and I think, Fuck it, if only I could have gone on for another hour, I could have got somewhere! It's this recognition, all the time, of being a person—of having animal qualities, y'know?"

Even the famous scene with Isabel and her dying cousin, Ralph (played in the film, with great sensitivity, by Martin Donovan), is eroticized by Campion. Touchett is an extraordinarily evolved, ironic, and nearly omniscient observer, like his creator—who in the novel assiduously protects the dear boy from any pressure to have a sex life by giving him a slowly advancing case of tuberculosis. (In reality, some famous consumptives, like D. H. Lawrence, had no lack of drive.) Where Isabel's other suitors want to possess her like a trophy, Ralph is content to be a celibate soul mate, watching from the sidelines as she "affronts her destiny." It breaks his heart to see her contract her misalliance and take a husband who (like the settlers with the Maoris) makes it his mission to tame and colonize her mind.

The story of Isabel and her suitors is in large part about the confusion between sexual desire and the struggle men and women have for control and power. For the screen, Campion has turned the dial a notch on Osmond's sadism toward Isabel; he assaults her not just with psychological violence but with physical indignities as well. What's more, he is played by John Malkovich—with what will seem like too heavy a hand for many who have been chilled by the far more complex Osmond found in James. Indeed, it is almost as if, in a mirror of the characters' power struggle, the actor had tussled with the director and come away with the right to play not Osmond but himself.

Generally, Campion is known for the extraordinary and unpredictable performances she can get from actors. Many of those she has worked with claim that the experience has changed their lives. Campion's mother was a leading stage actress in New Zealand, her father an opera and theater director. The couple founded the first official theatrical touring company in their native land. Apart from her interlude as an anthropologist, she has been around the thespian tribe all her life. She must know its ways inside out: its vanities and insecurities, its antennae and its blind spots. "I felt really protected by her, yet also pushed really hard," Donovan told me, of playing Campion's Ralph. Harvey Keitel, whose scene of mutely noble nudity with Holly Hunter is one of the finest moments in *The Piano,* was once quoted as saying that Jane Campion is "a goddess."

It is a sign of her breadth and her courage that Campion—a female director whose movies are so loved by women and whose sets are full of women in key positions—has chosen to work with Keitel and Malkovich, two actors associated with male energy at its most demonic and dark. Before directing Keitel, she cleared the air by admitting to him she was intimidated. With Malkovich—a fellow who admits to having a bad temper, and like Keitel a brilliant actor whose experience in making movies is far greater than Campion's own—she was scared at first, but she says she got over it. "I'm not frightened of anybody," she told me. "Unless they're going to hit me or hurt me. And I don't think he ever did that!" The documentary about making *The Portrait* gives a remarkably intimate view of her at work with her stars. With Kidman, she is maternal—hugging her between takes, wiping her tears, and gently, with the balls of her thumbs, stroking her eyebrows, disarrayed from copious weeping in her scenes with Malkovich. But she squares up to Malkovich with her chest and looks him in the eye, as if confronting him man-to-man.

Sophisticated villains, Campion says, are part of her fantasy world. "Isabel fantasizes about men like Osmond, and so do I. I'm very interested in Osmond's power." I asked her whether she had ever been in a relationship with a destructive man. "It's so familiar," she said. Many women will identify with Isabel as she keeps trying to placate the husband who seems to hate her and whom she comes to fear. But she stays on, hoping that by fixing up a damaged man she can heal her own childhood shocks and wounds. She wanders through the dim and lonely terrain of what in current jargon is called "an emotionally abusive relationship." How bald that jargon seems beside the almost-breathing reality of Mr. and Mrs. Osmond, evoked by the pre-Freudian Henry James.

Campion, the would-be anthropologist, sees Isabel Archer as a case history of a group of humans not generally viewed as an abused minority: beautiful young women. If they are also sensitive and clever, she says, it is ten times more difficult for them than for other women to find their path in life. If Isabel had not been lovely, she would not have been first elevated and adored, then humiliated and abused. "You see it all the time," Campion says indignantly. "Who approaches a beautiful woman? Insensitive men!

They're the ones who can handle it if they're rejected. The really sensitive, gorgeous ones, like Ralph Touchett, stand back."

At this point in my conversation with her, I may have sighed. At this very moment, bright-faced new versions of Isabel are undoubtedly finding their Osmonds and warming up for the familiar dance. I asked Jane Campion whether she thought that women had made any progress at all since the days of Henry James. "I don't believe in progress!" she said with a laugh. "It's such a short life we all have. We're here only to explore our humanity. Each one of us starts at the beginning. It's not as if we can start where the ancient Greeks left off."

She aspires, like James before her, to look at life through the widest possible lens. She bristled at my suggestion that James might have followed his father's example and been, in *The Portrait,* at least, a closet antifeminist—punishing poor Isabel for her aspiration to feel free. "He was a realist," Campion said firmly. "Whatever you might want for women or for men, the important thing is to see the truth and be a commentator on that." Her feminism, she says, should speak for itself, but she resists anything that smacks of feminist pieties or of unfriendliness to men. Henry James, she added, isn't interested in small questions of whether women should be working outside the home. She points to the character of Isabel's friend, Henrietta Stackpole, a prying American journalist whom he treats with "chiding affection" and permits to grow up by "going against her feminist principles by marrying an Englishman." The director seemed surprisingly happy at this thought. "I've seen that so many times," she added. "Some of the strongest lesbian feminists I know married some of the macho-est guys."

In spite of her open-seeming manner, Campion has succeeded in guarding the details of her private life almost as closely as James, who abhorred publicity and laid false trails for his biographers. She is known to be married to Colin Englert, a well-known Australian television director. (She is said to have practiced on him—being self-assertive without being bossy—before directing Keitel.) In the years between the filming of *The Piano* and that of *The Portrait,* she is known to have had a pregnancy that ended in her baby's tragic death. (Isabel Osmond also loses a baby; in the film there is a poignant "extended moment" with the hands of a grieving woman fingering a replica of an infant's hand.) Then Campion gave birth to a baby girl, Alice, who was old enough to toddle about the set as her mother was making her new movie. "I've got a daughter now," an exhausted Campion told the documentary-maker halfway through. "She's just a baby. So it's a scary balance of trying to have enough time with her—to feel that I'm doing any kind of mothering and also that I'm doing the work well enough to satisfy myself."

It isn't easy for young women to find their truth and the opportunity to speak it in art, the way Jane Campion did, from *A Girl's Own Story* on. "I think both women and men are afraid to speak their own truth," she told me with her habitual conviction. If anything, she added, women are more fortunate, because they are used to telling truths among themselves. "That culture of private truth-speaking is the compensation for not having power," she said. "You shut up, you see what's going on. Growing up as a woman—without power—is very interesting. You learn to get around it. To work without power but still feel expressed. It makes you very observant."

Portrait of a Lady and Her Films

SUSAN SACCOCCIA/1997

THREE YEARS AGO, FILM director Jane Campion was known to few beyond arthouse and film-festival audiences. Then millions watched the 66th Academy Awards bestow three Oscars on her 1993 film, *The Piano,* including Best Screenplay for Ms. Campion.

Her new celebrity sprinkled gold dust on the compelling and quirky films that came before—just two features, a telefeature, and a handful of film-school shorts. Her fame also fired immense anticipation for her next film, an adaptation of the Henry James novel *The Portrait of a Lady,* recently released in theaters.

"It was a cross to bear that it was another frock drama," says Campion, in Manhattan to première the film, which is, like *The Piano,* set in the 19th century.

Her hair is cut in a short blond shag, and she wears a black knit jacket, burgundy silk trousers, and stylishly chunky oxfords. She is tall and radiates ebullient energy and warmth. One gets the impression she brings down-to-earth enthusiasm to activities, whether hiking on a trail in her native New Zealand or discussing her work in a suite at the Drake Hotel.

In fact, with a two-year production in Italy and England behind her, she is about to take "a big holiday" in the New Zealand bush with her husband, Colin Englert, a television director and producer, and their two-year-old daughter, Alice. Campion is building a hut on a remote sheep station in the alpine region of New Zealand's South Island.

From *The Christian Science Monitor,* 13 January 1997. Reprinted by permission of the author.

Home is across the Tasman Sea, in Australia, where she and Mr. Englert recently bought "the most beautiful house in Sydney," on a tranquil Mediterranean-like bay. "We'll camp out for a while with our old tacky furniture," Campion laughs. "I don't want to get all caught up with finding curtains."

Instead, Campion is captivated by the contemporary dilemma of Isabel Archer, the heroine of Henry James's novel, who is a free-spirited, idealistic girl until cynical Gilbert Osmond, a fortune-hunting dilettante, lures her into a bleak marriage.

"Isabel wakes to the discovery of how things are," Campion says. "Her insight is her reward. Hers is a tragic rite of passage. Through suffering, she finds her real self. She didn't realize how tough the journey was going to be. She is beautiful, tall, intelligent, arrogant, courageous. But, like women who are not as beautiful, not as sought after, she also experiences the hardships of life.

"Growing up, the expectation is that life will turn out sweetly," Campion says. "When it doesn't, you handle it. It's very 20th century."

As Campion's film opens, young women wearing soft white sheaths describe their expectations of romance and love. The scene echoes the final moments of *A Girl's Own Story* (1983), Campion's 27-minute film about a girl's passage from innocence to experience. In the surreal closing scene, a chorus of girls dressed in white are chanting, "I feel the cold." "It's a mini *Portrait of a Lady,*" says Campion.

Campion draws from her own experience. "I'm a romantic-obsessive," she says. "I love to fall in love." One relationship left her "unable to trust for two years," but she got over it. "I fell in love again," she laughs.

Mining terrain she knows well, what it means to grow up female, she trains a keen and darkly comic eye on the losses, betrayals, and excesses of control and neglect within families and the decisive moments on which lives turn.

"I tell little stories," she says of her films, which portray coming-of-age crises with the close-up, intimate detail of miniatures.

Campion's TV movie, *Two Friends* (1986), portrays the unraveling of a friendship between two teenage girls in poignant flashback.

Her first feature film, *Sweetie* (1989), is a black comedy that contrasts wild and impulsive Sweetie with her passive sister, Kay. Sweetie descends into madness while her oblivious father dreams that she will be a singing star. "It's both funny and tragic," Campion says of the film, booed at the 1989 Cannes International Film Festival for its seeming heartlessness. "Sweetie's song at the end is about fallen promise. Her father was unable to love her well and was complicit in her illness. Fantasy can be destructive. It's hard to grow up and be real, and come to see things as they are."

Campion speaks of trusting her instincts as she brings "little stories" to the big screen. "I'm grateful to my parents," she says. "Our strong family gave me the freedom to explore."

Born in Wellington, New Zealand, she grew up among actors. Her parents, Richard and Edith Campion, founded New Zealand's first touring theater company in the '50s.

After graduating with a degree in anthropology from Victoria University of Wellington in 1975, Campion earned a degree in painting at Sydney College of Arts in 1979. While at the Australian Film, Television, and Radio School in the early '80s, she wrote and directed a nine-minute film, *Peel* (1982), which won the Golden Palm (Palme D'Or) for short films at Cannes in 1986.

Campion credits Australia's government-supported film industry for promoting equal opportunity, particularly the Women's Film Unit, where she worked after film school.

She found her way to filmmaking, she says, "by daring to fail, first in art and printing, then with film. Discovering film was an incredible high. I never thought I would be directing features. It would have terrified me. I didn't have the confidence. First, I made movies that lasted three minutes, then seven minutes, then 27 minutes. My commitment is to each story, not to a career. I do exactly the same thing now."

Campion's *An Angel at My Table* (1990) conveys the tenderness, humor, and heartbreak in the autobiographies of New Zealand author Janet Frame, including her richly observed rural New Zealand childhood and harrowing stay in an insane asylum (she was misdiagnosed as a schizophrenic). First a TV movie, the theatrical film version won the Silver Lion and seven other awards at the 1990 Venice Film Festival.

Next, Campion wrote and directed *The Piano,* her story of erotic awakening from the perspective of a willful Scotswoman who is mute by choice. The film received more than 30 awards, including the Golden Palm at Cannes in 1993. Campion was the first woman to take the Cannes top prize.

But these triumphs coincided with a great personal loss. After Cannes, Campion gave birth to her first child, Jasper. He lived for only 12 days. "It was the most dire chapter of my life," says Campion. "The success of *The Piano* escaped me completely."

Alice was born a year later. Her elfin face beams forth from a publicity photo shot during a production break in Italy, where lunch with Alice was Campion's daily treat. "I couldn't survive if work was my only world," says Campion. "My identity as a big-time director is not enough. . . . When Alice walks into the room, that's the best thing."

Campion's successes have given her a larger palette, but she still paints miniatures. Her canvas is not Hollywood, she says, but the independent film industry, which targets a "huge" audience not satisfied by standard big-studio fare.

Yet she is working on a large scale. *Portrait* cost $24 million, more than threefold the $7 million budget of *The Piano*. "I work to my own vision," she says. "If I thought about the millions, it would be scary."

Campion's next projects are already on the drawing board. Susanna Moore's novel *In the Cut* will be her third adaptation with screenwriter Laura Jones. And Campion is writing a screenplay with her sister, filmmaker Anna Campion. "It will be a *Sweetie*-like comedy with no holds barred."

Jane Campion Is Called the Best Female Director in the World. What's Female Got to Do with It?

LIZZIE FRANKE/1997

A COUPLE OF YEARS AGO, a film magazine described Jane Campion as "unquestionably New Zealand's top woman director." It was meant to be a compliment. At the time the director had to her name *The Piano* (complete with Cannes's Palme d'Or, and three Oscars), as well as *An Angel at My Table,* which won the Grand Jury prize at Venice a few years before. Would the same magazine have described Tarantino, at the time of *Pulp Fiction,* as California's top male director?

For Campion is one of the few women to leap over the barrier and join the pantheon of great filmmakers. The critic David Thomson puts the record straight when he hails Campion as one of the best young directors in the world today, describing *The Piano* as "a great film in an age that has nearly forgotten such things."

Indeed, her films stretch the possibilities for cinema—both in terms of visual scope and subject matter. Her first feature, the extraordinary *Sweetie,* was shot from a host of weird angles, as she surveyed the lives of two sisters from a family whose world was askew. Dedicating it to her sister Anna, who is herself now a film-maker, she has unnervingly described it as "loosely autobiographical." (One suspects this is her own playful, pre-emptive gambit in a climate that attempts to forge connections between a film-maker's work and personal history). Shot with a garish palette while at the same time affecting a drab realism, *Sweetie* intended to make one uncomfortable in its bittersweet depiction, particularly its sly intimation of father-daughter

---

incest. Certainly the smart set at Cannes, where it debuted, slammed their seats in disgust, though the more discerning put the film on the map.

Campion's desire to find poetry in the rawness was evident in her next film, *An Angel at My Table,* which was unflinching in its depiction of the life of the New Zealand novelist Janet Frame who spent much of her young adulthood in a mental hospital. As with *Sweetie,* there was a desire to underpin uneasy family relationships, to portray a female willfulness that had gone awry. One of the most haunting images is that of Janet (Kerry Fox) trying on her dead father's boots. It's a mirthful moment that also weighs heavy. Campion's heroines are women at odds with the world—no more so than with the elective mute Ada in *The Piano,* or now *The Portrait of a Lady*'s Isabel Archer, one of 19th-century literature's most complex heroines.

This complexity is important to Campion. She has little time for traditional costume drama and has dismissed the recent rush of Jane Austen adaptations as "'very soft." By contrast, she says, James "is very modern because he's already tearing apart the fairytale. He's saying, 'Be real. Life is hard . . . No one's going to get the right person.' "

Campion is quick to say what she doesn't like. Interviews, for example. She doesn't suffer fools—and the questions relevant to her work and life—gladly. She is also highly skilled at steering a conversation in her preferred direction: Henry James, George Eliot, her favourite fictional heroines Isabel and Dorothea Brooke. She visibly relaxes as the interview lapses into chat.

Campion's *Portrait* explores the darker elements of James's text as Isabel, a seemingly bold and vivacious heroine from America, makes her way through a Europe that proves to be a dangerous labyrinth in which she encounters the monstrous as personified by the aesthete Gilbert Osmond. Campion has been a fan of the novel since she was a teenager. Indeed, she seems to see something of herself in the heroine.

For the 20th-century Antipodean, the experience of coming to Europe has been like that of the 19th-century American. Like Isabel, Campion came to Europe as a young woman, living for a while in England and studying art in Italy. She calls it both the best and darkest time of her early life. She talks of the time she was living just outside Venice and a friend was arrested for cocaine trafficking. "I had no idea that was even going on. I just thought, I'm going to be arrested and put in jail, and no one is going to listen to me. I felt that I really had the confidence knocked out of me . . . I think I was close to a breakdown." Her time in Italy, she says, helped her understand Europe's "winter spirit," its darkness. It prepared her for Isabel Archer.

Nicole Kidman, who plays Isabel in *Portrait,* told Howard Feinstein in a perceptive piece in *Vanity Fair*: "I think all that Isabel has experienced Jane has also experienced at some stage in her life. Isabel said that what she wants from life is chances and dangers. And I think that's also Jane."

Like Isabel Archer, Campion lost a baby. Jasper died when he was 12 days old, just after Campion had won the top prize at Cannes. She says the two experiences taught her a lesson, made her reassess her life. "The irony of Jasper dying at the moment of winning the Palme d'Or is that you learn that what you want is not always under your control." *Portrait* is dedicated to Jasper.

Others have suggested 42-year-old Campion is closer to another of the book's characters, the manipulative Madame Merle. But the documentary *Portrait: Jane Campion and* The Portrait of a Lady, made by her friends Peter Long and Kate Ellis, reveals that rather than coercing actors, she wins them round with encouragement ("Just have faith, OK?" to Kidman), care (wiping raindrops off Barbara Hershey's face), hugs a-plenty, and the occasional confrontation (ordering Shelley Winters to stop whingeing).

Darkness, strangeness, madness have always been important to Campion's vision. Not so much an analysis of strangeness, just an acknowledgement that it is there, stirred in with the apparently normal, inseparable. Perhaps it's not surprising, then, that she is now planning to produce, along with husband Colin Englert (a former television reporter and director) and Nicole Kidman, Susanna Moore's violently erotic novel, *In The Cut.* Her mother, Edith Campion, has described Jane as idiosyncratic, a mischief-maker, "with a peculiar eye on the world." She says: "If Jane hadn't done anything I think she might have become a great criminal. She likes to set things into action and see what happens. But, then, that's rather like being a movie director."

One might, to be contrary, go back to that film magazine quote and ponder: is it because Jane Campion is a woman and from the Antipodes that she has fashioned such a unique approach to film? Australia (where she moved to study film after doing a degree in Anthropology in Wellington) and New Zealand loom large in her films, particularly the latter, which provides the sombre psychic landscape for *An Angel at My Table* and *The Piano.*

Campion herself says that New Zealand fashioned her way of seeing. She points to a tiny country on the edge of the world, a country where personal matters are kept personal (hence her delight in showing characters on the toilet?), a country founded on a Utopian ideal of equality that ended up flattening out difference. Campion talks of the uncelebratory nature of New Zealand. You know, she says, "they used to have a programme on TV in New Zealand called That's Fairly Interesting. That's the title of it. In America, it's That's Incredible! New Zealand is really a country of enormous understatement."

Meanwhile, the young Campion's imagination was allowed to run riot at a time when Australian cinema was high on the new wave that had produced such film-makers as Peter Weir and Bruce Beresford. She evolved as a film-maker during a particularly enlightened period in Australian film-making. In the late 1970s and early 1980s government-funded agencies actively encouraged young women film-makers.

From her early shorts, Campion took a very particular, uncensored slant on what she observed, never shying of the stranger or abject elements of life. *Passionless Moments* (1984) strings together a series of vignettes focusing on obsessions both hilarious and tragic, such as the fear of treading on the cracks in the pavement.

In *A Girl's Own Story,* a 1960s-set coming-of-age short, pubescent desires turn dangerous as a brother and sister experiment with each other. When she made her first featurette, *Two Friends,* for Australian TV, Campion turned story-telling inside out as she ran back to front the tale of two schoolmates who fall out, with the film starting at the final bust-up.

Her pursuit of new ways of seeing things is no less evident than with her version of James's *The Portrait of a Lady,* her first film to be shot in Europe. I say version, since this film spikes expectations of the literary adaptation genre. Campion's movie is like an intense, intimate reading that explores the darker elements of James's text.

"What I love about James, who in turn was so influenced by Eliot, is that he plots a life in terms of the spiritual journey as much as anything else," explains Campion. "Isabel Archer starts out on a false journey—in the pursuit of wordly knowledge, and she can't even imagine what it is she wants to be knowing and learning. What she does find out is who she is."

Campion identifies closely with Isabel's journey. "I really love Europe. But I tried to live in England and got very depressed. I know this sounds ridiculous but I began to wonder whether it was something to do with my relationship with the sky. One can have a very psychic relationship with the sky." In this, she says, she is very much an island girl.

Indeed, one thinks of her as wild to nature, and fearless. She strips through the heavy undergrowth of emotions, uprooting the primal even in the poised milieu of James's novel. In *The Portrait,* drawing-rooms become bloody battlegrounds as treacherous as the dark woods of the more obviously tempestuous *Piano*. Once again, Campion has reshaped our perception of the world.

INDEX